THE MARKET RISK AMENDMENT

Understanding the Marking-to-Model and Value-at-Risk

DIMITRIS N. CHORAFAS

McGraw-Hill

New York   Chicago   San Francisco   Washington, D.C.   Auckland   Bogotá
Caracas   Lisbon   London   Madrid   Mexico City   Milan
Montreal   New Delhi   San Juan   Singapore
Sydney   Tokyo   Toronto

Library of Congress Cataloging-in-Publication Data

Chorafas, Dimitris N.
    The market risk amendment : understanding the
        marking-to-model and value-at-risk / Dimitris N. Chorafas.
        p. cm.
    ISBN 0–7863–1224–6
    1. Financial futures. 2. Risk management.
        3. Futures—Law and legislation.
  HG6024.3 .C48 1997
  361.63/2—dc21

                                       97–8664
                                       CIP

McGraw-Hill
A Division of The *McGraw·Hill* Companies

1 2 3 4 5 6 7 8 9 0 DOC/DOC 9 0 2 1 0 9 8 7

The acquiring editor for this book was *Steven Sheehan,* the editing supervisor was *John M. Morriss,* and the production supervisor was *Suzanne W. B. Rapcavage.* It was set in Times Roman by *Hendrickson Creative Communications.*

Printed and bound by R. R. Donnelley & Sons Company.

McGraw-Hill books are available at special quantity discounts to use as premiums and sales promotions, or for use in corporate training programs. For more information, please write to the Director of Special Sales, McGraw-Hill, 11 West 19th Street, New York, NY 10011. Or contact your local bookstore.

CONTENTS

v

Chapter 9

Policies and Procedures against Systemic Risk   153

PART TWO

UNDERSTANDING MARKING-TO-MODEL   173

Chapter 10

The Calculation of Value-at-Risk (VAR) with Parametric Models   175

Chapter 11

The Calculation of Value-at-Risk through Simulation   193

Chapter 16

The Development and Use of Proprietary Models for Pricing the Trading Book   285

PREFACE

This text grew out of an intensive research project in the United States, England, Continental Europe, and Japan. The project—in which the Basle Committee on Banking Supervision, Federal Reserve Board, Bank of England, Banque de France, Swiss National Bank, and Bank of Italy, as well as accounting standards boards, commercial banks, investment banks, and some of the foremost technology vendors participated—had the objective of providing a basis for evaluating and appreciating the 1996 Market Risk Amendment.

- This book is for bankers, financial analysts, treasurers, investors, and traders—in short, potential practitioners of effective risk management.
- The primary aim is to help the reader understand the new regulations, as well as to assist in the appreciation of methods and tools permitting to mark-to-model.
- The second goal is to explain how to calculate value-at-risk (VAR), presenting the reader with modelling concepts and techniques that have gained the regulator's approval.

The directives included in the 1996 Market Risk Amendment by the Basle Committee on Banking Supervision have enormous potential in the financial industry. The concepts and the tools it promotes are well positioned to revolutionize many aspects of current banking practices.

Therefore, the book explains tools such as *value-at-risk* from both a conceptual and an applications viewpoint, but in a way presupposing no mathematical background to understanding the text. To gain the full benefit of the material in this book, the reader is advised to work through all of the chapters because each chapter has a specific message for the practitioner. The 16 chapters are divided into two parts.

- Part One explains the Market Risk Amendment, and presents the information banks need to comply with it, as well as the possible aftermaths of such compliance the way the Federal Reserve and other central banks look at them.

■ Part Two concentrates on value-at-risk, presents its two alternative methods of computing, and extends this discussion to cover other models currently used in the financial industry.

Chapter 1 is based on the presentation given by Sarah Dahlgren of the Federal Reserve Bank of New York to the First International Conference on Risk Management in Banking, which I chaired.[1] The pleasant surprise of that conference was that on the same day Sarah Dahlgren of the Fed delivered her lecture, Daniel Schutzer of Citibank demonstrated how fast and effectively the Fed's advice can be implemented.

Chapter 2 is an introduction, intended to provide the reader with a valid definition of the trading book and the banking book. It also provides background on market risk and credit risk; the notions of risk capital, replacement value, and net present value; and the concept of position risk.

Chapter 3 examines the most fundamental clauses of the 1996 Market Risk Amendment, targeting the risks that are inherent in the trading book. It also brings into perspective the Capital Adequacy Directive (CAD) of the European Union.

The central theme of Chapter 4 is how to implement the Market Risk Amendment. It does so by starting with the development of internal proprietary models (eigenmodels) and proceeding to the ways and means necessary for testing these models—since this is what central banks will be after in terms of regulatory action.

Chapter 5 expands upon this subject, introduces backtesting and control by central banks, explaining what the green, yellow, and red zones mean to the commercial banker in terms of model results and possible penalities. It also discusses current regulatory action by securities and exchange commissions.

Chapter 6 includes some of the opinions contributed by the Federal Reserve and the Bank of England in the course of the research meetings regarding the implementation of the Market Risk Amendment. It also incorporates the directives by the Financial Accounting Standards Board in the United States, particularly FASB Statement 119; and by the Accounting Standards Board in the United Kingdom, placing emphasis on the Statement of Total Recognized Gains and Losses (STRGL).

Chapter 7 is a case study based on the reorganization of accounting standards in France and the new structure of accounting regulation and banking supervision. These are problems every country of the Group of

---

1 London, March 17–19, 1997.

Seven (G–7) and the Group of Ten (G–10) will eventually face. How G–7 and G–10 look at the Market Risk Amendment is the subject of Chapter 8.

Part One concludes with Chapter 9, which addresses policies and procedures currently followed against systemic risk. Propelled by the central banks' new directives, the integration of balance sheet and off-balance sheet exposure currently taking place should be seen from the perspective of a new, global regulation promoting a methodology for the control of market risk.

Value-at-risk—its concept and the algorithms used for its calculation—is the theme of Chapters 10 and 11. Chapter 10 concentrates on parametric models, discussing their strengths and weaknesses. Chapter 11 explains the sense of simulation, and why nonparametric VAR models can provide more dependable results.

The Black–Scholes formula for option pricing is presented in Chapter 12, along with the Sharpe Index and the Olsen utility formula. Chapter 13 concentrates on the concept of hedging and hedge accounting. It also incorporates important metrics for derivative financial instruments: delta, gamma, theta, kappa, and rho.

The core matter of Chapter 14 is the assessment of counterparty risk, interest-rate risk, currency risk, country risk, and equity risk. These are the basic risks a bank faces in its daily transactions. Each is explained in terms of the requirements it poses in regard to a successful implementation of the 1996 Market Risk Amendment by the Basle Committee.

Commodity software for marking-to-model the trading book occupies the better part of Chapter 15. The Morgan Bank's RiskMetrics, with its strengths and weaknesses, is offered as an example. The text also emphasizes that neither models nor financial theories last forever. This field is too dynamic to accept solutions that remain valid for the long term.

Chapter 16 is of interest to those banks that develop, or plan to develop, their own proprietary models for pricing the trading book. It concentrates on the importance of abstraction and simplification in model building, emphasizes the vital competitive advantage provided by intraday financial time series, discusses nonlinearities, and underlines the need for model testing.

The structure of this text has been chosen in the belief that the future development of risk-management tools, methods, and procedures should be of great importance to *all* banks. The fact remains, however, that money-center banks and generally the larger financial institutions have so far shown more extensive interest in developing and using eigenmodels for compliance with the Market Risk Amendment. They have done so well before it becomes compulsory, which is at the end of 1997.

I am indebted to a long list of organizations and knowledgeable people for their contributions to the research that made this book possible (cf. the Acknowledgments in the back of the book). I am also indebted to several executives and experts for their constructive contribution during the preparation of the manuscript; particularly Dr. Frederik C. Musch of the Basle Committee, Patricia Jackson of the Bank of England, Alan Brown of Barclays Bank, A. V. C. Cook and Sandra Thompson of the Accounting Standards Board, Martyn Taylor, chairman of the Banks Working Party, European Federation of Chartered Accountants, as well as Sarah Dahlgren of the Federal Reserve of New York and Dr. Daniel Schutzer of Citibank.

I also want to thank Steven Sheehan and Kevin Thornton of McGraw-Hill, for steadily steering this book through the publishing process; Pamela Sourelis for her careful editing and attention to detail; John Morriss for the production of this book; and Eva-Maria Binder for compiling the research results, typing the text, preparing the figures, and compiling the index.

Valmer and Vitznau   Dr. Dimitris N. Chorafas
July 1997

Xenophon (430–354 B.C.) once wrote: "Whoever wants to keep alive must aim at victory."

This book is dedicated to those banks and bankers who aim at victory over global risk.

PART ONE

Impact of the 1996 Market Risk Amendment

CHAPTER 1

The Market Risk Amendment and Beyond*

1. INTRODUCTION

The goal of this book is to present to its readers a comprehensive and easy-to-follow account of the 1996 Market Risk Amendment by the Basle Committee of Banking Supervision. The Basle Committee is made up of the central bankers of the Group of Ten (G–10) countries: the United States, Britain, Germany, France, Italy, Japan, and Canada, which make up the Group of Seven (G–7), as well as Switzerland, Sweden, Holland, and Belgium, and Luxembourg as an observer.

Beginning at the end of 1997, the Market Risk Amendment must be applied by all G–10 central banks to the supervision of commercial banks as well as other financial institutions under their jurisdiction. It is the law of the land. But between January 1996, when it was published, and December 1997, when it will be applied, many other events have taken and will take place.

These events were covered by the First International Conference on Risk Management in the Banking Industry, which I chaired in London March 17 to 19, 1997. Distinguished lecturers from central banks, as well

---

* Portions of this chapter are based on a presentation made by Sarah Dahlgren, assistant vice president of the Federal Reserve Bank of New York, at the First International Conference on Risk Management in the Banking Industry, March 17–19, 1997. The opinions expressed are those of Ms. Dahlgren and Dr. Chorafas and are not to be construed as the opinion or policy of the Federal Reserve Bank of New York.

as executives of securities commissions, stock exchanges, and commercial banks, participated in this conference. The following is a list of the
lecturers in alphabetic order:

- **Central banks:** Sarah Dahlgren, Federal Reserve Bank of New
  York; Dr. Werner Hermann, Swiss National Bank; Particia D.
  Jackson, Bank of England; Michel Martino, Commission
  Bancaire, Banque de France.
- **Securities commissions:** Beata Stelmach, Polish Securities
  Commission; Andrew M. Street, Securities and Futures
  Authority, UK.
- **Stock exchanges:** Jean-Pierre Paelinck, Federation of European
  Stock Exchanges; Dr. Rüdiger von Rosen, Deutsche
  Aktieninstitut e.V.
- **Commercial banks:** Brandon Davies, Barclays Bank; Stephen F.
  Myers, Bankgesellschaft Berlin; Dr. Daniel Schutzer, Citibank;
  Dr. Yves Wagner, Banque Générale de Luxembourg.
- **European authorities:** Nick K. Cook, European Commission
  DG XV; Martyn Taylor, European Federation of Chartered
  Accountants.

To a significant extent, the text of this chapter is based on the concepts conveyed by Sarah Dahlgren of the Federal Reserve Bank of New
York and Dr. Daniel Schutzer of Citibank. Ms. Dahlgren's concepts are
hers alone and should not be construed as the opinions of the Federal
Reserve Bank of New York. What retained my attention in these two lectures was their synergy.

Chapter 2 will explain all terms discussed in this chapter: credit risk,
market risk, operations risk, financial asset, financial liability, fair value,
and more. The goal of this chapter is to make the reader aware of Federal
Reserve policies relative to the 1996 Market Risk Amendment, as well as
to provide an appreciation for how fast and how well tier-1 banks can
implement them.

2. ONGOING IMPROVEMENTS IN RISK CONTROL
AND REPORTING PRACTICES

Many of the basic concepts underpinning the way senior bank managers
look at comprehensive risk control have been elaborated by the lecturers
from the Federal Reserve, the Bank of England, the Banque de France,

and the Swiss National Bank—as well as the British Securities and Futures Authority and the Polish Securities Commission—at the First International Conference on Risk Management in the Banking Industry. It comes as no surprise that, as was revealed during the discussion period connected to these lectures, while some of the better-known commercial banks have in place a sophisticated risk-management system that they continue to develop and focus on, for a large number of financial institutions risk management is simply not there. Hence, for compliance purposes everything has to be done from scratch.

This has many implications, both in terms of how well the bank itself is being managed and in terms of supervision. To make things more complex, even if there is a system that reports on the positions taken by traders and quantifies exposure, this does not mean that the appropriate internal controls are in place.

One of the approaches the British Securities and Futures Authority uses to test what is in place in terms of risk management is to ask traders "If you were to price something you have not handled so far, what would you do?" A surprisingly small number of those questioned passes the test.

Similarly, a good way to evaluate how well a bank is prepared for recognizing exposure in its *trading book*[1] is a thorough audit of the systems and procedures that are in place in connection to marking-to-market. The principle is that, for risk-management reasons, dealers should mark their derivatives positions to market on at least a daily basis—though *intraday* is preferable.

In the better-managed banks most portfolios are marked-to-market daily, and some banks mark-to-market intraday, because they have the culture, the technology, and the models to do so. However, exotic portfolios are still marked-to-market weekly or even monthly. This may change because of the increasing appearance and use of *automatic pricing feeds,* particularly for liquid financial instruments. Ms. Dahlgren suggested that the Federal Reserve Bank of New York looks at pricing feeds as a means for improving the commercial bank's ability to obtain prices even for exotics.

All central bankers who lectured at the London Conference on Risk Management in the Banking Industry stated that there is plenty of room for improvement in internal controls, modeling methods, and ways and means of prudential supervision. An example is the establishment of policies and procedures distinguishing between portfolios that are marked daily and intraday and those that are marked at less than daily frequency.

---

1 For the definition of *trading book* and a description of its contents, see Chapter 2.

Another improvement, which in some countries (such as Germany, as of January 1997) has become the law of the land, is that when automatic pricing feeds are not practical or available a middle-office function should be responsible for pricing. The Bundesbank specifies that the middle office should operate quite separately from the front office, controlling the prices established at the front desk and exercising bankwide risk-management responsibilities.

An equally significant improvement over current practices discussed by the central bankers is going beyond marking-to-market by means of independent price testing, followed by a steady revaluation. This poses a number of requirements, which to be met, require a significant change in the bank's culture:

- Developing models and checking their accuracy.
- Assessing the adequacy of valuations under volatility and liquidity conditions.
- Verifying if gains and losses in trading positions reflect fair value and net present value.

A significant contribution was made by Sarah Dahlgren during the London conference through the emphasis placed on the calculation of risk with major clients. A distinction was made between the risk with major counterparties and the risk involved in loans and in trading with smaller parties. Credit risk and market risk with major counterparties should be integrated on an individual basis. By contrast, credit risk and market risk with small parties should be subject to statistical analysis.

No doubt this policy has been under development for some time at the Federal Reserve. The concept is a good one, but it is not yet widespread. What impressed me is that Sarah Dahlgren, of the Federal Reserve Bank of New York, made this statement in the morning, and in the afternoon of that same day Dr. Daniel Schutzer, of Citibank, presented a practical example on how it has been effectively implemented.

Such a policy has very important implications for the banking industry. First and foremost, only banks that are way ahead in technology can put it into practice. We will see what this means in Sections 7 to 9, which review the Citibank example.

Second, and just as important, the calculation of compound risk calls for homogeneous procedures. It is no longer possible that *market risk* is marked-to-model (as stipulated by the 1996 Market Risk Amendment) while *credit risk* remains inflexible at the 8 percent level, as it was set by the 1988 Capital Accord. We will see what could be done when in Section

9 we discuss dynamic credit analysis and in Section 10 J. P. Morgan's CreditMetrics is briefly introduced.

3. RETHINKING THE BASIC RISK-MANAGEMENT RESPONSIBILITIES

In Section 2 the statement was made that there is an evolution in the central banker's thinking regarding risk management, a trend most clearly seen in the Federal Reserve's approach. No doubt, this evolution has been influenced by the new culture in supervision reflected in the Market Risk Amendment. What is suprising is the speed with which the change in culture has come.

Take as an example the reference that for complex financial instruments and relations with important counterparties there should be internal verification by control area, with the goal being significant improvement in terms of strategy and structure concerning internal controls, and an increasing sophistication and divulging of pricing methods.

Since the advent of the Black–Scholes options pricing formula in 1972, pricing models are not new. What is new is the consistent application of pricing methodologies across products and business lines. Also very recent is the process of independent reevaluation of positions by means of marking-to-market or model daily, including fairly illiquid and exotic transactions.

Reading between the lines of what was said by the Federal Reserve and the other central bankers, in the coming years these reevaluations will occur with a greater frequency than ever before. But they should not benefit from *volatility smiles*[2] and they should be substantiated by audits. For this reason, it is necessary to have a *corporate memory facility* serving the valuation process.[3]

Internal controls must be characterized by a *solid structure* and exercised with *independence* and *authority*. Only then will they be able to assure that a number of internal supervisory responsibilities are carried out effectively.

What the Federal Reserve and other major central banks have been saying is that the best results are obtained when independent risk-management procedures are conducted by a control area of the bank using

---

2 A volatility smile is a bias towards lower volatility estimates, with the result being underpricing of instruments and transactions.

3 See D. N. Chorafas, *Risk Management* (London: Butterworths, 1992).

sophisticated models. Leading financial institutions now increasingly use the Monte Carlo method in connection to complex products. Also, people assigned to control the modeling process must not only analyze the model, its algorithms, and its variables but must:

- Evaluate the bank's internal controls.
- Assure that P&L manipulation is avoided.
- Guarantee there is an overall risk-management system solution.

Basic risk-control responsibilities include the development of risk-limit policies as well as the monitoring of transactions and positions for adherence to these policies—followed by corrective action. Equally important, the central bankers said, is the implementation of *stress scenarios* to do the following:

- Measure the impact of market conditions, however improbable.
- Evaluate what might cause market distortions and gaps.
- Identify volatility swings, liquidity squeezes, and disruptions of major relationships.

Practically all central bankers lecturing at the London conference said that an early warning system is needed to indicate what might reduce liquidity in the face of unfavorable market swings, lead to concentrated market-making, or result in credit exhaustion.

Quite similarly, market-risk measures, such as value at risk,[4] require the monitoring of variance between actual volatility of portfolio value and predicted future volatility. Failure to do so leads to the mispricing of financial instruments and the distortion of valuation systems used by front-desk, middle-office, and back-office personnel.

Just as vital to rigorous risk management, the central bankers suggested, is the development of reconciliation procedures. This is particularly important if different systems are used in the front desk and the middle office, and it is part of *model risk*—the risk that something is wrong with the model. In several cases, the pricing models developed and used by the front desk are more sophisticated than those in the middle office or the back office. Furthermore, independent risk management by the middle office has not yet clarified itself in terms of policy and structure.

The loss of £90 million ($150 million) by NatWest Markets, the fully owned subsidiary of the National Westminster Bank, which was announced mid-March 1997, dramatizes what is meant by this statement.

---

4 See Chapter 10.

Only rigorous risk management can enable the bank to make well-reasoned trading decisions.

Beyond this, the central bankers advised that the review and approval of pricing models and valuation systems used by front-desk and middle-office personnel, as well as the development of reconciliation procedures, should take place every time new products are introduced or computers and software change. This brings the need for independent model validation into the picture.

The overall strategy, Dahlgren suggested, should be one of increased scrutiny of calculations underlying modeling procedures and the models themselves, the implementation of rigorous controls for all crucial activities, and the establishment of schedules for periodic model reviews. Both the Fed and other central banks advise an enhanced use of model review triggers followed by corrective action.

4. EXAMINING MARKET-VALUATION METHODS

The principle discussed by central bankers during the March 1997 London conference is that derivatives portfolios should be valued based on midmarket levels, less specific adjustments. Midmarket levels can be obtained through the appropriate bid and ask. Valuation adjustments must account for expected future costs, such as unearned credit spread, investing and funding costs, closeouts, and other administrative costs.

If midmarket levels are the nearest thing to fair value, as defined by FASB 105 and FASB 119, the add-ons lead to net present value (NPV) calculations. Most of the top-tier banks have practiced NPV since the 1988 Capital Accord by the Basle Committee, which introduced the present value concept, but over time its implemention has become more sophisticated.

Even the more complex NPV models, however, do not erase the need to fine-tune valuation techniques. The forecast made by the Federal Reserve and other central banks during the London conference is that in the coming years we are going to see methods and models that are much more sophisticated than those recommended by the Washington-based Group of Thirty (G–30).

The way reserve bankers look at this issue is that there might be some distortions by valuing positions at bid/ask rather than at midmarket. Therefore, a bank's policies and procedures should clearly indicate which valuation methodology management considers appropriate for different types of transactions. This leads to the requirement of *model literacy,* which is a step beyond computer literacy.

Not only are tier-1 banks and bankers becoming aware of what model literacy implies, they are also beginning to take action. Model literacy leads to much greater sensitivity to high-frequency financial data (HFFD) streams[5]—a process already used by top-tier banks. "We see some intraday activity," said Sarah Dahlgren, "and we also see the desire to move marking to more automated systems."

But the assistant vice president of the Federal Reserve Bank of New York also added that the central bank sees some weaknesses in the lack of clear-cut policies and procedures by the top management of commercial banks. These typically relate to valuation adjustments in regard to:

- Market risk.
- Liquidity risk.
- Model risk.
- Credit costs.
- Administrative costs.

Awareness of credit costs and administrative costs is a novel issue. In the United States and Britain, a growing number of financial institutions are considering valuation adjustments to recognize the costs of transactions, for instance, valuation adjustments targeting recognition into income, more consistency across business units within the bank, and critical evaluation of appropriateness of reseves and reserve levels.

Not only are sound policies necessary for recording procedures and for public disclosure, but a higher degree of automation is needed because daily and intraday valuations cannot be done by hand. The leading information providers (IPs) are aware of this. Therefore, knowledgeable people expect to see a boom in *pricing feeds* from the IPs.

With regard to recording and reporting procedures by the banking industry, Sarah Dahlgren stated that the Fed recommends clear-cut time of valuation, even if instruments are traded on different locations. The Fed also expects an evolution to *intraday* financial series, including profit and loss (P&L). This fits well with a recent trend in American industry towards *virtual balance sheets.*[6]

In conclusion, as far as market-valuation methods are concerned, the Fed expects to see established policies and procedures that clearly indicate

5 D. N. Chorafas, *How to Understand and Use Mathematics for Derivatives,* Volume 1: *Understanding the Behavior of Markets* (London: Euromoney, 1995).

6 See *Business Week,* October 28, 1996, pp. 58–60.

which banks have a valid risk-management system and which do not. Though this development comes in stages, looking back over the last 10 years the careful analyst will appreciate that there have been quite significant developments that, in all likelihood, will continue. It is not only the money center banks that feel the need to improve their management; the central banks have also become quantitatively oriented.

5. PROVIDING A HIGHER LEVEL OF EXPERTISE

More sophisticated models and valuation methods require a higher level of professional expertise, both for development and for implementation. The background for such expertise should be polyvalent in terms of skills, and it should also be interdisciplinary. In terms of skill, the know-how possessed by rocket scientists is definitely required as a basic ingredient. But traders must also be closely involved in the development of models and methods, so that the resulting solutions are fundamental and solid.

Traders and other end users must be sure their activities are well understood by the rocket scientists. Management should guarantee that mathematical/analytical skills are available in sufficient number, enriched with appropriate experience.

Among the contributors to the restructuring of the risk-management system should be professionals who transact risks and information scientists responsible for data capture, processing, and interactive visualization of computational results. Fine-grain data streams must be manipulated, leading to the identification of patterns of risk.

Several of the central bankers and securities commissions' executives at the London conference suggested the need for an enhanced understanding and overall awareness of risk models by board members and senior managers. Without this, the policymakers of a financial institution have difficulty catching up with developments in derivatives and other instruments as they occur.

When they understand what is involved with derivatives, and only then, board members can be independent from the trader's expertise. Otherwise, board members are not able to control the traders. Model literacy at the board level is not unthinkable. The Fed has evidence of an increasing quality level in the senior management of financial institutions.

To reach this higher quality at the board or management level, banking industry executives, securities experts, and derivatives specialists, as well as risk controllers, have to work together. Areas that still need improvement include:

- A general consistency among international regulators and the rules they apply.
- Explicit policies on accountability based on more disclosure for risk management.

Not only should ways and means for controlling risk become a focal point of attention, so should solutions for identifying new revenue processes at a given level of confidence. To do this, the board must ensure that portfolio valuation is reasonable and exposure is properly reflected, leading to documented revenue with enough provisions to cover the risks being taken.

The good news in this connection is that among boards there is a reduced tolerance of *unexplained P&L*. In their lectures, the central bankers insisted on the fact that during the last three years, tier-1 banks have become very keen in identifying revenue sources and their associated exposure. They are asking that dealers measure the components of revenue, regularly and in sufficient detail to understand the sources of risk, and they have put increased emphasis not only on realized P&L but also on recognized gains and losses that will show up in the income statement at a future date.[7]

The central banks said that, among the better-managed commercial banks, boards look after diversification, targeting P&L attribution across a greater number of products. Chief executives see to it that senior management enhances its ability to identify P&L drivers and start to require an independent P&L evaluation procedure. This, however, is still an area needing further improvement.

Implied between the lines of what was said by central bankers at the London conference was that reserve institutions should look favorably at the processes described by the preceding paragraphs. A similar statement can be made regarding a policy of exercises that can help uncover areas of weakness and unpreparedness.

- Is top management and the risk-control group developing procedures to check exposure?
- Is the bank able to carry these procedures intraday? What does it learn from them?
- Does the bank have the technology to look for patterns? What do the patterns reveal that looks abnormal?
- How is top management judging normality? What is the bank's definition of *outliers?*

---

7 See also Chapter 6 on STRG by the British Accounting Standards Board.

Both central bankers and the executives from the securities commissions expressed the opinion that, as current evidence suggests, skilled management among a number of top-tier banks also asks increasingly similar critical questions in terms of the analysis of credits. Are our credits and our trades diversified or concentrated? Do we know them by product? Interest rate? Currency? Do we know our exposure by desk? By dealer? Do we have an above-normal number of weak credits? of sour derivatives?

6. BETTER ACCOUNTING PRACTICES, HOLDBACKS, AND DISCLOSURE

There is still a great deal to be done in terms of international harmonization of accounting standards for loans and for derivatives. During the London conference, this was not discussed much by the central bankers, but it was a focal point of the lecturers currently working on new accounting standards. However, the central bankers did refer to the growing need for a whole system of real-time accounting and auditing to track derivatives, manage risks, and achieve a consistency of income recognition.

Closely associated to accounting standards are the expected rewards to be derived from better management of exposure. If the risk is accounted for as a cost, changes in the value of risk and return would be visible at all levels and to all levels of management.

If the risk under control is marked-to-market with changes in value being taken to income, amounts due to and from counterparties would also be more manageable. This has led tier-1 banks to the policy of *integrating* credit risk and market risk in relation to important counterparties, as we will see in Section 7 with Citibank.

Significant areas for improvement exist within the framework of a new internal management accounting system, for instance, greater consistency across internationally active banks, explicit internal accounting policies that address marking-to-market and deferral accounting, new disclosure requirements where accounting standards don't allow marking-to-market, and the case of holdback reserves.

The way Ms. Dahlgren presented the issue, *holdback reserves* can be associated with transactions with a long time horizon. This is important because holdbacks are not released into income until the close of the transaction. Alternatively, holdback reserves could be released on an amortization schedule, their role being to cover the following:

- Market risk and liquidity risk.
- Counterparty risk (as discussed in Chapter 14).

- Model risk (inaccuracies and uncertainties).
- Credit cost (based on counterparty rating).
- Administrative costs.

Some of these costs were discussed in Section 4. The reason for repeating the reference is to underline that a new accounting system able to map market realities must reflect them. The market realities constitute the justification for holdback reserves.

The approach taken by central banks differs from one jurisdiction to the next. The Federal Reserve considers valuation reserves as separate from administrative costs. It also tries to restructure the holdback issue since some banks have up to 20 different references (and reasons) for such reserves.

The main argument here is that, although holdback reserves constitute a welcome capital cushion, they are also an element leading to reduced taxation because they are essentially deferred income. The balancing act must reflect the fact that while *excessive reserves* may result in underreporting earnings, *inadequate reserves* leave the bank exposed to market gyrations.

Therefore, Ms. Dahlgren suggests that the bank's risk-management authority look into holdbacks to assure they are reasonable, and that they follow homogeneous procedures and do not bias balance-sheet reporting.

This is no different from that of other central banks which also look at inducing more transparency by commercial banks on holdbacks, therefore to a factual and documented disclosure of reserves, and explanation of their reasons. This leads to rethinking rules and regulations regarding disclosures.

As everyone knows, disclosures are financial statements containing sufficient information about the transactions the bank enters into as well as their aftermaths. In practically all jurisdictions, their aim is to provide an understanding of:

- The purposes for which a transaction is undertaken.
- The financial extent of each transaction.
- The degree of risk involved.
- How the transaction must be accounted for and reported.

Disclosure to control authorities should be subject to harmonized accounting standards. This is an activity to which the Basle Committee addressed itself right after the 1996 Market Risk Amendment, including accounting policies and procedures, accounting standards, and norms for the analysis of positions at the balance sheet.

Not covered by this effort are the analysis of credit risk inherent in trading positions, and information about management's attitude about financial risks. Also not covered are, how instruments are used, how risks are monitored and controlled, and the extent of dealers' activities in connection to the financial instruments they are handling.

Here is how, during the London conference, Dahlgren characterized the ongoing evolution in disclosures: "We see progress, but it is not consistent across the board." Between the lines of this statement lies the fact that most progress is made in market risk disclosure but not in operations risk, liquidity risk, and risk resulting from deficient internal controls.

"What we see most often is lack of disclosure in regard to internal controls," the Fed advised, adding that, "We see a need to continue the improvements, including detail and clarity." The FDIC now requires (FDIC 112) that it is management's responsibility for attesting to internal controls (and the ensuing reporting requirements that stem from that legislation).

With the 1996 Market Risk Amendment, value at risk, stress analysis, simulation, and other models for market risk and its disclosures now seem to be well launched in a developmental sense. But as the following sections explain, there are reasons to look for enhanced disclosure across internationally active firms by rethinking credit risk, as well as integrating market risk and credit risk into one comprehensive figure.

7. INTEGRATING COUNTERPARTY RISK AND MARKET RISK: A CASE STUDY OF CITIBANK

With relationship banking and assets management, a financial institution usually adopts a long investment horizon. This is as true of its portfolio as it is of its customers, particularly those who are the most important in loans, trading, and asset management. It is therefore essential that the bank's management tries to decide two things:

- How much exposure the institution should have with each customer.
- How to steadily measure that exposure to provide for an effective control of risk.

This poses two problems, which so far, in the vast majority of cases, have been handled independently from one another: (1) assessing the creditworthiness of the counterparty in a quantitative sense and (2) quantifying the exposure taken with the counterparty both in loans and in trading.

The challenge comes from the fact that even if the forementioned two problems are treated as separate, there is evidence that in the bottom line they are tightly connected.

Assessing creditworthiness is not new. The procedure is based on careful analysis of a firm's financial health. This is primarily a human decision process, which over the last dozen years has been greatly assisted with expert systems.[8] The challenge lies in integration and in the requirements this implies. Banks that have been using expert systems for over a dozen years have found that through practice they are able to offer consistent results. These systems also help enforce corporate policy.

Another major contribution of knowledge engineering is that it effectively assists less experienced officers in making better decisions. At the same time, it relieves the best officers from routine tasks, allowing them to handle bigger loads more accurately and to concentrate on more difficult aspects of the business, including the analytical tasks confronting them. A good approach is to embed into the expert system's knowledge bank the creditworthiness factors. These typically include profits, cash flow, debt burden versus revenues, and a comparison with previous years in terms of consistency and growth problems.

Much more difficult is the quantification of intangibles. A very important element in judging counterparty risks is the perception of management capability, which should be integrated with the input received from industry analysis. General political and economic considerations also play an important role.

As Daniel Schutzer of Citibank emphasized in his lecture at the first international Conference on Risk Management in the Banking Industry, building and implementing expert systems for creditworthiness is a problem that can be nicely solved. But this is not necessarily the case with *exposure management,* which constitutes the new frontier.

In a consolidated sense, exposure management is a newer and more mathematically oriented activity than market risk and credit risk alone. A number of assumptions come into play. We typically use past market prices to evaluate a portfolio—or, more precisely, to determine a present valuation distribution, which is necessary to proceed through simulation. By means of simulation we evaluate the portfolio over many runs, typically 5,000 or more. The goal is to find worst-case loss if the counterparty

---

8 See D. N. Chorafas and H. Steinmann, *Expert Systems in Banking* (London: Macmillan, 1991).

forfeits. This computation takes place at the 99 percent or 99.9 percent level of confidence.

Unlike creditworthiness, which provides a single number, the simulation's result is repeated for different scenarios, permitting "what if" experimentation. For instance, how are our credits distributed with the counterparty? by type of commitment? by currency? by maturity? Other critical questions include:

- What is the pattern of our credits by credit officer? by branch? by foreign subsidiary?
- Is the same credit officer always dealing with the same counterparty?
- Is there an abnormal number of "weak credits"? Have they been detected?

Let me add another critical question for "what if" analysis, once discussed by another lecturer at the London conference. Are our credits diversified or concentrated in a few names? A British bank had a dealer who mostly traded with the same client company, a hotel chain. No one questioned this relationship until the hotel company went bust and the bank lost £30 million.

The knowledgeable reader will appreciate the sophistication demanded by credit-risk models once the management of credit exposure moves out of the 8 percent capital accord and into the simulation domain. The solution we see in this section is Citibank's internal model, but Section 10 briefly reviews CreditMetrics by J. P. Morgan.

If credit modeling is tough, an integrative approach to market risk and credit risk is even more challenging—but it is necessary. It is a matter of good internal controls to analyze credits for risk management, from examining why the same dealer follows a given pattern in trades with the same counterparty, to asking the following questions:

- Is the counterparty a steady user of OTC, or does it balance its pattern with exchange-traded products?
- Why is *this* counterparty dealing in billons of dollars in swaps?

In short, what is the net and gross exposure with this counterparty? Is the account executive aware of the exposure? What is the account executive doing about it? The target of an individualized exposure analysis is to find out worst-case loss if a given counterparty goes bankrupt. The goal of a global analytical exposure study is to compute the general worst case—and both are necessary.

8. CUSTOMER RELATIONSHIPS, EXPOSURE OVER TIME, AND PORTFOLIO PERFORMANCE

Citibank's Daniel Schutzer explained in his lecture during the London conference how rewarding it is for the function of the risk-management group to compute exposure over time. Both accuracy and precision are vital. There should be no averaging out, and "what if" scenarios must be performed in repeated steps:

- What if the German mark dissociates itself from other European currencies?
- What if interest rates rise by 1, 2, 5, or 10 basis points?

Accuracy requires that we simulate the portfolio on a per-contract basis, subsequently simulating the entire portfolio's performance. This provides better estimates of true exposure. On the other hand, analyzing a contract independently of all the other commitments could lead to inconsistent assumptions about customer relationships and changes in market prices.

Also, measuring exposure over time is a process that gives a great deal more information regarding the nature of the exposure, making better decisions feasible. Another reason for simulating the entire portfolio rather than computing only on a per-contract basis is that worst cases do not necessarily happen per contract. But they do take place in the larger portfolio context.

The other side of this argument is that portfolio-based calculations are computer-intensive. This is a technology issue. Therefore, while measuring exposure over time provides management with valuable information, it also requires the leading edge in technology—not Cobol programs and mainframes. The technology is available, but many banks don't know how to use it. As Daniel Schutzer underlined, opportunities exist for greatly improving portfolio performance and for significantly reducing risk taken by the bank.

There is simply no excuse for not having the necessary information—or, for that matter, the needed technology and methodology. The methodology can be gained by visiting, analyzing, and learning from what tier-1 correspondent banks are doing. Citibank is a good example.

The same recipe—visit, meet the people, and analyze—is valid in terms of collecting qualitative data about the counterparty. Quantitative insight can be gained through statistics and careful study of the accounts. The principle is this: "If you want me to extend credit to you, then I am entitled to know your people and to inspect your books."

For large accounts, clearance and hand-holding must be individualized and customized. For small companies and individuals, clearance is usually done through statistical sampling. This is precisely what Sarah

Dahlgren of the Federal Reserve said in her lecture, and I was pleasantly surprised to see how fast it has been implemented, following the 1996 Market Risk Amendment.

What is new with quantitative metrics in credit modeling is that besides the classical overall credit rating and exposure estimation, the bank must have access to the detailed trading history of the counterparty. This should not be applied informally and in reaction to events but in anticipation, proactively and analytically. Top-tier banks use transaction history to detect anomalies, leading to possible alerts, and adjust their exposure requirements. Such anomalies may be an unprecedented growth in trading exposure, an unusual transaction activity, greater use of margins, or speculative trades.

The principle is this: Look at the trading partner and try to comprehensively express both creditworthiness and market risk. The crucial questions are: How much exposure do we currently have? How much exposure can we afford to have? Do we wish to take that much more exposure with the same counterparty?

Citibank said that credit-risk and market-risk problems must be combined and the cumulative result brought to the attention of traders, senior credit officers, and relationship managers. Both top-management policies and knowledge-enriched systems are needed to provide links between the credit-risk and market-risk problems.

A major difference from past practices is that in the past such linkage was usually done by the relationship manager on an informal basis. Modeling can make the linkage more formal, integrating the following into a control framework:

- The counterparty's stability in a banking relationship.
- The pattern suggested by the counterparty's trading history.
- Potential business perspectives, with P&L projections at a given level of confidence.

This integration leads to a more sound policy on how to treat a counterparty. Simulation also helps to evaluate business linkages made over time, usually in an informal way. But the automation of complex relationships is possible only through sophisticated software.

A legitimate question for any bank is: Can we provide *agents*[9] able to automate the credit-risk/market-risk linkage? Knowledge artifacts can make an important contribution because, as Daniel Schutzer emphasized,

---

9 D. N. Chorafas, *Agent Technology Handbook* (New York: McGraw Hill, 1997).

expert systems have a knowledge bank enriched by the experts' know-how. They also learn by working online with their master because of ongoing knowledge acquisition.

Models also lead to mathematical optimization, which is what many banks are currently lacking. But, though necessary, algorithms and heuristics alone will not do the whole job. An integral part of what has just been explained is *database mining,* for instance, mining the counterparty's *trading history* and *loans history.* This can be done by asking well-focused questions:

- How is the client making his or her payments?
- Have there been delays and minor defaults?
- Are the client's trades getting more speculative?
- Has the change of treasurer changed the trading pattern?

In conclusion, Citibank has demonstrated that time-based measures significantly improve exposure management. As Daniel Schutzer has shown, through expert systems and simulation, risk is better controlled, and portfolio management improves. There is plenty of opportunity, but the question remains whether the bank for which the reader is working is able to capitalize on high technology.

9. DYNAMIC CREDIT ANALYSIS AS AN ALTERNATIVE TO THE 1988 CAPITAL ACCORD

The example we saw in Sections 7 and 8 is Citibank's, and it rests on two pillars: (1) the integration of credit risk and market risk by major counterparty and (2) a number of factors and processes to be considered in evaluating future business. *Dynamic credit analysis* looks at the client relationship over a number of years and is asking questions such as:

- In five years, should I handle the customer relationship as I do now?
- Will my current credit estimate be good for the next five years?
- Which is the most likely trading pattern by this counterparty over the next five years?

The answers to these questions will not be precise, but they may be accurate. They could, for instance, lead to the conclusion that we should perform a rating of the client *over time* because the current static rating is not the best estimate of creditworthiness over a five-year period.

The establishment of *time-based estimates* for loans and trading relationships is new in the banking business. The same is true about developing agents and expert systems to help in the linkage between creditworthiness and exposure management. Case histories can be of assistance, and case-based reasoning has given good results in banking. Knowledge artifacts help develop a more structured decision analysis, particularly in connection to database mining.

As Sections 7 and 8 have shown, knowledge engineering is a significant factor in developing and using sophisticated models, though not all banks really master this art. Also (contrary to dumb software), from agents to expert systems, knowledge artifacts must be specific to the job they execute.

If these prerequisites are fulfilled, a bank positions itself against the market forces, and at the same time, it is much better able to handle counterparty risk. Daniel Schutzer did not say so in his lecture at the London conference, but a good example of what more can be done through agents and simulation is the revamping of the 1988 Capital Adequacy accord.

Let me return to the fundamentals in order to explain what I mean by a post-mortem analysis of the 1988 accord by the Basle Committee of Banking Supervision. Since 1988 when this accord was made, the Basle capital adequacy rules have become a universal benchmark. As such, they influence the banks' decisions on the management of credit risk and on the capital required to face such risk.

But as every alert banker knows, the rules guiding management's hand in the control of risk evolve over time. During the last couple of years, among senior bankers there is building dissent regarding the 8 percent capital requirement. Many believe that the 1988 Capital Adequacy accord unfairly penalizes low-risk lending, while favoring much more dangerous types of business.

The essence of the Basle 8 percent capital adequacy formula, which has been well integrated into the European Union's Capital Adequacy Directive (CAD), was to require banks to hold a capital cushion. The decision that this should amount to at least 8 percent of their total assets was in essence a compromise—some banks did not even have a 5 percent cushion.

With the 1988 Basle Accord, assets (principally loans and securities) are weighted according to risk. Commercial loans are counted at their full value. Because mortgages are backed by physical property, they are weighted at 50 percent of the risk of a commercial loan. Debit from governments is counted at zero risk on the hypothesis that governments don't go bankrupt. Ten years ago, these credit-risk weightings were a step forward from earlier formulae used by bank regulators. Old standards typically measured capital as a percentage of total assets, with no weighting factors whatsoever.

The good news is that over the last decade at least some of the commercial banks have become much more sophisticated than they used to be. They can measure risk much more accurately than in the past. As a result, they look at the 1988 Capital Adequacy accord as high school stuff.

The problem is that an 8 percent flat rate makes no distinction between loans to a company rated by the international credit rating agencies as AAA and those to an A company, a BB company, or an owner-operated new venture. Nor did the 1988 formula offer the bank a credit for spreading its risks over a diversified portfolio of loans. As a result, the 1988 rule produces relatively crude formal capital requirements. This gives nothing more than a level ground of minimum capital standards.

By contrast, today we have the know-how and the technology to do better than that. The answer is *dynamic credit analysis* supported through simulation and agents, as has been explained in Sections 7 and 8. Fuzzy engineering, among other models, can be instrumental in dynamic credit analysis, as I have demonstrated in one of my previous books,[10] based on a real-life financial project.

10. CREDITMETRICS BY THE MORGAN BANK

Section 9 referred to the fact that there is dissent in regard to the 1988 Capital Adequacy accord. This dissent got louder after the 1996 Market Risk Amendment by the Basle Committee on Banking Supervision, which permitted, indeed promoted, the use of models for the calculation of value at risk.[11] Citibank is not alone in seeking a better solution. In April 1997, J. P. Morgan launched a model for measuring credit risk, known as CreditMetrics.[12]

"We Citibank," Dr. Daniel Schutzer suggested, "want to improve credit management effectiveness—whether or not this leads to change in the Basle formula." At least one central bank and some money center banks have calculated that *if* credit risk is modeled according to real exposure, accounting for diversification in counterparties, financial instruments maturities and other crucial risk factors, *then* the capital requirements will tend to be *about half* those imposed by the 8 percent ratio for credit risk by the 1988 Capital Accord.

---

10 See D. N. Chorafas, *Chaos Theory in the Financial Markets* (Chicago: Probus, 1994).
11 See Chapter 10.
12 See also in Chapter 15 the discussion of RiskMetrics by Morgan.

The bet with credit risk modeling efforts is that regulators may one day accept the modeling of credit risk as a substitute for the 8 percent Basle formula. The key is to be able to quantitatively integrate credit risk and market risk per client, obtaining as a result a compound figure of exposure. This makes the management of risk much better focused. At the same time, it avoids penalizing the financial institution that has diversified its risks while, relatively speaking, rewarding the banks that are not careful enough to avoid concentrating their risks.

Precisely for these reasons, both the credit risk/market risk integration per important client done by Citibank and the CreditMetrics model by J. P. Morgan aim to build a more rigorous approach to risk management. They do so by developing and using a quantitative standard for measuring credit exposure.

The aim is to qualify and quantify how much a bank stands to lose on a portfolio of credits that have very different characteristics. Once determined, this exposure derives the calculation of the level of capital the institution ought to hold in reserve, for the combined effects of credit risk and market risk.

CreditMetrics has a desktop version known as Credit Manager. Both models measure changes in portfolio value expressed as a function of upgrades and downgrades in counterparty credit rating, not just defaults. They also incorporate correlations among credit quality changes and make it possible to quantify the risk of overconcentration in terms of counterparties, instruments, and other factors.

Bank of America, UBS, SBC, BZW, Deutsche Morgan Grenfell, and the KMV Corporation are Morgan's partners in this effort. The target is to permit management to handle the bank's portfolios more accurately but also more actively. The deliverable is a comprehensive presentation of value at risk. This is critical for loans, trading analyses, and investment decisions.

Top-tier banks are increasingly eager to consolidate credit risk across the organization by means of a statement of value at risk expressed in function of credit quality. CreditMetrics and similar models integrate a number of instruments including:

- Loans to businesses
- Personal loans
- Other similar commitments
- Commercial credits and receivables
- Fixed income instruments
- Forwards, swaps, and other derivatives

CreditMetrics includes a simulator permitting the user to estimate the distribution of a credit portfolio. The model can be extended to include rating changes that result in crossing *default thresholds*.

Assuming that default likelihood is given by the credit rating, it is possible to work backward to thresholds in asset values delimiting default. Based on the Moody's and S&P rating systems, CreditMetrics utilizes transition matrices which include historically estimated one-year default metrics. The drivers of the model are:

- Default likelihood, and
- Probability of credit rating migration.

Both Moody's and S&P publish a one-year transition matrix, which is essentially a square matrix of probabilities. In Moody's case this ranges from Aaa, to Caa and default. In S&P's, it ranges from AAA to CCC and default.

CreditMetrics works on the hypothesis that default correlations actually exist, and investigates the possibility of modeling joint rating changes through historical rating change data. Actual rating and default correlations can be derived from rating agency data. These provide an objective measure of actual experience, but suffer from sparce sample sets.

Alternatively can be used bond spread correlations, which give a fairly objective measure of actual correlation in bond values and, by extension, credit quality. These, however, suffer from data quality problems, particularly in connection to low-quality issuers.

A third alternative is equity price correlations. Equity prices offer forward-looking, efficient market information as well as the advantage of good time series. The disadvantage is that they require much more computing time to yield reliable information about likely credit quality correlations.

Another disadvantage seen by a number of regulators, commercial bankers, and financial analysts stems from the fear that there might be over-reliance on advanced statistical techniques. This could lead people toward avoiding the use of their own judgment—and therefore, if it happens, it will be counterproductive.

Simulation and knowledge engineering will only be accepted by regulators if they are convinced that commercial bankers know what they are doing. True enough, the dual impact of new regulation and losses on lending over the last dozen years have been instrumental in inducing bankers to apply a greater focus on credit risk. However, not all do so with the same vigor.

An approach to the dynamic credit-risk analysis, discussed in Section 9, can be strengthened by market pressure to deliver good value to the bank's shareholders by producing an acceptable return on the capital the institution employs. Better organization also plays a crucial role, as many of the most successful international banks are delegating responsibility for credit to individual business units, requiring at the same time an increased transparency. At the holding level, management demands that each unit produces a return on the capital allocated to it that meets the group's criteria. Independent business units that cannot do so are sold or closed, with all this means in personal accountability.

Every one of the references I just made has an impact on the conversion of senior management of financial institutions toward more dynamic organizational structures as well as experimentation and modeling. Most banks are aware of the distortions a blunt application of the Basle 8 percent formula could bring to business decisions, further pronouncing the emphasis on modeling credit risk. Examples are solutions such as the following:

- Risk-adjusted return on capital (RAROC).
- Return on economic capital (ROEC).
- Return on risk capital (RORC).[13]
- Risk-adjusted return on risk-adjusted capital (RARORAC).
- Actuarial Credit Risk Accounting (ACRA).

Another potent factor in this transition is the profit motive with market risk, requiring a much more sophisticated control of exposure through eigenmodels. This sees to it that a bank dynamically manages its capital requirements, as opposed to using the level ground formula applicable to everyone.

At the First International Conference on Risk Management in the Banking Industry, the executive of the Bank of England said that, according to a recent study, the so-called standard method for market risk by the Basle Committee requires up to seven times more capital than eigenmodels do. The 1996 Market Risk Amendment stipulates that any bank wishing to use eigenmodels must multiply by three the amount of capital its models say it needs. Even so, given the above one-to-seven ratio, the use of models helps reduce capital requirements by more than half.

In a similar vein, Barclays, a bank that has made great progress in using risk-adjusted measurements for calculating its treasury and its invest-

---

13 See D. N. Chorafas, *Managing Derivatives Risk* (Burr Ridge, IL: Irwin Professional Publishing, 1996).

ment banking business, finds through models that it needs a capital base less than half of that set by the Basle Committee. However, its business banking division requires more capital than the 8 percent rule stipulates.

The sense of these references, and of the entire chapter, is that banks who are versatile in mathematical modeling and experimentation can smooth out differences in capital requirements for credit risk at a group level. Therefore, banks can allocate more capital than formally required to their business loans portfolio or to other activities in order to compensate for the extra risk these businesses involve. But they cannot allocate less than the rules dictate to the overall credit-risk target.

By contrast, as we will see in Chapters 2 to 16, the 1996 Market Risk Amendment offers a far more flexible and controllable frame of reference regarding exposure. The integration of credit risk and market risk must stand on a similar dynamic platform. Therefore, it would be a good exercise for the reader to think of the Market Risk Amendment as the forerunner of new credit-risk rules.

Management's Responsibility with Market Risk and Credit Risk

1. INTRODUCTION

Management responsibility in regard to market risk, credit risk, operations risk, legal risk, and all other risks the bank takes is to assure the profitability and survival of the financial institution—in spite of the exposure the bank assumes. This requires much more than knowing risk in global figures. Detail is very important. So is appreciating:

- The relationship between equity capital set aside to cover risks, its allocation between product lines, and risk-related returns expected from trades and investments.
- The amount of exposure taken by instrument, client, interest rate, and currency—as well as country and region in which the bank operates.

Classically, issues connected to supervision, regulations, and the reporting procedures associated with them have been established by national supervisory authorities, for instance, in the United States the Federal Reserve Board, the Office of the Controller of the Currency (OCC) of the Treasury Department, and the Federal Deposit Insurance Corporation (FDIC). Acceptable reporting practices are also detailed by authorized bodies, such as the Financial Accounting Standards Board (FASB) in the United States and the Accounting Standards Board (ASB) in Britain.

But globalization, deregulation, and technology have made the financial industry transnational. It is therefore increasingly important to have a coordination of regulations and of reporting practices and procedures at least among the Group of Ten (G–10) countries. This coordination is done by the Basle Committee on Banking Supervision at the Bank for International Settlements (BIS).[1] The first important piece of transborder regulation by the Basle Committee was the Capital Accord of 1988. Its goal was to provide adequate reserves for credit risk. Market risk was addressed by the Basle Committee's 1996 Market Risk Amendment, whose provisions become mandatory at the end of 1997.

This book looks into the Market Risk Amendment, the requirements it imposes, and what it implies for the banking industry. But before doing so, and in order to make its provisions comprehensible, this chapter will address the notions underpinning financial instruments, their present value, and their risks as well as the difference between the trading book and the banking book.

2. DEALING IN FINANCIAL INSTRUMENTS AND VALUING FINANCIAL ASSETS

A *financial instrument* is any contract that results in both a financial asset for one party and a financial liability for another. In the broad sense of the term, financial instruments include primary products, such as receivables and payables; equity securities and debt obligations; and derivatives: options, futures, forwards, interest-rate swaps, currency swaps, and others.

In FASB Statements 105 and 107, the definition of *financial instrument* excludes several types of commodity-based derivatives contracts, such as futures contracts for oil products. By contrast, it includes other commodity contracts, for example, most oil swaps because they must be settled in cash.

The concept of a *financial asset* is more focused. It may be cash, a contractual right to receive cash or another financial asset from a counterparty (at terms potentially favorable), or the possession of equity of another entity.

Each country has its own rules and directives governing financial instruments and associated reporting practices. For instance, according to the bank accounts directive of the European Union (EU), regulatory reporting on assets includes cash in hand, treasury bills, loans and

---

1 We will talk much more about the Basle Committee in Chapter 3, in connection to the 1996 Market Risk Amendment.

advances to credit institutions, loans and advances to other customers, debt securities, equities in portfolios, participating interests, and shares in affiliates as well as derivative financial products and other assets.

Correspondingly, a *financial liability* is any liability that is a contractual obligation. For instance, the Financial Accounting Standards Board defines a financial liability as the delivery of cash or another financial asset to a counterparty or the exchange of financial instruments with another entity under conditions that are potentially unfavorable. The EU bank accounts directive includes the following as financial liabilities:

- Amounts owed to credit institutions.
- Amounts owed to customers.
- Debts evidenced by certificates.
- Subordinate liabilities.
- Equities.
- Derivatives.

Whether it concerns assets or liabilities, *dealing* is the activity of standing ready to trade, by buying or selling, for the dealer's own account. This process helps provide liquidity to the market. The term *trading purposes* includes activities reported in a trading account and measured at *fair value*. Such activity ends up in gains and losses recognized in earnings.

FASB Statement 121 defines the fair value of an asset as the amount at which this asset could be bought or sold in a current transaction between willing parties in a case other than forced liquidation. In this sense, current *market value* is fair value. In Section 6, we will talk about replacement value and net present value. Dealers hold contracts with customers for debt, equities, derivatives, and other financial instruments for indefinite periods. They enter into contracts to manage the risks arising from assets and liabilities in their trading account, not only to make immediate profits.

Several definitions underpin the concept of *financial risk*. One of the best definitions is a *hazard* because of the exposure the bank has taken. A good way of approaching the issue of exposure is to relate it to the expected reward from the positions that are open if these positions originate from any of the following:

- Loans being given.
- Bonds issued or bought money.
- Interest-rate instruments.
- Currency-exchange operations.

- Equity positions.
- Derivative products.
- Commodity prices.

In this sense, risk can be appreciated as a potential negative change in conceived and projected reward(s), as a consequence of an unforeseen, unexpected, or uncontrollable market event. The bank has locked itself into that event because of past decisions and actions.

Each one of the channels of business the bank enters, as well as each operation it executes, has its own risk characteristics. Most product lines influence one another, as shown in Figure 2–1. Loans get securitized; they can also be given in one or more currencies. Currencies are bought and sold spot or forward. Bonds are underwritten at different interest rates and (often) in different currencies. Interest-rate derivatives are used to swap interest-rate risk out of the banking book, among other reasons.

When risks can be measured, they can be managed. Therefore, the first important responsibility of the bank's management is to identify and measure the risks, tracking them in *real time*. This is a business that must be not only properly analyzed and planned, but also done steadily and in a rigorous manner, in full observance of rules and regulations.

FIGURE 2–1

Financial Instruments Become Complex Because They Can Be Combined in Many Ways

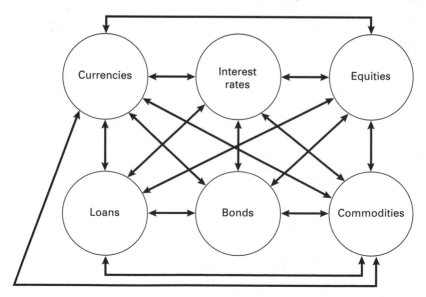

Rules and regulations don't need to say, and they rarely if ever do, how risk will be kept under control. All they say is how exposure should be reported to the supervisory authorities by bank management. This includes credit risk, market risk, and operations risk.

Credit risk has to do with default and bankruptcy of the counterparty and is the better-known type of risk because it is the more classical. Our loans or other claims may not be repaid or be only partly repaid because of credit risk, country risk, or other reasons.

Market risk is not one but a whole family of exposures primarily concerned with price volatility and liquidity prevailing in the financial market. Market risk is connected to interest rates, currency-exchange rates, commodity prices, and other events influencing modern financial instruments. Market risk is magnified by derivative products because of their gearing.

Operation risk constitutes a fairly recent concept, which because of its nature, can be more under management control than market risk. Operation risk is diversified, ranging from board decisions to internal controls. It includes technology risk, which is the bank's own doing, but also risks resulting from the payments and settlements system, which is typically operated by independent agencies.

In all these cases, and in many others, there is plenty of management responsibility for risk control, starting with metrics and proceeding with the determination of the capital needed to cover risks. This responsibility includes the dynamic allocation of capital to individual risk categories, the establishment and follow-up of limits per instrument class, and the corrective action necessary to right the balances.

3. THE NOTION OF RISK CAPITAL AND OF WORST CASE

In the sense it has been used in Section 2, *risk* is the chance of injury, damage, or loss. In banking and insurance, risk is expressed quantitatively as the *degree* or *probability* of loss, but it can also be given in absolute numbers. The probability of a hazardous outcome is a function of the type of loss it represents, the market factors creating the hazard, and the risk involved in a transaction.

Examples of *the type of loss that it represents* are credit risk, with loans, but also interest-rate risk with loans; credit line(s) given to a customer; paper profits connected to derivative instruments and other commodities; or life, fire, and accident insurance.

The *market factors* creating the hazard may be due to unexpected fluctuations in exchange rates, major changes in interest rates, default risk due to exceptionally adverse economic conditions, or the particular situation in which a counterparty finds itself because of rules and regulations beyond its control.

Every financial transaction has some amount of *risk,* but some have more than others. A major risk may result because of the type of person or company with whom the bank does business as well as the nature of the commercial or financial operation being transacted.

Statistically, risk is the measure of variance around an expected value or outcome.[2] Its calculation involves some uncertainty, but it also provides a basis for the prognostication of an *outcome* in a financial transaction which we know is probable but not certain. Therefore, we are willing to pay the cost of this uncertainty.

Generally, risk and opportunity (or return) are related because there is no significant gain without our ability to overcome adversity. Such adversity results from a situation, position, or choice that involves possible loss or danger.

An implied loss or danger might be contained, or it might be substantial because risk events do not have a well-defined or sure outcome. Hence, loans, investments, and derivatives deals should not be calculated on face value but on the basis of a *risk-adjusted return on capital* (RAROC). This is a term developed by Dr. Carmine Vona of Bankers Trust in connection to a mathematical model for risk evaluation.

Theoretically, all of the equity of a financial institution is available to cover risks. Practically, if all of the equity were actually depleted by losses, this would result in liquidation. Therefore, there are legal equity requirements that specify the capital adequacy for risk reasons—the balance of the equity being essential for continuing the current volume of a bank's business.

Since the 1988 Capital Adequacy accord by the Basle Committee, banks have been very careful about meeting capital adequacy requirements, particularly in tier-1 capital. Figure 2–2 presents statistics in the public domain from the Union Bank of Switzerland, covering the period from 1991 to 1995. Tier-1 capital is shareholders' equity and retained earnings (see also Section 6 in Chapter 2).

Prudent management sees to it that, from an operational standpoint, only part of a financial institution's equity is employed to cover risks into which the bank has intentionally entered. This part of the equity can be seen as having been set aside to cover exposure across all risk classes. Hence, it constitutes *risk capital.*

---

2 D. N. Chorafas, *How to Understand and Use Mathematics for Derivatives,* Volume 2 (London: Euromoney, 1995).

FIGURE   2-2

Union Bank of Switzerland: Basle Committee Capital
Adequacy Ratio at Group Level

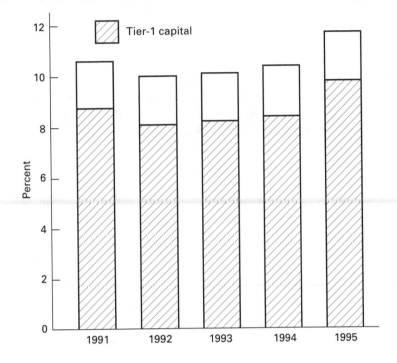

Risk capital must be distinguished from that part of equity that constitutes legal or residual requirements. No bank wants to lose its risk capital; but because of transacting business, part of the equity must be available to cover entrepreneurial risks.

As explained in the chapter introduction, risk capital is directly connected to expected return. Any transaction into which the bank enters has
an expected benefit. Therefore, for all practical purposes, risk capital is
conditioned by two basic factors:

- The nature of the business activity and latent risks (potential
  losses) related to it.
- How much equity can be set aside to cover possible losses in a
  worst-case situation.

Seen in this dual light, risk capital constitutes a frame of reference
consisting of the allocation of money to cover potential risks taken by the

bank across risk categories. Risk and return calculation should permit an assessment of profit potential related to each risk class—hence of expected gains.

An intriguing concept in modern financial analysis is the *worst case,* which factors into the equation the most pessimistic estimate of future risk potential. Fundamentally, worst case represents the greatest projected change in market prices—currencies, interest rates, default probabilities, and so on—that has to be taken into account.

Worst-case scenarios serve to convert risk capital into the overall *limits* for each risk category and are usually calculated, for each risk category, on the basis of goals and of experience. The goals are set by the board of management. The experience is contributed by everyone in the line of command—and it should be qualitatively and quantitatively expressed.

Risk factors based on worst-case scenarios essentially help produce estimates reflecting a conservative policy. Therefore, some financial analysts chose to use metrics, which, rather than targeting the worst case, look at *expected risk.*

The usual thinking is that market risk characterizes the trading book and that credit risk characterizes the banking book. The concept of expected risk applies to both books. But before going further on this issue it is proper to examine what a bank's trading book and banking book contain.

4. THE TRADING BOOK AND THE BANKING BOOK

The 1996 Market Risk Amendment by the Basle Committee targets the trading book. The division of a bank's assets and liabilities between the two books is not new. The problem, however, is that no two banks exactly agree on the details of what should go in each book. Part of the reason is that the concepts underpinning the dividing line are in full evolution. Figure 2–3 gives a birds-eye view of the principal contents of the trading book and banking book. These contents are based on the most frequent responses I received in my research and don't necessarily satisfy every bank's definition.

The *trading book* has assets bought and held principally for selling them in the near term. It comprises all debt securities, including fixed income, as well as shares and other variable-yield securities that are marketable. These do not form part of fixed assets and are held with the aim of achieving a short-term transaction profit.

If what is included in the trading book is strictly short-term assets and liabilities, then only a small part of the derivative financial instruments in the bank's possession should be registered in it. This is not, however, the

FIGURE 2–3

Characteristics of the Trading Book and the Banking Book

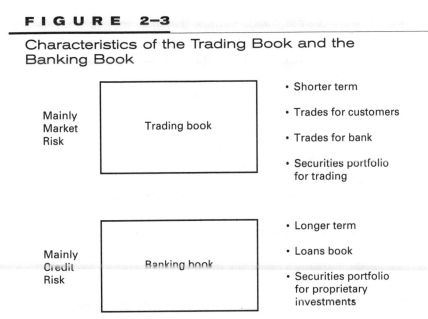

Mainly
Market
Risk

Trading book

- Shorter term
- Trades for customers
- Trades for bank
- Securities portfolio for trading

Mainly
Credit
Risk

Banking book

- Longer term
- Loans book
- Securities portfolio for proprietary investments

case. All derivatives are in the trading book, making its definition some-what elastic.

One of the disagreements among central banks, and by extension commercial banks, concerns the limits of the short term. The French believe that short term should mean less than six months. I subscribe to this definition, but once more underline that it does not apply to deriva-tives. Swaps and other less liquid assets are held in the trading book over long periods. They are not part of the active buying and selling done for profits on short-term price differences.

In FASB Statement 115, Accounting for Certain Investments in Debt and Equity Securities, *trading securities* are defined as "securities that are bought and held principally for the purpose of selling them in the near term" and therefore are held for only a short period of time. In connection to derivative financial instruments, FASB Statement 119:

Permits positions in swaps and other less liquid customized deriva-tives to be maintained for longer periods.

Requires reporting them as part of the trading portfolio: in the income statement when profits and losses have been realized, and in *comprehensive income*[3] when recognized but not yet realized.

---

3 Statement of Total Recognized Gains and Losses (STRGL) in the United Kingdom.

It is therefore correct to keep in mind that there are exceptions to the statement that the trading book contains only short-term assets and liabilities, subject to active and frequent buying and selling. Items held with the objective of generating profits on short-term differences in price are part of the trading book, but they are not its exclusive contents.

While activities connected to derivative financial instruments are generally characterized as concerning products held or issued for trading purposes, longer-held positions may also fall under this concept. We will return to this notion later.

The contents of the *banking book* include deposits, loans, and the investment portfolio of the financial institution. The latter comprises all debt securities, including fixed-income, as well as shares and other variable-yield instruments. These are held as fixed assets, and a bank's policy typically looks at them as longer-term investment instruments.

In classical banking theory, the main risk involved in loans is credit risk. But because loans are usually made at fixed interest rates and there is volatility in interest rates, the loans book may also contain a significant amount of market risk.

Banks are increasingly concerned about this fact and, as Figure 2–4 shows, a recent policy among major commercial banks is to weed this market risk out of their banking book, switching it into their trading book. They do so through an internal swap.

F I G U R E   2–4

Weeding Interest-Rate Risk out of the Banking Book for Internal Accounting Reasons

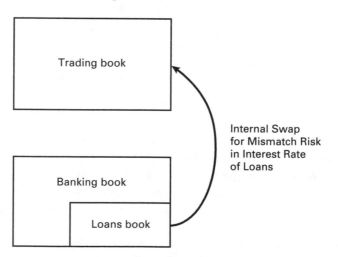

Trading book

Internal Swap
for Mismatch Risk
in Interest Rate
of Loans

Banking book

Loans book

The Bank of England welcomes this practice of internal swaps for management accounting reasons, but not for regulatory reporting. This brings attention to the distinction between general accounting and internal accounting management information system (IAMIS).

In regard to a bank's internal risk-management procedures, the calculation of risk capital is an internal matter. This can be done effectively if and when management knows credit risk and market risk in a timely and accurate manner. For this reason, the bank must be in a position to value the content of its trading book and banking book by *marking-to-market* or *marking-to-model.*

In conclusion, internal management accounting and reporting to the central bank for regulatory reasons are two different issues. As we saw in the preceding example, an internal swap done to weed interest-rate risk out of the banking book is admissible for management accounting purposes. But it is not acceptable for central bank supervision.

The Market Risk Amendment by the Basle Committee outlines regulatory reporting for reasons of bank supervision. However, the treatment of the trading book that it specifies, and the concept of value-at-risk, can also make valuable contributions to internal management accounting. How to implement the value-at-risk system is explained in Part Two.

5. POSITION RISK AND THE ESTABLISHMENT OF A RISK-MANAGEMENT CULTURE

Tier-1 banks base their leadership in risk management on two concepts: the computation of risk per transaction, instrument, counterparty, and place of operation, down to the trader level; and the development of powerful mathematical models in order to make this feasible. Neither is necessarily part of the more widely held current banking culture.

The first and foremost issue to comprehend regarding the control of exposure is the need to appreciate (and calculate) *position risk* (also known as *inventory risk*) for every position in the financial institution's *trading book* and *banking book*—whether or not this is required by the regulators.

In the majority of banks worldwide, position risk is either not being managed because they lack both the concept and the tools, or it is taken into account only rudimentarily, which does not provide a valid basis for control.

Yet, position risk is a vital statistic, and it should definitely become a moving gear of the risk-management system. In terms of definition, position risk is assessed as the *sensitivity* to changes in market parameters of the position in each transaction, counterparty account, and instrument, such as currency, interest rate, or equity.[4]

The punctual establishment and follow-up of position risk and the implementation of interactive computational finance permit the management of the bank to work on a decentralized basis within allocated limits. By means of worst-case evaluation, the limits for each risk class can be converted into risk capital or derived from the risk capital allotted. This allows not only real-time reporting, but also experimentation on assumed risks. It facilitates the comparability of results derived from the management of exposure per risk class—doing so in relation to the capital earmarked to cover these exposures.

Position risk, which is essentially market risk, should be complemented by *default risk*. In the large majority of banks, the adversity resulting from default risk is taken into consideration only in cases of realized loss. There are historical reasons for this.

Classically, risk-related income has been included in the different types of business without a kind of insurance for credit risk. Until the 1996 Market Risk Amendment by the Basle Committee, in the majority of cases market risk did not even come into the picture in terms of needed reserves.

This policy is definitely wrong on both counts. Because default risk is a permanent feature of all financial transactions, it is correct to account for it through a *virtual insurance policy*. This means accounting for default risk by means of a risk premium to be deducted from product-related income.

Once approved through a decision by the board, this strategy becomes fairly simple to implement. In a growing number of banks, standard risk premium rates are centrally determined per credit-rating category and country rating. This is done by the division responsible for counterparty risk. The currently established credit-risk rating forms the basis for provisions when the deal is made.

Typically, if the risk premium determined by those responsible for counterparty and country risks is equal to or lower than the centrally stipulated risk premium, the premium rates are applied. If it is higher, the rate should be higher, with the extra amount going to a reinsurance fund.

On this concept rests the risk-adjusted return on capital method to which reference has been made in Section 3. At the same time, in the internal accounting management information system of the bank, the extra

---

4 See also Chapter 14, The Assessment of Counterparty Risk, Interest-Rate Risk, Currency Risk, Country Risk, and Equity Risk.

premium should be credited to the account of those responsible for counterparty risk, and bad debt failures, whether in loans or in derivatives, should be debited to that same account.

This is part of the system of balances connected to rigorous controls. IAMIS is a long-term proposition, and the risk premium actually applied must be valid for the entire period of a transaction.

Default-risk premiums should be delivered by the operative units responsible for the products to those responsible for risks. With a risk premium, the department responsible for risks takes over the risk of the parties responsible for the products. This is comparable to what I have called a reinsurance.

The party responsible for risk is also responsible for the creation of provisions equal to the sum of required risk premiums. In the case of default risks, it becomes possible to establish a risk position comparable with the position risks in the form of an aggregation of risk premium.

Exposure can be computed within the credit-rating class or country class. The volume of trades is multiplied by the corresponding risk premium rate per annum, accounting for the time to maturity. Then we can integrate default risks in the overall risk-management system.

The ideas outlined in this section were not specified by the Basle Committee. They are a distillation of the best practices I have observed among commercial banks that participated in this research.

The reason I bring these practices to the reader's attention is that they constitute some of the mechanics of the implementation of the Market Risk Amendment, which we examine in detail in Chapters 3, 4, and 5. Commercial banks must develop their own solutions. The Basle Committee has not yet outlined the accounting infrastructure that is necessary; though, as Dr. Frederik C. Musch, the secretary general, has confirmed, "Accounting issues will in the future be receiving additional attention as a newly established accounting group starts its deliberations."[5]

6. CREDIT EQUIVALENCE, REPLACEMENT VALUE, AND NET PRESENT VALUE

Fair value, credit equivalence, replacement value, net present value, accruals, lower of cost or market, value-at-risk, capital-at-risk, and risk-adjusted return on capital are concepts that, though they differ from one another, have in common the aim of providing a factual and documented

---

5 In his letter of October 25, 1996.

valuation method for position risk. I have chosen to address these issues in Chapter 2, at least in their fundamentals, because I see them as prerequisites to appreciating what the Market Risk Amendment stipulates.

Let me put it this way. The 1988 Capital Accord by the Basle Committee of Banking supervision brought into banking practice the concepts of replacement value, fair value, and present value (PV). These were subsequently enriched by net present value (NPV), which is equal to PV plus add-ons.

New concepts and processes have been introduced by the 1996 Market Risk Amendment by the Basle Committee. These are marking-to-model, value at risk/parametric approach (VAR/P), value at risk/simulation (VAR/S),[6] stress analysis, 99 percent confidence level, backtesting, and the green/yellow/red zones for the classification of model-derived results.

Once these notions became understood and accepted by the banking industry—and this happened in record time—some central banks softly advanced further requirements that can make supervision much more effective. A good example is the integration of credit risk and market risk for each important counterparty. The Federal Reserve of New York is one example regarding the promotion of this approach. Citibank is an example of a tier-1 commercial bank that was happy to oblige.

For internal management accounting reasons, the more sophisticated financial institutions produced risk-management eigenmodels that go well beyond what the Basle Committee advised. Examples are loans-equivalent exposure (equal to notional principal amount divided by a demodulator), the calculation of intrinsic value based on cash flow, capital at risk (CAR), and earnings at risk (EAR).

Fair value was defined in Section 2. The concept of *credit equivalence* makes it possible to compare claims arising from various instruments. However, to be really of value, the approach we choose should take into account the period of utilization of the instrument and the credit rating of the counterparty. These elements must be contained in the *risk premium rate.*

A one-day credit-equivalent loan expresses current exposure. Its principal components are *replacement value* (RV) and an add-on factor. Many banks take as RV the *present value* of a financial transaction, which tends to coincide with fair value, as defined by FASB. Other banks, however, do not follow this approach. Instead, they calculate PV to represent the costs

---

6 See Part Two.

at present time for the replacement of this transaction in the event of default. We will further explore this issue.

The add-on factor, which is chosen in connection to RV, is an additional charge for presently *recognized future changes* in the replacement value. Possible future changes in the replacement value may be due to the volatility of market prices in currency-exchange rates, interest rates, or other factors that are not presently recognized.

An additional add-on clause may be necessary because of uncertainties in the financial market. Some banks (correctly, to my judgment) make a distinction between two add-on factors in calculating the risk premium rate over and above credit equivalence:

- Add-on for recognized future changes.
- Add-on for future changes not presently recognized.

While the exact procedures vary between banks, the trend is that a model for replacement value will account for everything related to instruments, business types, and clients. Such a model should be calculated by a uniform method throughout the bank; otherwise, the results will not be comparable from one branch or subsidiary to another.

Alternatively, the bank may choose a slightly different method: the *net present value*. The NPV is calculated as the sum of the *present market value* or, in the case of some instruments such as forward contracts, of *future cash flows*. In this computation, the risk premiums for default risk and deferred earnings—as well as the cash account—should be taken into account.

Whether the risk premium rate is considered separately or in conjunction with future cash flows, some basic principles need to be observed. For instance, it is necessary to account for the fact that risk increases variably with *time to maturity* according to the credit-rating category. There is a higher risk premium rate in the case of longer time to maturity of the loan. A similar statement is true about derivatives.

Figure 2–5 shows how a major financial institution classifies its derivatives contracts into three time periods, and shows the financial instrument dominating each one of them. Different banks are using different approaches.

Another approach is the *accruals method* used in conjunction with different financial products, including, for example, interest rates in foreign-exchange operations. Many banks favor the accruals method. In the interest business, this involves the discounted future margins on fixed-interest assets

F I G U R E   2–5

Contract Volume of Derivatives at a Major Financial Institution

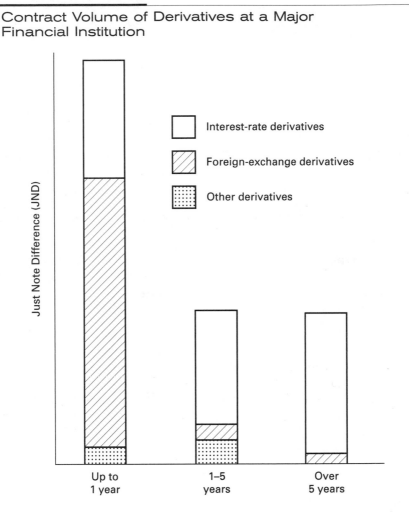

and liabilities. In currency exchange (foreign exchange) this includes the sum of accrued foreign-currency interest.

In foreign exchange (forex), this position is closed through an internal transaction with currency trading, as nontrading lines are typically not permitted to maintain currency positions. The result from internal hedges in the interest business is offset with the foreign-exchange result from interest earned and interest paid.

Many merchant banks apply the *lower of cost or market value,* including funding costs. Several commercial banks, particularly continental

European, follow the same approach with equities. The difference between the purchase price of equities, including funding costs, and higher market value becomes effective only upon sale of these equities.

Value-at-risk is extensively discussed (and defined in detail, including its two alternative notions) in Chapters 10 and 11. In a nutshell, it is the expected loss from an adverse market movement with a specific probability over a period of time.

After replacement value and add-ons—or some other method—have been computed for the trading book, derivatives book, loans book, and any other transactions concerning counterparties, the time comes for the calculation of total credit exposure. This should be comprehensive of counterparty risk exposures in the following:

- Bonds
- Equities
- Repo agreements
- Underwriting
- Merchant banking

Such exposures must be added to those managed in connection to trading lines in order to provide an integrated picture for counterparty risks. My advice is that the chief risk management officer (CRMO) calculate the entire exposure per counterparty upon inclusion of all relative exposures by activity sector. The results are a matter of interest well beyond senior management.

Through interactive computational finance, such results should be available at least daily and, even better, *intraday*. For trading lines, the results must be available at any time, with gains and losses calculated monthly or, better, more frequently. When this is done, there will be many surprises.

Even five years ago, intraday financial time series and the concept of *microseasonality* were not popular. But this has radically changed. Not only the more technologically advanced commercial banks but also information providers and stock exchanges now exploit intraday data streams. NASDAQ is on the Internet, and it provides intraday statistics.[7]

Using Microsoft's back-office product family, with its Internet development tools, in just nine weeks NASDAQ put together a web site that earned a Magellan four-star rating. This is the highest award given in the industry for significant technological advances.

---

7 See also Chapter 16.

With over a million hits each day, NASDAQ's web site proves to be both versatile and current. It assures up-to-the-minute market summary information and quotes as immediate as regulations allow. The microseasonality provided by NASDAQ's Internet site is quite comprehesive and focuses on microseasonality.

By exploiting this microseasonality, top-tier banks see to it that traders and executives responsible for product lines are presented with documented evidence on unexpected events and/or undesired large exposures. My research also demonstrates that there is a connection between notional principal amount involved in derivatives trades and replacement cost. We will return to this issue when we talk of the attention that should be paid to the *notional principal amount.*

7. A BANKERS ASSOCIATION LOOKS AT THE MARKET RISK AMENDMENT

There is one more issue we should examine before looking in detail at the 1996 Market Risk Amendment by the Basle Committee. How are the bankers and their associations looking to the new regulation and to the practice of marking-to-model?

In the opinion of Paul Chisnall of the British Bankers Association, the Market Risk Amendment, with its marking-to-market and marking-to-model directives, is an open-minded approach gaining favor with European bankers. Already, 8 out of 15 member states of the European Union (EU) accept the new regulation and do their best to apply it. The same is true of the United States and Canada.

During the London meeting, the British Bankers Association stressed that in the United Kingdom the majority of senior bankers now believe that derivatives in the trading book should be marked-to-market or marked-to-model, whether they are held for trading or hedging.

The challenge is to establish a realistic market price, and to do so through a generally valid methodology that can be replicated. In February 1996, the British Bankers Association published a statement outlining this opinion.

The more general issue regarding the valuation of the trading book, and the associated measures to be established, is now the object of a recommendation to the European Parliament. The leading concept regarding methodology generally follows FASB Statement 119, which gives the latitude to develop models and implement them.

"Imposing a unique model will be synonymous to applying a lower standard than if the banks develop models by themselves," said an executive of the British Bankers Association during our meeting in London. Not only are universal models for risk management not available, but different banks have different values. I have heard the same argument from senior American bankers.

It is important that each bank and its regulators satisfy themselves that the model(s) being developed and used meet(s) minimum requirements of accuracy in terms of exposure. During our meeting, Chisnall explained that the British Bankers Association has no competence to develop pricing models for its members, but that it can help develop the framework; the Association can also assist in getting the banks together to share information and know-how.

In terms of marking-to-model, I have found no difference in opinion between the regulators and the commercial bankers. There is, however, a difference of opinion between the Accounting Standards Board and the British Bankers Association concerning how to integrate balance sheet and off-balance sheet items. "We have two concerns," said Paul Chisnall:

> The approach proposed by the British Bankers Association is to have the trading book marked-to-market. This follows the Basle Committee directive and it meets with general agreement.
>
> To the contrary, regarding the non-trading book the Association proposes using the historical accrual method after transferring market risk into the trading book.

As we will see in subsequent chapters, this transfer of risk between banking book and trading book will take place through internal interest-rate swaps. The goal is to weed out of the loans book the fixed interest-rate risk. Therefore, in the opinion of the British bankers, it is no longer necessary for financial institutions to apply current value to the banking book. Beneath this procedure is a dual goal:

- Switching exposure.
- Generating a rate of return.

Switching exposure makes the banking book market-risk neutral. What mainly remains is credit risk. The market risk that exists today in the loans book of the typical bank is due to *source of funding,* and it originates from the fact that in a decentralized organization the different business units are free to lobby for funding their functions.

The mismatch risk in loans and fixed-income securities is real. It has wrecked the savings and loans in the United States and many banks in other countries. But by moving interest-rate risk out of the banking book, its embedded market risk is transferred to the trading book—where it must be marked-to-market or marked-to-model.

The British bankers have discussed this internal swaps approach with the European Accounting Standards Board and with the EU Commission, in Brussels. There are no decisions yet on this matter, and a key question asked by practically everyone is whether the Americans will come on board.

When, starting with Chapter 3, we talk of the 1996 Market Risk Amendment, we should keep in mind that it addresses the trading book—not the banking book. The financial industry still has some way to go until all assets and liabilities are marked-to-market or marked-to-model. Even so, what has been accomplished so far by the Basle Committee is a big step forward.

FASB Statements 105, 107, and 119 will be soon substituted by a new FAS comprehensive of all clauses concerning the reporting of realized profit and loss in the body of the financial statement—or recognized but not yet realized gains and losses reported in the accompanying notes.

This new FAS was originally scheduled for realease in the second quarter of 1997. In this case, it would have been fully reflected in this book. FASB says that the new FAS is now sheduled for release at the end of August 1997, or thereafter.

C H A P T E R   3

The 1996 Market Risk Amendment by the Basle Committee on Banking Supervision

1. INTRODUCTION

Top-of-the-line financial institutions have already implemented, or are in the process of implementing, risk-management policies. They have instituted systems and procedures that, to a significant extent, fulfill the requirements outlined in the Market Risk Amendment. But the majority of banks are way behind, and some institutions don't even have the basics necessary to control market exposure. They lack a homogneous way to measure market risk, and they don't have well-established global standards in place.

This led the Basle Committee on Banking Supervision, Bank for International Settlements (BIS), to take the initiative. I personally view this as most welcome. It is an initiative that puts to the test (and to rest) old concepts about risk. It also complements the Capital Accord of 1988, by the Basle Committee.

As a brief background, the Basle Committee on Banking Supervision was established in 1975 by the governors of central banks of the Group of Ten (G–10)[1] countries and other authorities with responsibility for the supervision of banks. About five years after the Capital Accord of 1988 and in recognition of the fact that it addressed only *credit risk,* in April 1993 the Basle Committee issued for comment by banks and financial market participants a package of supervisory proposals concerning *market risk.*

---

1 The United States, United Kingdom, Germany, Japan, France, Italy, and Canada (which constitute the group of Seven [G–7]), plus Switzerland, Sweden, Holland, Belgium, and Luxembourg (as an observer)—12 in all, as noted in Chapter 1.

Elaborated on by representatives of banking supervisory authorities, this first document suggested the application of algorithmic solutions and procedural approaches that could lead to *capital charges* because of market risks incurred by banks. It also advanced the concept of *netting.* In April 1995, after the first responses were received, the document was redefined, refined, and reissued.

The concept of capital charges to be taken because of market risk has in its background the possibility of losses in on-balance sheet and off-balance sheet positions[2] arising from movements in market prices. Added reserves are meant to face this challenge. The Market Risk Amendment was finalized in mid-January 1996. It took effect immediately, but capital standards for market risk will be implemented by the G–10 supervisory authorities by the end of 1997.

The Basle Committee has left a considerable amount of flexibility to the central bank of each of the G–10 countries in terms of the control of market risk. But while national rules and regulations concerning supervision continue to apply, the Amendment provides a common frame of reference, which in turn assures a reasonable level of homogeneity among national regulatory policies.

2. TARGETING THE RISKS OF THE TRADING BOOK RATHER THAN OF THE BANKING BOOK

As explained in Chapter 1, a bank's trading book includes its proprietary positions in financial instruments intentionally held for short-term dealings or resale. Alternatively, such products may be taken on by the bank for benefits in the short term from expected differences in their buying and selling prices.

Chapter 1 outlined what enters into the bank's trading book, as well as the time horizon of these instruments. To make this chapter self-contained, and to refresh the reader's memory, Figure 3–1 includes the main groups of instruments that constitute the trading book.

As has already been explained, a financial institution's banking book contrasts to the trading book in the sense that it is medium- to long-term. The banking book typically contains loans of all sorts—mortgages, personal loans, business loans, longer-term corporate loans—and is often

---

2 See D. N. Chorafas and H. Steinmann. *Off-Balance Sheet Financial Instruments* (Chicago: Probus, 1994).

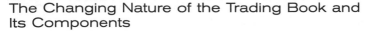

F I G U R E   3–1

The Changing Nature of the Trading Book and
Its Components

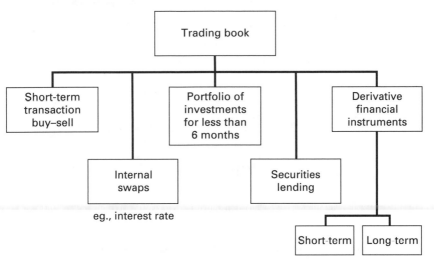

referred to as a *loans book.* It also includes the portfolio of proprietary securities in stocks and bonds.

The point has also been made that not all banks have a clear-cut dichotomy in terms of the contents of each book. Nor are commercial banks following exactly the same terminology. In principle, transactions should transit through the trading book, which apart from being short-term also plays the role of the *memorial,* invented by Luca Paciolo in 1494.[3]

One of the problems with definitions is that even if they are more or less generally accepted, the concepts underpinning them don't necessarily become universal rules. Also, the borderline between short- and medium-term (therefore the trading book and the banking book) can be fuzzy, as there are some degrees of freedom in establishing the short-term limits, and banks tend to exploit them.

The G–10 central bankers will be well-advised to settle in a comprehensive and unambiguous manner the limits separating trading book and banking book. After all, they all address the transactions happening and positions taken in the same financial markets outlined in Figure 3–2.

---

3 See D. N. Chorafas, *Financial Models and Simulation* (London: Macmillan, 1995).

F I G U R E   3-2

Three Financial Markets That Work in Unison and
Complement One Another

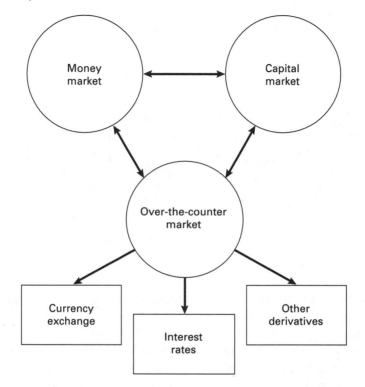

For the purpose of our discussion, the trading book will be taken as comprising all securities and derivatives with short-term maturity marked-to-market—except that in some countries, regulations oblige banks to value at market some instruments not falling into the trading book.[4] At the same time, other regulators require that trading activities must be accounted for at book value or at the lower of cost and market.

Given these differences in definitions and in reporting practices, the trading book and its valuation are not exactly the same from one country to another. Other differences are those dividing the banking book from the portfolio of the bank's own holdings in securities and other assets.

The 1996 Market Risk Amendment by the Basle Committee does not enter into these differences, leaving it to national regulators to iron out

---

4 The differences existing in transborder regulations will be discussed in Chapters 4 and 5.

matters. Cornerstone to the Amendment, in connection to the trading book, is the concept of marking-to-model its positions if marking-to-market proves impractical. Marking-to-model is fully explained in Part Two.

Also included in the Market Risk Amendment is the concept of *backtesting*.[5] This is done by means of post-mortem comparisons between results obtained through modeling and actual market performance in assets pricing.

The bank should regularly conduct backtesting, comparing the risk measures generated by models. Connected to the results of modeling are the green, yellow, and red zones discussed in Chapter 3. Marking-to-model has become necessary because the largest parts of derivatives deals are over the counter (OTC). OTC positions typically have no active market and therefore cannot be marked-to-market according to established banking practice.

To assure that no abusive switching aimed at minimizing charges occurs, the Market Risk Amendment foresees that central banks will be vigilant about preventing gains trading in securities not being marked-to-market. Supervisory authorities will also take precautions against cherry picking between the standardized approach by BIS (which essentially is netting) and the banks' own, proprietary models (eigenmodels) for risk management.

The Amendment also stipulates that positions of less than wholly owned subsidiaries will be subject to generally accepted accounting principles in the country where the parent bank is supervised. In a way similar to that regarding credit risk, capital requirements for market risk are to apply on a global consolidated basis.

As the Basle Committee apptly suggests, in order to effectively control risk, an independent review of risk-measurement systems should be carried out regularly in the bank's internal auditing. Besides risk auditing, senior management must be actively involved in risk control and must review the daily or ad hoc reports produced by the independent risk control unit. In other words, risk-measurement models must be closely integrated in the day-to-day management of the bank, and the results of experimentation on exposure should be not only reviewed by senior management but also reflected in policies and limits set by the board of directors.

In order to avoid conflicts of interest, the bank should have an independent risk-control unit responsible for design and implementation of

---

5 See also Chapter 4.

risk-management systems and procedures regarding internal controls. Sound management practice would see to it that this unit reports directly to senior management and that it is given the authority to evaluate relationships between measures of risk exposure and trading limits.

3. BASLE COMMITTEE, EUROPEAN UNION, AND THE AMENDMENT OF THE CAPITAL ADEQUACY DIRECTIVE

The 1996 Market Risk Amendment is not the first piece of regulation targeting Market Risk. Published in 1993, the Capital Adequacy Directive (CAD) of the European Union did not make reference to marking-to-model. But it did require marking-to-market for reasons of market risk.

However, after the 1996 Market Risk Amendment by the Basle Committee on Banking Supervision, the EU executive added a clause to CAD promoting models at the discretion of central banks. With this modification, known as the Amsterdam Accord, after the city in which it was signed, the two directives on market risk have converged.

In 1993, when it was issued, the Capital Adequacy Directive did not address any other approach to risk management than the so-called standard method. But the work being done by the Basel Committee brought into evidence the need to incorporate eigenmodels into the rules for bank supervision.

Under pressure by some of the countries of the EU, and most particularly by American money-center banks operating in Europe (which are masters in proprietary models), Brussels finally gave its accord to the use of internal algorithms for marking-to-model. In terms of eigenmodels, it has been specified that their use is subject to control by the supervisory authorities. While models can serve in the computation of most risks, this does not necessarily include all risks; the eigenmodels cannot be used to calculate the proper funds necessary for counterparty settlement.

In the broad sense of the term, *proper funds* include tier-3 type capital, and they must cover at any moment the highest amount indicated by the calculations being made. The Commission Bancaire of Banque de France, for instance, while it accepts eigenmodels—and indeed it assists commercial banks in developing them—it requires that periodically risk be computed and reported by the Basle Committee's standard method.

A different way of looking at this issue is that while all central banks of the G–10 countries have adopted marking-to-model, some have added a twist. In the example just mentioned, the Banque de France requires that commercial and investment banks using *value-at-risk* (VAR) models[6] twice per year in official reporting to the supervisory authorities employ both the standard method of BIS and VAR. Furthermore, banks must follow the maximum capital adequacy requirement for market risk, specified by either of the two methods.

In other words, day-to-day risk control can be done by bank management, for internal accounting purposes, by marking-to-model. But for reporting reasons, calculations must be based on both the standard method and the eigenmodels.

Keeping in mind the amendment of the EU Capital Adequacy Directive as well as the fact that the Market Risk Amendment by the Basle Committee evolved considerably between its first draft in 1993 and its release in 1996, we can see that new regulations have gone through a period of incubation. The effort to control market risk came in steps rather than one shot. The fact that more than one supranational authority got involved with market risk is positive.

There is plenty of scope in international collaboration, as Figure 3–3 suggests.

Marking-to-market or marking-to-model the trading book is now a process well under way, and there is no turning back. Furthermore, on the horizon looms the need for marking-to-model, or to marking-to-market, the banking book. When it comes, this will most likely happen in two steps. The first step will probably be for internal accounting management information system (IAMIS) purposes.

Most of the knowledgeable people who participated in my research believe that this risk-oriented information in connection to the banking book should be provided to management. Most likely, the regulation addressing the next step in marking the banking book will see the light by the end of this decade or thereafter. Hence, the second step is marking the banking book for supervisory reporting reasons will come after the year 2000.

Some central banks believe that because there is no precedent and there are many unknowns, for the time being marking-to-market or marking-to-model the banking book might provide more inconvenience than advantages. Nevertheless, the Basle Committee continues to work on this matter. One of the current projects under way is how to handle fixed interest-rate risk. No firm solutions have come forward so far.

It would be wise to pay attention to the fact that while they are necessary and helpful, research projects undertaken by the Basle Committee

---

6 See Chapter 10.

F I G U R E   3–3

The Role Played by International Collaboration of Central Bankers Can Be Expressed in a Three-Dimensional Frame of Reference

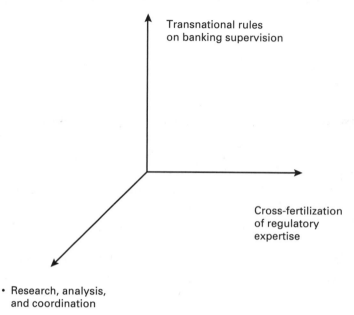

Transnational rules
on banking supervision

Cross-fertilization
of regulatory
expertise

- Research, analysis,
  and coordination

- Closing of gaps in
  model's armory

and the European Union have aftermaths. They are obliging the banks to develop the tools that are needed, and will be needed, for the control of risk—and not all banks are up to this task. While some commercial banks are now going well beyond the rules advanced by the central banks of the G–10 and the Basle Committee, others are hopelessly behind because of the many years they did not change their culture from vanilla banking.

Personally, I consider the most important part of the new regulation the methodology that has been introduced in terms of prudential management of market risk. The direction is now clear, though it is still too early to have a definite opinion on how this system would work. There are organizational as well as technical challenges, as we will see in Section 4.

With the possible exception of the New York Federal Reserve Board, none of the G–10 central banks that have entered into the 1996 Market Risk Amendment have experience with the new rules of prudential management and supervision of market risk. Only three to four years from now, there will be enough evidence to permit a critical analysis of the method that has been followed and of the obtained results.

4. PROCEDURAL ISSUES CONNECTED TO THE MARKET RISK AMENDMENT, INCLUDING MATURITY AND DURATION

Let me begin with the statement that many of the existing definitions in the banking industry are parochial, and this makes a homogeneous approach to market risk evaluation difficult. Also, the fact that the Basle Committee's Market Risk Amendment of January 1996 does not address positions in the banking book creates some problems.

One of the problems is *organizational*. Because, as has been already explained in Section 2, not all financial institutions clearly differentiate the same way between books, unavoidably there is the temptation to switch some items between trading book and banking book—where, for the time being, no marking-to-model is required for reporting reasons.

The 1996 Market Risk Amendment does not address issues of an internal organizational nature. It only notes that in some banks trading activities are carried out in quite separate units from normal banking business. This leaves some degrees of freedom in identifying those transactions falling within the trading book.

Another one of the problems is *technical*. Commercial banks need rocket scientists to develop tests and implement eigenmodels.[7] The same is true of central banks for supervisory reasons. The technical issue comes from the fact that at present there are few of them available, though this siutation is improving.

Central banks are moving faster than commercial banks in acquiring such skills. The Federal Reserve of Boston, for example, currently employs a dozen rocket scientists. Their skills are largely used in risk-management models and in prognosis—not in writing software that a computer vendor or software publisher should be able to provide.

A third problem with market-risk management concerns regulatory reporting because of evolving practices. Chapter 2 made reference to the fact that some of the larger banks in the United Kingdom make an internal interest-rate swap to weed mismatch risk out of their banking book

---

7 See D. N. Chorafas, *Rocket Scientists in Banking* (London: Lafferty Publications, 1996).

and into their trading book—where it will be marked-to-market or marked-to-model. It was also said that the Bank of England welcomes this practice in connection with the commercial bank's internal management accounting system but not for regulatory reporting purposes.

These are some of the issues that still need to be addressed by the Basle Committee in order to promote universal practices in risk control. The Amendment, however, has strong points as it currently stands, starting with the fact that it is quite comprehensive in regard to the type of transactions that should be targeted and the way in which they should be handled. The main frame of reference consists of four domains where market risk definitely applies:

1. Interest rates
2. Foreign exchange
3. Equity positions
4. Commodities risk

A separate section sets out methods for measuring price risk in connection to options.

From the day on which commitments are undertaken, all transactions, including forward sales and purchases, should be included in the calculation of capital requirements to compensate for market risk. Supervisory authorities will assure there is no window dressing on specific dates in such reporting.

The Amendment stipulates that capital charges for currency-exchange risk and commodities risk will apply to the bank's total currency and commodity positions, subject to some discretion. Two processes are necessary to calculate capital requirements for foreign-exchange risk[8]:

1. The measurement of exposure in a single currency position.
2. The measurement of risks inherent in a bank's mix of long and short positions in different currencies.

Gold is to be dealt with as a foreign-exchange position rather than a commodity because its volatility is more in line with currency exchange. When gold is part of a forward contract, any interest rate of foreign-currency exposure from the other leg must be reported.

The Amendment also weights the fact that banks incur an increasing amount of interest-rate risk, which, other things being equal, is greater the

8 Computational methods are discussed in Chapter 4.

longer the maturity of the contracts into which it enters. The Basle Committee Amendment offers two alternative methods for measurement: *maturity* and *duration*. Under the maturity approach, long or short positions in debt securities and other sources of interest-rate exposure are slotted into a maturity ladder composed of 13 to 15 time bands. With the duration method, banks can more accurately measure their general market risk by separately computing the price sensitivity of each position through Macauley's duration algorithm.[9]

Duration is the result of a calculation based on the timing of future cash flows. It can be considered as the life in years of a notional zero-coupon bond whose fair value would change by the same amount as the real bond or portfolio in response to a change in market interest rates.

The usefulness of information about the duration of a portfolio or bond might be enhanced by also disclosing the convexity. *Convexity* is the extent to which duration itself changes as prices change. Tier-1 financial institutions know well how to use convexity to sharpen management decisions.

Banks should welcome the regulators' flexibility in regard to the method used. While this tends to make comparisons between banks difficult—which is the homogeneity problem mentioned on several occasions—the choice of method helps differentiate the more sophisticated bank from the others. In this specific example, the duration approach is the more advanced.

5. GENERAL MARKET RISK AND SPECIFIC RISK

The 1996 Market Risk Amendment distinguishes a *specific market risk* in the case that an individual debt, equity, or other security moves differently than the general market in terms of day-to-day trading. This has to be measured and reported.

In a way that follows reporting practice in the United States, the Amendment says there is a link between specific risk and the standard method proposed by BIS. Let's therefore define *general market risk* and *specific risk.*

General market risk is relatively easy to understand. In the case of interest rates, for example, a general risk results from the change in the yield curve because of higher interest rates than those contracted, or from the change characterizing the stock market index.

---

9 See D. N. Chorafas, *Financial Models and Simulation* (London: Macmillan, 1995).

Specific market risk is connected to the instrument and/or the issuer of the instrument. In the case of interest rates, different issuers and different instruments have a different spread. This spread is defined by the market on the basis of the information it possesses on that particular instrument and/or the rating of the issuer.

Other factors can influence the spread as well, for instance, the possibility of a corner, whereby a small number of players affect the market, or liquidity reasons relating to the type of the instrument and independent of the issuer.

In terms of volatility, the specific risk can be significantly greater than general market risk because it is influenced by so many factors involving unknowns. A good example is *event risk,* such as a leveraged buyout (LBO), which can happen at any moment. Therefore tier-1 banks have developed expertise on how to simulate event risk.

In the Market Risk Amendment, the factors that represent specific risk are not outlined in detail. The Amendment does, however, say that the specific risk being computed by the eigenmodel must be equal to or greater than 50 percent of the specific risk calculated by the standard method.

Another clause of the Market Risk Amendment addresses repo deals. For supervisory purposes, a security that is the subject of a lending or repurchase agreement will be treated as if it were still owned by its lender.

The Amendment has chosen not to treat *anticipatory hedges,* which are made in connection to future positions, or cash flow, that are not yet recognized in the balance sheet. For instance, a hedge of interest-rate risk is expected to occur on future lending or borrowing transactions.

Key to the use of anticipatory hedges is the assurance that the anticipated transactions will arise. This is an issue connected to management intent and prognostication. What it essentially means is that the transaction is part of an established business activity, with a counterparty unrelated to the bank doing the anticipatory hedge.

The essence of management intent is that the financial institution plans to create a hedge for anticipated exposure. In this case, the maturity, interest rate, and other factors of the hedged position—as well as the choice of the hedging instrument in an anticipatory sense—are highly correlated. The crucial point is that there is internal evidence on the intent of the hedge. But, at the same time, management intent is not evidence—a reason why many accounting standards boards don't accept simple "intent."

Typically, in everyday banking practice, recognized gains or losses of anticipatory hedges are deferred and included in the profit and loss account—when they are realized. This is done in conformity with, and over the period when, such gains and losses transactions are reflected in the income statement.

In terms of futures, options, and forwards in connection to commodities, the Market Risk Amendment advises banks to guard against risk arising when the short position falls due before the long position. The Amendment suggests that shortage of *liquidity* in some markets can aggravate this discrepancy. Therefore, liquidity should be part of the evaluation procedure.

The Basle Committee takes notice that banks may incur risks in interest rates, foreign exchange, commodities, and equities outside of their trading activities. The Market Risk Amendment, however, advises that the issue of explicit capital charges for price risk in such positions has not yet been addressed.

Swaps must be handled as two notional positions in securities with relevant maturities. To compute positions in the maturity or duration ladder, banks with large swaps books may use alternative formulae for the swaps into which they enter.

It is furthermore underlined that in certain cases there are circumstances where banks use derivatives such as swaps to hedge positions in their banking book. Instruments that theoretically qualify to be part of the trading book but practically are not part of it are excluded from the current market risk measures. According to the Amendment, such trades become subject to credit-risk capital requirements. This, however, constitutes a fairly major loophole, which will no doubt be exploited by many banks and eventually will be closed.

Finally, some risks are deliberately left out. For instance, traded mortgage securities and mortgage derivative products are not considered by the Market Risk Amendment because they have certain unique characteristics due to the risk of repayment. It must be admitted that it is far from easy to define all products in modern banking and to gain general acceptance of such definitions.

6. ADDING MARKET RISK TO THE CREDIT-RISK RULES OF THE 1988 CAPITAL ACCORD

One of the merits of the Market Risk Amendment is that it did not come out of the blue, nor was it written as a self-contained document. It is a directive that closely connects to capital agreements already in existence.

In this way, it supplements the 1988 Capital Accord, which has also been elaborated on by the Basle Committee.

The January 1996 market-risk document essentially confirms the April 1995 proposal by the Basle Committee to allow banks to issue short-term subordinated debt subject to a lock-in clause. Implemented at national discretion, this is *three-tier capital* rephrased to meet a part of the bank's market risk. Eligible capital will consist of the following:

1. Shareholders' equity and retained earnings, which is tier-1.
2. Supplementary capital, or tier-2, as defined in the 1988 Accord.
3. Short-term subordinated debt, which is tier-3.

However, tier-3 capital is now subject to a number of conditions explained in the Amendment. For all practical purposes, it is only eligible to cover market risk, including foreign-exchange risk and commodities risk—if the national supervisory authority judges this doable.

Insofar as the overall limits in the 1988 Accord are not breached, tier-2 assets may be substituted for tier-3 up to the preestablished limit of 250 percent. But tier-3 capital is subject to the *lock-in* provision, which stipulates that neither interest nor principal may be paid if such payment means that the bank's overall capital would then amount to less than its minimum capital requirement.

The Amendment registers the opinion expressed by central bankers from a number of G–10 member countries that the principle in the Accord about tier-1 capital calculated on a consolidated basis should represent at least half of total eligible capital to be retained. Because, however, other member countries objected to this clause, the Committee decided that the decision whether or not to apply such a floor should be left to national central bank discretion. I am not enthused about this compromise.

An algorithm is advanced in the Amendment to assist in calculating a bank's overall capital ratio. This algorithm provides an explicit numerical link between credit risk and market risk by multiplying the measure of market risk by 12.5 and adding the resulting figure to the sum of risk-weighted assets compiled for credit-risk purposes. The 12.5 multiplier is the reciprocal of the minimum capital ratio of 8 percent, from the 1988 Capital Accord.

The numerator of this calculation will be the whole of the bank's tier-1 capital. Its tier 2 capital will be considered under the limits imposed in the 1988 Accord. Plus, at national supervisory authority discretion, tier-3 capital elements will be added—if they can be used to support market risk.

Unused but eligible tier-3 capital may be reported separately. In other words, the Committee is favoring *capital requirements* over position limits as the appropriate instrument for international convergence in the treatment of market risk. But it also believes that limits can have an appropriate place in supervisory activities.

This approach has interesting characteristics because it could be algorithmically expressed. Hence, it is interactively confrontable. No doubt, it will take much more fine-tuning to develop from it a model that can be operational in the dual sense of a structured and of an unstructured information environment, as suggested in Figure 3–4. At the bottom of the pyramid is largely credit risk, which banks more or less know how to manage. At the top are exotic derivatives instruments so new and customized that very little experience exists in keeping exposure under control.

The Market Risk Amendment tries to combine the dynamic requirements of the coming years with those more static requirements that already exist. Individual national supervisors can maintain limits where they judge it appropriate to do so. Whenever and wherever they are applied, these limits can be used both as a means of imposing absolute ceilings on banks' exposures and for reinforcing *internal controls*.

I consider this emphasis on reinforcing internal control standards and procedures absolutely necessary. The same is true of the attention paid to the treatment of specific risk, which was discussed in Section 5.

Risk-management models must be elaborated in a way that makes it possible to capture elements of specific risk, for example, by modeling each equity as an individual risk factor. The Committee's opinion is, however, that some key elements of specific risk—such as *event* or *default* risk—are generally not adequately represented by internal models existing at various banks.

This shortcoming has led the Basle Committee to the conclusion that there needs to be a prudential cushion to address the fact that experience is still developing in terms of modeling and that a financial industry consensus has not yet emerged about how best to model the more stochastic elements of specific risk.

Even with these limitations, the objective of using the Market Risk Amendment to complement the 1988 Capital Accord is well-served. The market risk perspectives that opened in January 1996 can be instrumental in providing an *explicit capital cushion* for the price risks to which banks are exposed. This is true even if, at this stage, only market risks arising from trading activities have been treated.

FIGURE 3-4

The Information Environment within Which a Bank
Operates Is Structured at the Bottom and
Unstructured at the Top

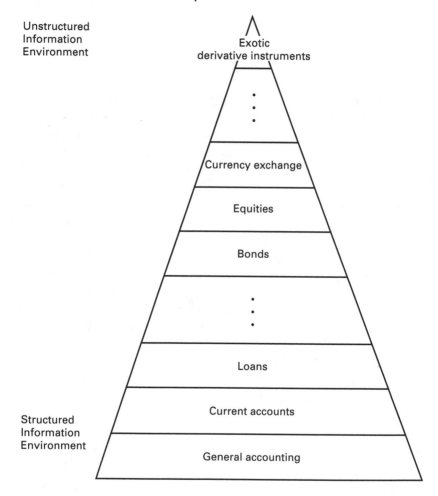

In conclusion, a discipline is now imposed in regard to tougher capital requirements. This is seen as an important step in strengthening the soundness and stability of the international banking system and of financial markets at large.[10]

---

10 See also the discussion on systemic risk in Chapter 9.

Part of the Market Risk Amendment is a set of qualitative standards for risk management, particularly important to banks basing their capital requirements on the results of eigenmodels—because they legitimize the concept of interactive computational finance. The Basel Committee has also underlined the need for top management coinvolvement on risk matters, at commercial banks—which is an excellent suggestion.

7. THE BASLE COMMITTEE ADVISES THAT A BANK'S TOP MANAGEMENT MUST BE ACTIVELY INVOLVED IN RISK CONTROL

While practically all banks have a risk-management system of sorts, generally it suffers from three major deficiencies. First, it is too oriented toward loans and credit risk, leaving out of serious consideration market risk, legal risk, settlement risk, operations risk, and other risks. Therefore, it does not respond to the characteristics specified by the Market Risk Amendment of the Basle Committee.

The second deficiency is more serious and is of an organizational nature. It starts with the fact that most current risk systems for loans have not coinvolved top management in their design, nor are they oriented toward board decisions. This violates the very spirit of the Market Risk Amendment because the traditional reporting procedures on risk neither necessarily reach the board level, influencing its decision process, nor are they handled by an executive with board status, as is the case of the chief risk management officer (CRMO)—a post that presently exists in only a very few, well-managed banks.

Over and above these deficiencies, reported risk is usually seen from the narrow band of a given department—such as credit, forex, or the international division. This skews results. The international division, for instance, may have a conflict of interest between intensive marketing with business expansion as the goal and risk control.

The third deficiency with current systems and procedures is that risk management largely constitutes a batch exercise without the benefits of *real-time simulation* and of interactive ad hoc reporting. It does not use models, or when it does, the models have not been appropriately tested for dependability in terms of their prognostication features.

As we will see in Chapter 4, precisely because models may not be accurate, the Market Risk Amendment stipulates backtesting as one of the prerequisites. It also advises independence of opinion, underlining that each bank should have an autonomous risk-control unit responsible for the design, testing, and implementation of its risk-management system. The unit should do the following:

- Produce and analyze daily reports on the output of the bank's risk-measurement model.
- Make evaluations of the relationship between measures of risk exposure and trading limits.

The results must be interactively presented to most top managers. This is a job the chief risk-management officer must perform. Therefore, his or her function should be independent from that of trading units or marketing departments, reporting directly to the chief executive officer (CEO).

Furthermore, the Basle Committee aptly suggests how and why the board of directors, chief executive officer, and senior management should be actively involved in the risk-control process. They must regard risk management as an essential aspect of their personal accountability, a business to which significant resources and skills need to be devoted.

It is also the opinion of the Basle Committee that the risk-measurement system should be used in conjunction with internal controls, which dynamically adjust trading and exposure limits. In this regard, trading limits should be set not only in an absolute sense but also relative to the bank's trading book. We have already spoken of this requirement.

Banks with a rather large or complex options portfolio should establish and implement specifications relevant to prevailing *volatility* and *liquidity* conditions. Connected to this is the need for measuring volatilities of options in the portfolio according to their different maturities.[11] These recommendations bring together the new culture of real-time simulation and the established principles of internal controls.

---

11 See also the distinction made between maturity and duration in Section 3.

CHAPTER 4

Implementing the Market Risk Amendment

1. INTRODUCTION

The evolution of rules in terms of bank regulation has changed the nature and competence of the Basle Committee. As long as the main subject was capital adequacy for loans, the principles guiding the hand of the regulators were fairly clear-cut, and they were largely based on experience. But since 1993, when the Basle Committee came into the domain of market risk, it became apparent that a detailed and fairly advanced technical competence is necessary, able to promote:

- International cooperation among central bankers.
- A quantitative evaluation of capital adequacy.
- A qualitative evaluation of derivatives exposure.

The qualitative and quantitative evaluations that led to the 1996 Market Risk Amendment have included risk-management requirements, modeling procedures, reporting practices, and disclosure guidelines. More recently, the Basle Committee effort orients itself toward new accounting standards that must complement the market-risk orientation.

One of the important issues to take notice of is that, with the Market Risk Amendment, marking-to-model has been legitimized as the solution to the valuation of the trading book. For valuation proper, banks can choose the so-called standard method by BIS or develop and use their own models. My advice is to apply their own sophisticated eigenmodels.

A bank's own models are usually derived from its internal risk-management systems and procedures. We will see how to develop and test pricing and risk-management models in Part Two. This will include the models that come under the cumulative name of value-at-risk (VAR), higher-order metrics and simulators, and algorithms that have become a standard reference in the financial industry, for instance, the Black–Scholes model for options pricing.[1]

The purpose of this chapter is to explain basic notions behind the concepts that dominate model development in the financial industry, within the perspectives set by the 1996 Market Risk Amendment. The careful reader will notice that eigenmodels come at different levels of sophistication. There is no unique approach or method that is best in all cases. But there is a need for accurate pricing of financial instruments as well as for the control of risk.

For this reason, as this chapter will demonstrate, the Basle Committee of Banking Supervision has been very careful to specify that eigenmodels must be subject to the observance of *adequacy criteria* and *stress analysis*. We will see what this means in the following sections.

2. WAYS AND MEANS OF MARKING-TO-MODEL THE TRADING BOOK

Let's start with the fact that whether or not banks mark-to-model their trading book, capital requirements for credit risk will continue under the terms of the 1988 Capital Accord by the Basle Committee on Banking Supervision, as modified by subsequent amendments. With respect to derivative products, the new element is that capital requirements for market risk are to apply on a worldwide consolidated basis, and market risk is add-on capital, over and above capital requirements for credit risk.

The second premise that is important in connection to the implementation of the Market Risk Amendment is that the eigenmodel approach follows a practice that has already taken hold in the United States, at least among tier-1 banks. The Amendment respects a bank's internal risk measurement system and uses it for applying capital charges. The generalization of this method offers banks of the G–10 countries the possibility of doing one of two things:

- Using their own risk-management systems, procedures, and models or
- Adopting the generalized netting/residual risk-measurement method of BIS.

---

1 In 1994, Dr. Fischer Black received the Chorafas Foundation award of the Swiss Academies of Sciences for the development of the Black–Scholes model.

The third critical issue in an implementation of modeling procedures is the sample space within which they will be exercised. The Market Risk Amendment (as well as CAD) specifies a holding period of the trading book of 10 days, but it accepts an interim measure, calculating for 1-day holding corrected by a factor that produces a 10-day equivalence in terms of embedded risk.

This method is approximate and works as follows. If t_{10} is the required holding period of 10 days[2] and the eigenmodel works on t_1 (or 1 day), then the risk $R(t_{10})$ can be computed from the risk $R(t_1)$ through the formula:

$$R(t_0) = R(t_1)\sqrt{\frac{t_{10}}{t_1}}$$

$$= R(t_1)\sqrt{10}$$

Indeed, one of the algorithms included in the Amendment is that banks can scale up their one-day, value-at-risk measurement for options by the square root of 10. They can do so for a certain period of time after the internal models approach takes effect at the end of 1997.

The sampling period over which this formula can be computed is equal to one year or more, whether the computation is for t_{10} or t_1. Eventually, the $R(t_1)$ approach should be abandoned in favor of a straight $R(t_{10})$ computation given that, generally, there can be autocorrelations that reduce the accuracy of Equation (1).

A different way of expressing the same concept is that the Basle Committee's quantitative criteria as well as those that will govern the use of proprietary models with the goal of determining capital charges require that value-at-risk (VAR) be computed daily, using a 99th percentile and one-tailed confidence interval.

Both the percentile method and the one-tailed distribution will be explained in Part Two. The Basle Committee intends to permit banks to use the correlations within and between markets that they deem appropriate, provided their supervisory authority is satisfied with this process.

An important point raised by the Amendment is that the central bank of the country where a financial institution resides must approve of the models developed and used by any given bank. The netting/residual method, also called the standardized method, was advanced by BIS in its April 1993 market-risk proposal (and revised in the April 1995 document) as a simpler approach than eigenmodels.

---

2 See also in Section 3 the requirement of the 10-day holding period, and in Chapter 11 applications concerning the holding period.

In order to assure a degree of prudence in regard to transparency and consistency of added capital requirements—in a way that is valid across banks and jurisdictions—the Basle Committee has proposed quantitative and qualitative criteria for those banks that wish to use proprietary models. By and large, these are sound guidelines.

Because it would have been a nightmare to control each eigenmodel individually, the Market Risk Amendment focuses on the control of the results but establishes criteria for the output of backtesting. We will talk about them when we discuss the green, yellow, and red zones.

To my knowledge, BIS is not planning to give a hand to individual commercial banks to develop their own pricing models, if for no other reason than it does not have the resources to do so. But central banks can take such an initiative, and some of them do. An example is the Commission Bancaire of Banque de France.[3] Commercial banks lacking the rocket scientists to develop their own models can always use the standardized procedure by BIS.

One of the problems with independently developed eigenmodels is that they will be heterogeneous among themselves, making the job of supervisors and regulators much more difficult. To reduce such differences between models, the Basle Committee aims to fix a number of the parameters that affect the way the models are specified and developed. The following are examples:

- A 99 percent one-tailed distribution defining the *level of confidence.*[4]
- The requirement to account for *nonlinear behavior* of option prices, which makes the model more sophisticated (see Section 5).
- The use of price changes over a two-week period, regarding fluctuation in *price volatility.*
- A minimum period of statistical sampling of one year in terms of historical information.

Another issue leading to diversity is the historical correlations used in value-at-risk algorithms, discussed in Part Two, which also explains two methods used to compute value-at-risk: the parametric and the non-parametric, or simulation, methods.

Banks are also given the choice of using eigenmodels in some cases and in other cases apply the netting method suggested in the BIS documents of April 1993 and April 1995. A precautionary measure taken by

---

3 See Chapter 7.
4 D. N. Chorafas, *How to Understand and Use Mathematics for Derivatives,* Volume 2 (London: Euromoney, 1995).

central bankers through the Amendment is that for the same financial products banks cannot switch from one method to the other—because this leads to cherry picking.

But the 1996 Market Risk Amendment does provide some degree of freedom in the calculation of risk, leaving it up to each central bank to decide if a new modeling approach is acceptable. As briefly stated in Chapter 1, a novel approach is the computation of *earnings at risk.* Another is the estimation of *capital at risk.* Still another is the use of a demodulator in conjunction with the notional principal amount of contracted derivatives deals.

For loans, capital at risk is the sum of capital committed in the loans, including the part of the line of credit used in authorized negative balances.[5] For derivatives, I use the notional principal amount divided by a demodulator, for instance, 30 for normal behavior of financial markets. This process of demodulation will be explained in Chapter 6.

As has been already stressed, a more precise approach with derivatives would be to compute and use one demodulator per instrument. The problem is that this approach is very complex because of the myriad of derivatives instruments. Therefore, it tends to become subjective and inaccurate. It is better to bet on accuracy than on precision.

3. SIMULATION, EXPERIMENTATION, AND INTRADAY TIME SERIES

Timing is everything in business, particularly in investments, and the same applies to financial analysis. Therefore, an important issue in an objective computation of market-risk exposure is the *time frames* to be observed in the sampling and testing procedure.

In the supervisory authorities' judgment, in the longer term a bank's models must have a proven track record of reasonable accuracy in measuring risk. As this will be statistically tested, it is advisable to establish a valid timing procedure, which eventually will be instrumental in conducting stress tests.

Supervisory authorities also retain the right to insist on a period of initial monitoring and live testing of a bank's eigenmodel before it is used for the calculation of capital requirements. This provision is a supplement to the basic objective followed with marking-to-model, and it constitutes a prerequisite for using the output as an emulation of capital charges. The

---

5 See also the discussion in Chapter 1 about the need to model loans risk, the CreditMetrics effort, and the integration of credit risk and market risk by counterparty.

Amendment advances methods of scaling up value-at-risk estimates. Scaling is taking account of potential weaknesses in the modeling process.

One of the issues examined by the Basle Committee is how to address different weighting schemes for the observation period. The conclusion has been that banks should have some flexibility in this area, subject to the constraint that, as noted, the effective observation period is at least one year.

The Basle Committee seems to have devoted considerable attention to the optimization of the observations period that will be used for the calculation of capital charges. The Amendment comments that the disadvantage of shorter observation periods is that they capture only recent market shocks. This could lead to the measurement of risk in a narrow bandwidth, with corresponding loss of accuracy. Particularly critical is the case when this period coincides with unusually long stable markets.

On the other hand, the disadvantage of a longer time horizon is that it is not very sensitive to rapidly changing market conditions, particularly in times of stress. This evidently creates problems in connection to the modeling process because simulation falls behind market shifts.

There is a great deal to be said about staying ahead of the curve in regard to market shifts. As we saw in Section 2, each bank must on a daily basis meet a capital requirement expressed as the higher of the following:

- Its previous day's value-at-risk measured according to specified parameters.
- An average of the daily value-at-risk measures on each of the preceding 60 business days, augmented by a multiplication factor.

Personally, I am not happy that value-at-risk must be computed on a daily basis. My regret is that daily statistics rather than *intraday* time series have been adopted.[6] While intraday time series or *high frequency financial data* (HFFD) require appropriate technology to be seen through, they provide a much more rigorous basis for simulation and experimentation. In procedural terms, the Market Risk Amendment:

- Specifies the employment of a minimum price shock equivalent to a holding period of 10 trading days.
- Instructs that the model incorporate a historical observation period of at least one year.

We have spoken of the minimum holding period of 10 days in Section 2 being used by employing Equation (1). If instead of days we

---

6 On intraday metrics, see D. N. Chorafas, *How to Understand and Use Mathematics for Derivatives,* Volume 1, *Understanding the Behavior of Markets* (London: Euromoney, 1995).

used five-minute intervals, in an eight-hour day we would have had two orders of magnitude more episodes on which to base our inference.

Given the rapid evolution in the financial markets, their globalization, the fact that there is practically 24-hour banking, and that a foreign exchange (forex) transaction happens practically every seven to eight seconds, intraday financial time series are a "must." The day will come when even the five-minute intervals are coarse-grain.

When we speak of 24-hour global banking, what we essentially mean is that the sun never really sets on the international bank—or the local/regional institution and its correspondent banks. The same is true of overdrafts that follow the sun. Therefore, the interday period and the 24-hour limits are totally arbitrary and can be misleading in terms of exposure.

The deregulation of banking, its global nature, and the impact of high technology have made many concepts obsolete. The Basle Committee has also looked into some other issues relating to eigenmodels, which means it has done its homework. The Amendment stipulates that, other things being equal,

- The capital charge for a bank that uses a proprietary model will be the higher of the previous days' value-at-risk.
- The risk factor should represent three times the average of the daily value-at-risk of the preceding 60 business days (see Section 4).

These regulations reflect the fact that not only has the landscape of commercial banking significantly changed over the last few years, it continues to do so. As Figure 4–1 suggests, the level of complexity is increasing in two dimensions: from the lower to the upper layer and from left to right. Hence, there is the need for prudent management of risk in appreciation of the fact that we deal with a system involving many unknowns.

4. THE x3 FACTOR SPECIFIED BY THE MARKET RISK AMENDMENT

This relatively short section has the goal of explaining the role of the x3 factor presented in the Amendment. At its core is the Basle Committee's standard that capital requirements should be equal to the higher of two measures:

- The current value-at-risk estimate.
- The average VAR estimate over the previous 60 days multiplied by 3.

Critics of this x3 factor say that no doubt central bankers at the Basle Committee were uneasy with the idea that capital requirements will be

F I G U R E   4–1

Liquid and Not-So-Liquid Products in a Complete Product Line

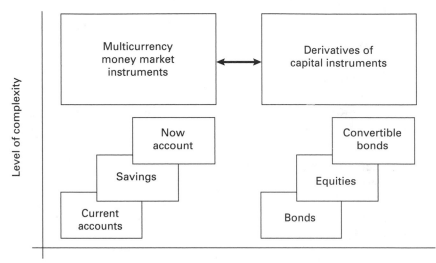

defined by a mathematical model—since they don't have extensive prior experience in this area. I don't think this is the case. Rather, prudential supervision requires one to be conservative until the new approach to market risk is tested, and this will take some years.[7]

As we will see in Chapter 5, when we talk of the green, yellow, and red zones, this x3 is not necessarily the maximum value of the multiplier. It can become bigger if the VAR model's accuracy leaves something to be desired. This is done by means of an add-on known as the "plus" factor.

Jackson, Maude, and Perraudin[8] looked at the important question of how much of a capital cushion the eigenmodel approach by the Basle Committee would deliver for real-life trading books, given the 99 percent level of confidence and the multiplier of 3. They examined this issue by comparing capital requirements generated by one part of the two-stage test, namely three times the 60-day average of VAR calculated to cover a 10-day holding period, using parameters laid down by Basle.

---

7 See also in Chapter 1 the discussion on credit metrics.

8 Particia Jackson, David J. Maude, William Perraudin, "Bank Capital and Value At Risk," a not-yet-published paper.

The researchers employed the parametric VAR algorithm in comparing 10-day returns that would have been secured on four model portfolios over the period July 1989 to April 1995. The capital requirements were based on three times the 60-day average, with a 24-month window of past returns data, equal weights, and a zero mean. With this, they calculated the capital requirement implied by multipliers of 2, 2.5, and 3—not just x3. The result was that, when the multiplier was either 2.5 or 3, none of the portfolios had a single loss outlier—which is good news.

The sense of a loss outlier is that losses exceeded the capital requirement. However, three of the four model portfolios had a marginal loss outlier for a multiplier of 2. This tends to support the x3 Basle Committee recommendation as a valid method.

In counterpart to these capital requirements, which tend to be somewhat stiffer than when BIS' own general netting model is used, banks will have more flexibility in specifying parameters for their eigenmodel(s). This freedom includes the possibility of recognizing correlation effects across and within broad risk-factor categories.

For supervisory purposes, however, the Basle Committee reserves the right to modify the specifications required for banks using eigenmodels, as more experience is gained with the marking-to-model approach in regard to dynamic risk calculation. As I have often underlined, a dynamic calculation of risk should be the goal of every well-managed financial institution.

It is conceivable that the outlined methodology will evolve over time and might simulate market events quite closely, which will be a welcome development. In the meantime, the fact that reserve banks have taken a stand in regard to market risk, and most particularly derivatives, has induced some commercial banks to bend the growth curve of their off-balance sheet business. Based on statistics from one of the best-known money-center banks, Figure 4–2 documents this reference. While this is far from being a general practice, I expect that the next few years will see more major banks taking the same approach.

Once the x3 factor is well established, central banks can use it as carrot and stick to guide commercial banks towards a reduction in gearing, because of derivative financial instruments, without shaking the market's confidence. The commercial banks themselves may reach a point of diminishing returns with derivatives, not only because of well-publicized losses such as the Barings Bank and Sumitomo Corporation, but also because there are no more fat profits with bread-and-butter derivatives, while the exotics involve nonlinear risks.

F I G U R E   4–2

The U-Curve in Contract Volume of Derivatives (in Notional Principal Amounts

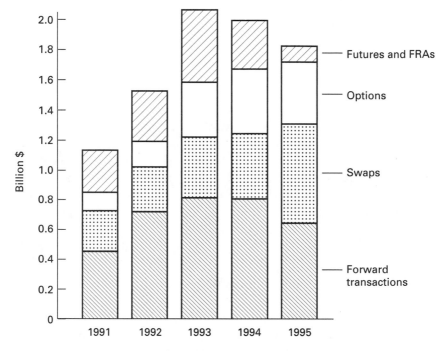

5. A NEW CONCEPT FOR BANKERS AND REGULATORS: NONLINEAR RISKS

In terms of reporting practices, the Market Risk Amendment provides some degree of freedom when it stipulates that banks may use value-at-risk numbers calculated according to shorter holding periods scaled up to 10 days. What is fixed is the choice of a historical sample period for calculating value-at-risk, as it is constrained to a minimum length of one year.

Banks will be allowed to scale their value-at-risk measure up or down to zoom in on a required 10-day holding period. The Basle Committee, however, is offering the financial industry new flexibility by introducing the concept of *nonlinear risks.*[9]

As will be explained in much greater detail in Part Two, nonlineari- ties are a nontraditional analytical solution to an industry accustomed for

---

9 See D. N. Chorafas, *Chaos Theory in the Financial Markets* (Chicago: Irwin, 1994).

a long time to treating market behavior as linear. The justification for using nonlinear models is in the fact that they represent with much more accuracy the interaction between financial instruments and markets—as well as that, under certain constraints, they make it possible to predict a forthcoming crisis.

The Market Risk Amendment does not explicitly say so, but nonlinear mathematics is today an integral part of *interactive computational finance,* which underpins the design of control systems addressing both business opportunity and risk connected to modern financial instruments. The complexity of new products requires the dynamic examination of financial time series, some of which are taken near a catastrophic threshold. As chaos theory teaches, systems that seemed to be random might actually be described by rules, which in turn makes feasible some degree of prognostication.

Tier-1 banks have been working for nearly 10 years on the implementation of chaos theory, fractals, leptokyrtotic distributions, feedback control, root locus, Nyquist criterion, auto-oscillations, heteroschedasticity, autoregression, autocorrelation, Brownian motion, and Weibull distribution. They do so in connection with the development of new financial products and for risk-control purposes.[10]

These analytical tools are not used today by every bank because of the cultural gap that prevails. Only the topmost financial institutions have the rocket scientists to develop state-of-the-art mathematical models. But the way to bet is that in the coming years a growing number of banks will acquire the ability to use real-life simulation, and the fact that G–10 regulators now think that marking-to-model is a good approach will stimulate many of the laggards to move forward.

What the Basle Committee essentially did with the integration of nonlinearities into the Market Risk Amendment is to legitimize these advanced solutions from the regulators' viewpoint. This is most significant and should be food for thought for all financial institutions. Nonlinear dynamics not only describe how complex systems change, they also suggest that a change in one input possibly has an effect out of all proportion to its size.

This is known as the *butterfly effect.* Any system that has some sort of sensitive dependence on initial conditions—be it a financial market or a weather pattern—is subject to its aftermaths. The point many people trained

---

10 For a definition and examples of each of these analytical tools, see D. N. Chorafas *How to Understand and Use Mathematics for Derivatives,* Volume 2 (London: Euromoney, 1995).

in traditional financial analysis fail to appreciate is that *discontinuous changes* require a sort of *discontinuous thinking.*

Figure 4–3 brings home the message that a time series that by all appearances seems to be predictable suddenly changes trajectory because of a certain event. The discontinuity that is temporarily present radically alters the landscape of the market, or of the instrument, from level of reference "A" to "B"—which may involve an altogether different ball game.

Another departure from past practices toward a higher level of sophistication in management planning and control is the concept advanced by the Market Risk Amendment that a better approach would involve a detailed attribution of *income by source,* including:

- Fees.
- Spreads.
- Market movements.
- Intraday trading results.

The greatest contribution rocket scientists have brought to the financial institutions for which they are working is the appreciation of the concept underpinning nonlinearities in pricing. This is also an example of the cultural change discussed in Chapter 1.

F I G U R E   4–3

Discontinuities Exist in Financial Markets because of Panics, Depressions, and Other Events That Change the Level of Reference

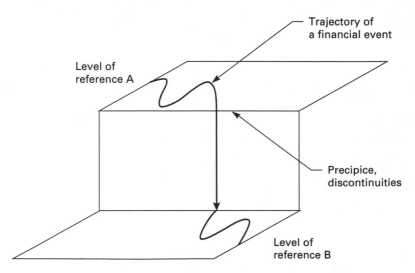

Because of its upside-down characteristics, discontinuous thinking has never been popular with the upholders of continuity and the status quo—whether bankers or mathematicans tied to classical theories. Today, however, it has become a fundamental ingredient of good management because it reflects the way in which choppy financial markets work.

This is the background reason why the Market Risk Amendment can have far-reaching aftermaths. Other parts of the Amendment are more conservative. Though it is feasible to define different price shocks for different classes of instruments, Basle Committee rules provide a fairly homogeneous method, which addresses the risk that portfolio losses can build up over a period of time greater than a day and therefore suggests a way of looking at market movements that may defy past know-how, but that correlates well with advanced practices.

Finally, let's keep in mind that, as already mentioned, there is a limitation in regard to switching between models—which makes sense. Save in exceptional circumstances, having adopted an internal model for one or more risk-factor categories, a bank will not be permitted to revert to the standardized approach developed by BIS. By contrast, those elements of market risk that are not captured by an eigenmodel will remain subject to the standardized measurement framework.

6. TESTING A MODEL FOR CONFORMITY AND IMPROVING ITS SOPHISTICATION

The development of algorithms and the elaboration of risk-measurement procedures for marking-to-model have to be calibrated against market data. Model testing helps as proof of accuracy and also permits the adaptation of algorithms and heuristics to develop conditions. The Basle Committee incorporates this notion into the Market Risk Amendment through the process of *backtesting*, to which reference has already been made. We must be very careful about this recommendation, because backtesting has aftermaths, and the concept underpinning backtesting is a cultural issue.

The notion rests on the fact that actual trading outcomes experienced by the bank could be different than those projected by the model. Therefore, given that real-life financial time series are the most relevant figures for risk management, models should be benchmarked against them.

The Basle Committee is proposing that, as a safeguard, banks applying the eigenmodel approach must use a rigorous and comprehensive testing procedure. It is also wise to conduct a priori tests covering a range of possibilities that could create extraordinary losses or gains. Examples of relatively recent historical stress events include the following:

- The October 1987 equity market crash.
- The suspension of the sterling's and Italian lira's membership of the ERM in September 1992.
- The bloodbath with leveraged bonds in the February to April 1994 time frame.

The need for testing is by no means present only in finance. Any mathematical model is based on abstraction and hypotheses. We may err on both counts. The abstraction might be too coarse-grain, and one or more of our hypotheses might be wrong; or the algorithm could be too approximate.

As Figure 4-4 shows, testing is an integral part of model development as well as of model usage. Testing as well as backtesting are concepts that are starting to be generally appreciated.

To help the commercial banks under their jurisdiction start on the right path with modeling, some central banks not only give advice but also help pretest the models. By contrast, other banks focus only on backtesting, as specified in the Market Risk Amendment. Senior executives at the Federal Reserve Bank of San Francisco said this is the paradigm they work with.

Whether pre- or posttesting, the job is not that easy because of the assumptions it involves. Maturity deposits are an especially thorny problem, and the same is true of modeling liabilities. When they approach the modeling of complex problems, some commercial banks work on the basis of hypotheses. In connection to interest rates, for example, these can be broadly classified into three classes:

1. What the reserve bank will do in response to an increase in interest rates.
2. What other banks will do in regard to the same variable.
3. How the customers will behave when interest rates go up.

The meetings with the Federal Reserve, the Bank of England, Bundesbank, Banque de France, and Swiss National Bank document that neither the Fed nor other central banks really rush the commercial banking industry toward increasingly sophisticated models. Even backtesting is introduced piecemeal, in order to allow time for the commercial banks to acquire the new culture and to tune their systems.

In the district of the Federal Reserve of San Francisco, for example, backtesting requirements will be imposed on 15 banks as the first implementation of the method. In this approach, emphasis is placed on identifying,

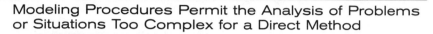

F I G U R E   4–4

Modeling Procedures Permit the Analysis of Problems
or Situations Too Complex for a Direct Method

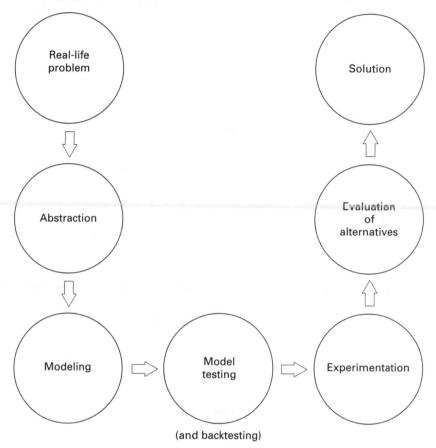

(and backtesting)

measuring, and monitoring risks. This is being done in consideration of the
size and complexity of the commercial banks' activities, and it regards both
American banks and foreign banks operating in the district's domain.

"Our responsibility for examining foreign banks operating in the
United States, shows that some are extremely sophisticated," advised a
senior executive of the Federal Reserve of San Francisco. What about the
green, yellow, and red guidelines of the Basle Committee?[11] The responsible executives at the Fed said that they don't yet have enough data.

---

11 See Chapter 5.

The value the Fed currently attaches is in the order of magnitude. "What we drive at is that there has to be segregation of risks," said another senior executive of the Federal Reserve Bank of San Francisco. Supervisory authorities also see to it that within the commercial bank there is an evaluation by someone other than the model designer.

The Fed actually advises banks to hire somebody from the outside for auditing the work of the internal rocket scientists, suggested the executives at the Fed of San Francisco. This is a very sound advice to be followed by the board of every commercial bank. After all, backtesting is an auditing procedure, and banks have the experience of using outside auditors.

Both the independent auditors and the central banks will learn how to deal with market-risk models through experience. Some central banks, such as Banque de France, are waiting for the results of the first years of application of the Market Risk Amendment to fine-tune their policies and procedures.

Correctly, Banque de France is also looking into the application of the Market Risk Amendment among commercial banks and investment banks not only in terms of deviations in the values calculated by marking-to-model but also in connection to the quality of the internal controls, the methodology being used, and management's understanding of what the control of market risk is all about.

This enlarges the concept of the Market Risk Amendment and brings into perspective the consistency of the effort put forward by financial institutions for managing their exposure. Quantitative results are only one aspect of the problem. The other side of the coin is qualitative.

7. PAYING THE NECESSARY ATTENTION TO THE RESULTS OF BACKTESTING

Backtesting essentially constitutes a statistical test of the integrity of the calculation of value-at-risk. The Basle Committee suggests it is appropriate to employ a definition of daily trading outcome. As already stated in Section 3, I would advise using intraday statistics.

Both for an analytical approach to risk management and for auditing reasons, my advice is to account individually for the different instruments in the trading book rather than averaging out pluses and minuses. In other words, it would be wiser to look at positions, deals, and exceptions, not in total, but by instrument, and to capture and exploit high-frequency financial data, not coarse-grain.

Backtesting should be made in connection to *profits and losses.* Not only is the bottom line quantitative, hence testable, but this is also a useful exercise since it can identify cases where the risk measures are not accurately capturing trading volatility. Another helpful type of test, or more precisely of experimentation, is based on the what if scenarios regarding changes in market value.

Apart from the income statement (profit and loss, P&L) the pricing of financial products is a good exercise in simulation. Different levels of detail may characterize a pricing model. For instance, a complete approach to risk calculation should include *fees* from clients, other income from correspondent banks, and corporate balances, as well as *costs* associated with trading. A rigorous solution would involve a detailed attribution of several factors:

- Income (by source), including fees.
- Prevailing spreads in the marketplace.
- Market movements and their aftermaths.
- Interday and intraday trading results as they are generated.

In each and every one of these areas of attention, *stress testing* is required to identify events or influences that could greatly affect the financial industry, but which might be *outlayers*. Therefore, banks with internal risk models must have a rigorous and comprehensive stress-testing program, backtesting being a special case of the overall test.

Stress scenarios should cover a range of factors, preferably examined parametrically, for instance, factors that might create extraordinary losses or gains in trading portfolios, or make the control of risk in those portfolios most difficult and/or uncertain.

Crucial factors may be not only high-probability but also low-probability events. Both high-probability events and outlayers (rare events) exist in all major types of risks, including the various components of market, credit, and operational risks—as discussed in Chapter 1. We will return to this issue in Chapter 4.

The results of stress testing should be presented in a way that sheds light on the impact of outlayer events on positions that display both *linear* and *nonlinear* market price-and-risk characteristics. Stress tests should be both of a quantitative and qualitative nature, incorporating liquidity aspects of market disturbances.

While the use of percentiles at the 99 percent level of significance is a good approach, and the same is true of the green, yellow, and red zones in which fall the experimental results when compared to real life,[12] it is no

---

12 See Chapter 5.

less true that in a rigorous mathematical method both the number of exceptions and the amounts per exception are important.

A change of the model to include amounts will alter it from being based on attributes (go, no go) to being based on variables, for instance, an $\bar{\bar{x}}$ chart with tolerances and upper and lower control levels.[13] I should also underline the use of modern methods such as fuzzy engineering and genetic algorithms for risk analysis.

- *Subjective criteria* used in fuzzy sets help identify plausible stress scenarios to which banks could be exposed.
- *Qualitative criteria* must emphasize the capacity of a bank's capital to absorb potential large losses.
- *Quantitative evidence* would lead to the identification of steps the bank can take to reduce its risk and conserve capital.

As a matter of principle in simulation, experimentation, and optimization, the more sophisticated the model, the more effective the what if evaluation can be. For this reason, the Basle Committee urges banks to develop the capability to perform backtests using trading outcomes that are both *actual* and *hypothetical.*

However, the Market Risk Amendment also takes account of the fact that national supervisors may differ in the emphasis they place on approaches to backtesting, as well as in what they believe to be the necessary frequency of the tests in reference.

One of the premises advanced by the Amendment is that for banks that use a weighting scheme or other methods for the prescribed historical observation period, the weighted average time lag of the individual observations cannot be less than six months. It is furthermore noted that a supervisory authority may require a bank to calculate its value-at-risk using a shorter observation period. This would happen if, in the regulators' judgment, it is justified by a significant upsurge in price volatility or for other reasons.

Another requirement outlined by the Market Risk Amendment leaves me unsatisfied. It specifies that, generally, banks should update their time series every three months or more frequently. This long period is utterly inadequate in a dynamic market even if the Amendment asks banks to reassess their data whenever market prices are subject to "material changes"—two words that convey a vague notion.

---

13 See D. N. Chorafas, *Statistical Processes and Reliability Engineering* (Princeton, NJ: D. Van Nostrand, 1960).

CHAPTER 5

The Days after the Implementation of the Market Risk Amendment

1. INTRODUCTION

Deliberately, one of the important components of the Market Risk Amendment by the Basle Committee, the definition of the green, yellow, and red zones, has been delayed until this chapter. While we have spoken of backtesting in Chapter 3, the concept of management's responsibilities regarding the results to be obtained through marking-to-model is an issue of capital importance, which has to be addressed in detail.

The responsibility for proper performance of risk management is, without any doubt, at the board's level. This is true even if the rocket scientists write the models, the party accountable for their performance is the bank's top management.

As a matter of principle, success or failure in trading operations greatly depends on top management's awareness of the need for a polyvalent approach to the control of risk.

Classically, the risks inherent in the trading business are managed through a system of market- and credit-risk limits that assures adherence of the operating units to ceilings set by management. A more sophisticated approach sees to it that, beyond the observance of limits, the trading units measure market-risk and credit-risk exposure of their positions using analytical techniques. In tier-1 banks:

- *Gains and losses* are determined by marking positions on a daily basis or, even better, on an intraday basis.

This does not cancel *position risk,* but it makes it visible. Hence, management can act on exposure in a timely fashion and in full knowledge of where the dangers lie.

■ *Advanced technology* rather than manual effort should be used in this process. Interactive computational finance is the best answer.

When the marking-to-market or marking-to-model is done, a virtual balance sheet, statement of total recognized gains or losses (STRGL), and income statement (P&L) can be constructed online and made available to authorized executives. The virtual balance sheets are discussed in Part Two, and STRGL is discussed in Chapter 6.

Model accuracy rather than precision is the critical factor in making this strategy possible. Therefore, the Basle Committee is right in insisting on a rigorous test of proprietary models. It is not enough that algorithms are available permitting online experimentation on exposure; they must also be dependable.

With every modeling solution, market volatility and liquidity must be steadily monitored to assure that the bank does not find itself confronted with serious, unpleasant surprises. But raw data on volatility and liquidity are not enough for effective action by the bank's management. Senior executives must be provided with a comprehensive view that over the longer run proves reliable.

2. TOP MANAGEMENT'S RESPONSIBILITY IN THE USE OF TECHNOLOGY

It is necessary but not enough to report to the bank's top management on the overall exposure. As Mies van der Rohe used to say, "God is in the details." The board should not only have available the global figure of risk and of risk capital to be set aside because of commitments in the transaction book and the banking book, it must also allocate that money by channel, instrument, and counterparty.

Senior management must have at its fingertips all the elements that permit it to determine worst-case scenarios for each class of risk, to distribute risk capital according to individual risks factors, to convert the risk capital into limits, and to calculate return on risk capital to assure that there is enough benefit to compensate the taking of risks.

The rules established by the reserve bank's regulation and supervision are only one of the four pillars on which rest top management decisions in terms of opportunities, limits, and risks. Figure 5–1 identifies

FIGURE 5-1

The Study of Business Opportunity and the Analysis of Business Intelligence Rest on Four Pillars

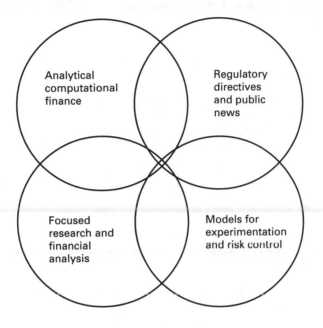

three other pillars whose foundations lie deeply in technology and without which a bank would find itself at a serious competitive disadvantage.

It is an integral part of top management's responsibility to clearly define the limits per instrument and counterparty for all lines of business.

With loans, this is traditionally done through credit rating and risk premiums. But it is no less a top management responsibility to establish similar procedures for market risks. This requires a comprehensive and flexible approach that enables interactive experimentation on embedded risk on the commitments being taken, as well as those already in the trading book, and that includes both risk and return in P&L evaluations, as well as the prepricing of new transactions.

Care should be taken to provide for experimentation able to assure that a conservative view of risk does not place *our* bank at an unjustified disadvantage when pricing transactions. This can happen if we fail to differentiate between *high-risk* and *low-risk* transactions because the system we have available cannot make that distinction.

Along the same lines, the concept of the green, yellow, and red zones established by the Basle Committee in connection to model testing for market risk should not be viewed as a burden. Rather, it is an opportunity not to be missed in connection with eigenmodels developed in conjunction with the bank's internal accounting management information system.

Top management will be justified if it says there are indeed missing links in the technology for controlling risk. What the board members and the CEO should understand is that this is the bank's own doing.

An example from a recent study is shown in Table 5–1. The result is disquieting, but the reader should know that the financial institution where this study took place is one of the better organized technologically. The average bank faces a much more disastrous situation in its information system, and it is doing very little to right the balances.

Interactive computational finance is not just the best way to calculate risk correlations. It is the only way to do so—and it has to be done *online*. Risk analysis, as well as the correlation among risk factors, is necessary for understanding the exposure *our* bank has taken.

A steady evaluation of model results in terms of their accuracy, along the lines suggested by the Market Risk Amendment for the green, yellow, and red zones, is the best strategy for developing and sustaining a mission-critical, rigorous risk-control system.

T A B L E   5–1

The Missing Technology for Controlling Risk at Most Financial Institutions

	Currently Is	Should Be
1. Global-market risk	Batch	RS*
2. Currency-exchange risk	Partially RT*	RS
3. Interest-rate risk	Partially RT	RS
4. Legal risk	Nothing	RS
5. Microseasonality risk	Nothing	RS
6. Credit risk	Batch	RT
7. Investment risk	Batch	RT
8. Event risk	Nothing	RT
9. Position risk	Batch	RS
10. Sales-conditions risk	Limits only	RS
11. Operations risk	Batch	RS
12. Funds-transfer risk	Nothing	RT
13. Settlement risk	Batch	RS
14. Transaction-processing risk	Nothing	RT

*RS stands for *real space;* RT for *real time.* See Section 8.

Internal controls must be in place that are able to ring real-time alarms about discrepancies between real-life and model results. The information system our bank puts in place should be able to follow the pulse of the market, reflecting exposure associated to the transactions that have been made.

Both credit officers and traders must be in a position to accurately assess market risk so that correct decisions can occur prior to commitments. This brings attention to another issue closely related to the dependability of the models our bank uses: They must be appreciated not only by top management but all the way down the line of command.

The knowledgeable reader will appreciate that this discussion constitutes a bridge between senior management's responsibilities regarding internal controls and those concerning technology. This bridge is vital because a bank is information in motion: "Information on money is as important as money itself," Walter Wriston, the former chairman of Citibank, once said. The topmost financial institutions seek to develop and sustain an autonomous information-processing system that actively and adaptively grasps incomplete, uncertain, and changeable data streams in the real world—massaging such information and presenting it in a decision-oriented manner. This can be implemented by rigorous models and high technology, provided we assure the model's dependability, as explained in Section 3.

3. THE GREEN, YELLOW, AND RED ZONES DEFINED BY THE MARKET RISK AMENDMENT

One of the most important clauses in the Market Risk Amendment is that not only the model itself but also the overall procedure to be used has to satisfy the requirements established by the supervisory authority in each country. The central bank will give its approval *if* it is satisfied that the bank's risk-management system is conceptually sound and implemented with integrity. Also *if,* to the regulators' view, the bank has a sufficient number of rocket scientists[1] and they work not only in the trading area but also in risk control, audit, and the back office.

As a check on the adequacy of the modeling approach, the Basle Committee proposed requiring banks to include information on the largest losses experienced during the reporting period. The resulting real-life capital requirements can thus be compared with the capital requirement for the same dates produced by the eigenmodel.

---

1 See D. N. Chorafas, *Rocket Scientists in Banking* (London: Lafferty Publications, 1995).

Every commercial bank that chooses to use its own models should appreciate that backtesting (discussed in Chapter 3) requires a statistically valid number of observations to make an accurate judgment about the model's accuracy. A model failure may be due to one of two reasons or to both:

- The algorithm is inaccurate.
- The data is insufficient and/or is subject to noise.

The Basle Committee projects that there might be a need for increases in capital requirements if over a 250-day period (that is, one year) the eigenmodel underpredicts the number of losses in a number of cases exceeding the 1 percent cutoff point—or 99 percent level of confidence. Calling such losses *exceptions,* the Market Risk Amendment stipulates that a procedure has to be established for continuous testing of the eigenmodel's performance. Regulators will not necessarily test the eigenmodels themselves, which may become a forbidding job, but they will test the results. This is the sense of the green, yellow, and red zones.

In other words, the Basle Committee and the supervisory authorities in each country reserve the right of interpretation of backtesting results and the responses to be obtained from the stress tests' signals. Three zones are distinguished: green, yellow (or amber), and red:

- A *green zone* corresponds to backtesting results that do not themselves suggest a problem with the quality or accuracy of a bank's model.

This case exists when the eigenmodel has generated zero to four exceptions per year. In the regulators' judgment, this represents an acceptable level of accuracy.

- A *yellow zone* encompasses results that do raise some questions, but not unsettling ones. Or, alternatively, the conclusion about a test is not definitive.

If during the whole year, with the result tested every working day, the model exhibits five to nine exceptions, it finds itself in the yellow (amber) zone and needs to be watched.

- A *red zone* indicates backtesting results that almost certainly reveal a problem with the bank's risk model(s) and its (their) accuracy.

Should there be more than 10 exceptions during the year, the eigenmodel is in the red zone, which is synonymous to low performance. The conclusion is that the model does not work properly.

If "exceptions" are viewed as failures in the eigenmodel's prediction, which they really are, the established system of quality control is fairly rigorous—as it should be. In terms of percent defective

- A zero to four failure rate means a 0 percent to 1.6 percent ratio in terms of *outgoing quality level* (OQL).[2]
- A five to nine failure rate corresponds to 2 percent to 3.6 percent in outgoing quality level.
- Ten or more exceptions in risk prediction correspond to an outgoing quality level with a failure rate equal to 4 percent or higher.

Capital requirements for banks whose models are in the red zone will surely be increased by regulators. If they are in the yellow zone, the capital requirements may be increased at the regulators' discretion.

This means that the Basle Committee's backtesting provisions will affect banks rather significantly. If a bank's eigenmodel underpredicts the number of large losses, the capital requirements will be adjusted upwards. If the failure rate is high, capital requirements will need to be adjusted fairly frequently. Therefore, banks must be very careful with the models they develop.

Some of the commercial bankers with whom I spoke about the green, yellow, and red zones think that the outgoing quality-level requirements established by the Basle Committee are tough. My opinion is different. Not only are they fair, they are also a sign of good management.

Let me qualify this statement. A bank's ability to compete effectively in a deregulated global market is not only a question of management but also of the risks being taken, the cost of operations, and the innovative products it provides. System solutions, too, play a crucial role. For instance, it is now possible within the same settlement day to:

- Buy securities for settlement in an exchange,
- Sell the same securities for settlement in a clearing house, and
- Resell the same securities for settlement in the exchange.

This is the so-called *back-to-back trade,* which is made possible because of advanced technology. If a bank is not able to develop and use sophisticated software, or to master the information systems it employs, then its future is bleak. A bank's weapon's system is technology.

---

2 A term borrowed from operating characteristics curves used in statistical quality control. See D. N. Chorafas, *Statistical Processes and Reliability Engineering* (Princeton, NJ: D. Van Nostrand Co., 1960).

If the rigorous testing procedures of the Market Risk Amendment have no other effect than to wake up the bank's management to the current technological challenge, they will do a great service to the banking industry. But there will be other effects. That's the way bankers should look to the green, yellow, and red zones.

4. A SOUND PROCEDURE FOR DAILY RISK MANAGEMENT

Because, as already noted, marking-to-model always involves some degree of approximation, as we saw in Chapter 3, Section 4, a multiplication factor has been established by the Basle Committee. Its exact value will be set by individual supervisory authorities on the basis of their assessment of the quality of the bank's risk-management system. This ×3 multiplication factor applies to the average of the daily value at risk over the preceding 60 days.

Banks are required to add to the multiplication factor a "plus" directly related to post-mortem performance of the model. This is expected to introduce an incentive to maintain and improve the predictive quality of simulation.

Based on the outcome of backtesting, the "plus" will range from zero to one, respectively increasing the base of 3—and therefore the exposure for which capital adequacy must be provided for market-risk reasons. This "plus" factor, however, could be zero if the backtesting results are satisfactory (green zone) and the bank meets all of the implied qualitative standards.

Some knowledgeable bankers suggested that this clause is somewhat curious because it does not take into consideration the nature of the distribution over 60 days of the value-at-risk. Yet such a statistical pattern is significant, and it might be quite revealing regarding risks taken by the financial institution.

I will bring this notion a step further by suggesting a daily management procedure using *intraday* time series, as explained in Chapter 10. This solution can capitalize on the fact that several banks, brokers, and corporate treasuries have systems in place able to explore the following:

- High-frequency financial data streams.
- Distributed databases through interactive mining.
- The results of experimentation permitting the judgement of exposure in real time.[3]

---

3 D. N. Chorafas and H. Steinmann, *Database Mining* (London: Lafferty, 1994).

One of the modeling weakness that is fairly generalized has to do with the fact that value-at-risk estimates are typically based on end-of-day positions and do not take account of intraday trading risk. While experience in intraday modeling is still limited, it is wise to bet on high-frequency financial data—particularly for currency exchange and exchange-traded securities or commodities.

It is, on the other hand, true that the majority of banks and other companies trading in high-risk instruments such as derivatives are still in the Middle Ages in terms of technology and financial reporting. Their traders don't have in place a system that permits them to generate daily balances. As a result, they are taking unreasonable risks.

Intraday market valuation of derivatives and other trading positions is the best practice for banks and dealers. A corollary to this best practice is to always understand what the bank, and the trader himself or herself, is trying to accomplish with higher-exposure trades.

Without a full understanding of how the technology works as well as the purpose for which *our* bank enters into a trade, it is nearly impossible to assess the effects of hedging in a risk-management sense. The sort of trading a bank is doing and the technology it is using are two closely related issues. Therefore, it is not enough to test only for one of them. Both must be examined for how they perform under stress.

In principle, the assumption that weaknesses in modeling may be unearthed through practice is correct. No model can be perfect, and it is wise to account for deviations and, therefore, for the need to proceed with corrections. But, once more, what leaves me rather perplexed is the forementioned flat "×3" to "×4" multiplier.

For instance, price movements in the market often display patterns that resemble a leptokyrtotic distribution with fat tails, rather than a normal distribution. Attention should also be paid to chaotic market activity, which possibly prevails. Both notions are shown in Figure 5–2. At the upper half of the figure is an example of a chaotic time series, characterized by great volatility. The lower half of the figure illustrates a leptokyrtotic distribution with fat tails, a pattern known as Hurst's exponent.

As with every real-life simulation, a great deal of attention must be paid to the filtering of the incoming time series,[4] the database mining activity, as well as the algorithms and heuristics we use. Accidents can happen everywhere. During modeling, too much attention might have

---

4 See D. N. Chorafas and H. Steinmann, *Virtual Reality—Practical Applications in Business and Industry* (Upper Saddle River, NJ: Prentice-Hall, 1995).

F I G U R E   5–2

The Number of Observations Is Particularly Important
in Complexity Theory—Whether We Study Chaos or
Hurst Exponent

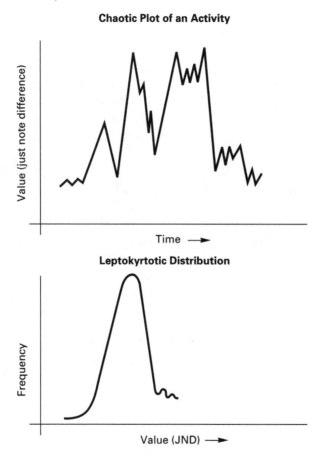

been given to historical data, and the past is not always a good predictor
of the future.

These facts are properly studied and taken into account by people
experienced in modeling, not by novices. When the model is sound, the
resulting pattern can be instrumental not only in prediction but also in
adjusting the model to keep it actual.

While all arguments about model weaknesses are real, it is just as
appropriate to add that marking-to-market is not free from from errors
either. Everything we do has only "so much" of a degree of certainty; the
rest is volatility and risk.

Even when it can be done, marking-to-market may be skewed because of local or temporary bias and the fact that asking a counterparty for a quotation does not always result in an objective answer. It is also much more difficult for the reserve bank to control the accuracy of such quotations, unless it follows the whole portfolio of each bank it supervises in all of the markets where the institutions under its control operate.

Therefore, we can make a fairly safe forecast that marking-to-model is here to stay. For this reason, I pay a great deal of attention to marking-to-model in Part Two.

5. RISK-ADJUSTED RETURN ON EQUITY

The development and use of dependable models can help well beyond risk management, in a compliance sense. The financial industry is characterized by a growing appreciation of the fact that there should be within the bank, as well as in major commercial and industrial organizations actively using financial instruments, analytical capabilities able to monitor and review all transactions in terms of the following:

- Business opportunities exploited and missed.
- Exposure assumed from deals being made.
- Position risk in the trading book and the banking book.

There is also a need for a uniform terminology to help in better communicating pertinent concepts. Market risks have different interpretations depending on the bank's internal culture and on which market its experts are analyzing. In the stock market, for instance, risk and return are associated with movements in the market index of portfolio returns.

Not all activities (transactions, positions, settlements) or all actions by the different parties (clients, traders, managers) involve every type of credit risk and market risk. However, in a number of cases, several of them are present in a stronger or in a weaker manner—and many tend to correlate. Banks typically try to control credit risk through overnight and interday limits. They consider interest-rate risk particularly important in connection to unmatched positions, and they tend to associate currency risk with currency risk, country risk, and credit risk.

However, as Chapter 3 and Chapter 4 have brought to the reader's attention, because the financial markets are very dynamic, static limits are absolutely inadequate in terms of protection. Therefore, I have advised using risk-adjusted return on capital, which is a good example of IAMIS metrics. Though the concept has been developed for loans, it is applicable to other instruments as well.

In the case of loans, for example, the typical case is that when a borrower (company or individual) goes to a bank for a loan, a binary decision is made: "Qualify/do not qualify." By contrast, risk-adjusted approaches are not binary. They stratify the level of risk, and they place a premium by risk ceiling.

We have spoken of this in connection to the concept of reinsurance. In an IAMIS sense, the process of *risk assessment* aims to quantify dangers so that responsible bank officers can decide if a particular risk is worth running. The quantification of qualitative issues is an approximation, but it is much better than guesswork. Calculated risks covered by premiums permit expanding money and securities trading activities without taking an inordinate exposure, and further building up and marketing personalized financial services.

But such solutions also require maintaining and selectively enhancing the quality and accuracy of the models we use. Service quality is vital both with old and with new financial products[5]—and it is inseparable from the process of developing new information-processing capabilities to sustain and enhance market presence.

Solutions such as risk-adjusted return on capital protect both the bank and the client against *default risk* and also serve in estimating *transaction risk* and *position risk*. As Figure 5–3 shows, these three issues overlap. At the heart of their common ground is *service quality*.

This interdependence requires an integrative view of default risk, transaction risk, and position risk. Dynamically established limits that are interactively readjustable through modeling help both the bank's professionals and management to decide where to draw the line. In terms of internal accounting management information systems, this requires:

- Online response to committed positions of the bank by credit line, client, instrument, and physical location.
- Interactive performance of profitability evaluations regarding exposure while accounting for liquidity and volatility.
- The use of intelligent networks to do away with geographic limitations and time-zone constraints.

Today, among tier-1 banks this type of real-time information is asked by general management and the divisions. To an increasing extent, it will be required by the rating agencies, the legislators, and the regulators—particularly in the case of large exposures. Banks that even temporarily

---

5 D. N. Chorafas, *Banking Strategy* (London: Lafferty, 1997).

F I G U R E   5–3

Service Quality Is at the Heart of Able Solutions to
Financial Risk

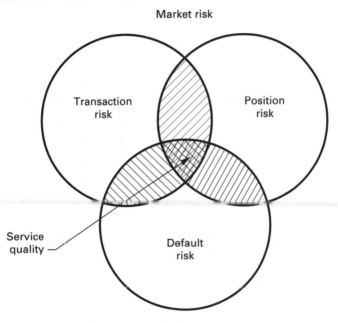

limit themselves to vague and inaccurate risk estimates take inordinate
risks while throwing away business. They lose the more lucrative part of
the market while they take on risks without an appropriate profitability.

Banks that are well managed are eager to develop a risk-control system able to assure that all known realized and unrealized profits and losses are consistently included in the results. Losses not recognized today—
such as future loss potential owing to market risk and credit risk—must be
covered by an additional charge on a risk-free investment rate when targeting the return on equity (ROE).

While it is good to know that ROE is a two-digit figure, as shown in
Figure 5–4, a result achieved in 1993 by the Union Bank of Switzerland,
it is also important to introduce into the equation the risk being taken. In
the evaluation of ROE, both risk and return are important references.

A way of fulfilling this objective is the concept of a reinsurance policy that virtually offers a (simulated) risk-free investment and transaction
environment. By introducing the notion of risk-adjusted return on equity,
business transactions that entail position risk and default risk will both
contribute a premium to the risk-capital fund and use risk capital.

FIGURE   5-4

Union Bank of Switzerland: Return on Equity

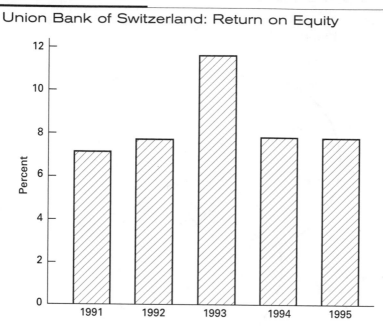

6. EQUITIES, SECURITIES AND EXCHANGE COMMISSION, AND PLAYERS IN ASSET MANAGEMENT

The May 20, 1996, meeting between G–10 central bankers and securities regulators in Frankfurt proposed to provide an even level in risk management between commercial banks and investment banks. The Securities and Exchange Commission has been instrumental in regard to the use of risk models by securities houses.

In a manner that closely emulates the Market Risk Amendment by the Basle Committee of Banking Supervision, securities firms will calculate the change in value of all positions as a result of changes in market prices. A similar approach has been recently set out in the Framework for Voluntary Oversight by the Derivatives Policy Group.

As with commercial banks, models will cover losses calculated over 24-hour and two-week holding periods with a 99 percent confidence level. However, in contrast to the Basle Committee initiative, some eigenmodels used in connection to internal management accounting include a number of specified core risk factors to watch out for.

With stock markets in the United States, Britain, and Continental Europe at all-time highs, securities houses generally show significantly improved results. But the best time to prepare for a rainy day is when profits are high. According to an article in the *Financial Times:* "Under the ownership of Swiss Bank Corporation, Warburg now flourishes, as does Barings under ING. But they will all be severely tested in the next bear market. The ultimate return on these global ambitions may well prove disappointingly small."[6]

A similar statement is valid about financial institutions and treasuries particularly active in derivatives. In a 1994 survey, the Washington-based Group of 30 found that 96 percent of dealers and 99 percent of end users who participated in this project believed they should measure actual exposure and potential exposure of derivatives.

The same study[7] found that 93 percent of dealers and 74 percent of end users use, or plan to use in the near term, solutions that permit the measurement of credit exposures with derivatives. Furthermore, 87 percent of the dealers surveyed have established, or planned to establish in the near future, credit limits that reflect the sum of current and potential exposures.

This growing trend toward the use of models for risk-management purposes is significant because it reveals a change in culture among financial institutions. But at the same time, the senior management of these institutions should be aware of the fact that risk models that are not subject to constant reevaluation tend to decay in terms of performance. This is why it is so important to generalize the use of the green, yellow, and red zones even among algorithms that are not used for regulatory reporting.

One more reason for paying attention to the outgoing quality level from models is the concentration taking place in asset management—and with it the concentration in risks. Goldman Sachs has predicted that within five years there will be only 20 to 25 asset-management companies, each with at least $150 billion in assets under control. There will also be numerous small companies that have established themselves as niche operators, serving particular needs by offering specific personalized products.

Globalization is a very important part of this transition. Size is also a key, and so is technology. Videoconferencing and E-mail have not stopped the need for face to face business meetings but have made them

---

6 October 31, 1996.

7 Group of 30, *Derivatives: Practices and Principles, Follow-up Surveys of Industry Practice* (Washington, DC, 1994).

more effective. Management information systems have improved focusing, provided the algorithms and heuristics they use are up to the risk.

Mathematical models are now permitting rigorous financial analysis, and researchers are trying not only to identify investments that have competitive advantages but also to find those with advantages that can be sustained for several years. This is something of a novelty in a fast-buck business.

The overriding idea is to translate economic theories about competitive advantages into something one can invest in. In a deregulated and globalized financial market, four factors matter most in shaping the competitive terrain in which investment firms operate:

1. Currency values.
2. Interest rates.
3. Know-how about manipulating them.
4. Technological prowess.

Asset managers destined to survive select their instruments in three stages. First, they examine each industry for factors leading to long-term competitive advantage because different things matter in different industries. Then, they concentrate on companies that are active in more than one region of the world. Finally, they compute the risk-adjusted return on equity, as explained in Section 5.

The clients of asset managers use similar criteria as well as growth in value and management quality, including steady restructuring. There are also some other factors. An asset manager has got to be very small or very big, but in either case it must be a leader in technology.

7. THE BUSINESS ASPECTS OF NEW TECHNOLOGY FOR RISK CONTROL

What the topmost commercial banks and investment banks have found during recent years is that leadership in technology makes sense, not only because it permits capturing business opportunities and better control of risk, but also because it is appreciated by their customers. Typically in the financial industry

- One percent of customers represent 20 percent of profits.
- Two percent of customers bring home 50 percent of profits.
- Twenty percent of customers account for 80 percent of profits.

Therefore, there is an understandable rush to capture the top of the customer pyramid. The example I have chosen in this section is State

Street Bank and Trust of Boston, regarding its development and use of new technology in business opportunity analysis and in risk management.

The meeting with James J. Darr started with a statement that set the pace for the whole discussion. He said, "Our primary concern is what *our customers* expect from us in information technology." This is how a provider of financial services should think, and the answer that is given can make or break the financial institution and its impact on the market.

The executive vice president of State Street Bank and Trust stated that as far as the nature of technology is concerned, a lot of change is not perceptable from where they were three or five years ago. The new tools that will be used will be enhanced versions of what is known. This misses the point. The point is that not the tools by themselves, but the speed and accuracy of the information we feed in makes the difference.

The reasons underpinning this very significant evolution in technological thinking is that the meaning of time has changed. Five years ago, having daily information on assets, liabilities, and risks was leading edge. A bank that was able to know its accounts weekly was among the best. Today this is utterly inadequate.

What is today at a premium is the ability to have a risk-adjusted strategy—and this means that assets and liabilities information must be intraday. I have steadily underlined this need throughout this chapter. Some banks have reached this status. For instance, State Street Bank and Trust has fully updated assets, liabilities, and risk information available every 30 minutes. The system works with preestablished parameters, and the next goal is to have this information on tap every five minutes.

This is essentially a *virtual balance sheet* (VB/S) operating as a real-time management information system. We will discuss virtual balance sheets and virtual financial statements in much greater length in Part Two, because they constitute the top technology of the end of this decade.

"Is there a risk that outsiders get hold of the contents of the virtual balance sheet," I asked, "or maybe of some of its information elements?"

"No," said James Darr. "It is hard for an outsider to look at and understand what is on a virtual balance sheet."

The thesis of State Street has been that behind the need for intraday VB/S solutions is not only the bank's management but also, if not primarily, the bank's clients: "Our customers are a source of demand for such tools and methods because they want us to help them in managing risks in a strategic way."

This statement should be written in block letters and be at the desk of every chief executive officer. Examples of clients with such requirements are pension funds and mutual funds. State Street is working with Morgan Bank on a pension fund account. The project promotes an improved version of RiskMetrics.[8] The most significant value-added characteristics are the personalization of the risk-management tools and a much greater sophistication in terms of their implementation.

A greater sophistication is necessary not only for reasons of competitiveness but also to account for the fact that the typical pension fund is a *long-term investor* but at the same time faces many short-term requirements. Examples of solutions for the short-term needs are:

- Sophisticated tools for arbitrage and
- Tactical asset-allocation models.

These are subject to personalization, which considers a lot of factors, among them currency-exchange risk. With this pension fund, currency risk is currently at 8 percent to 10 percent of investments. But because of increasing investment abroad, it is a foregone conclusion that currency risk will increase. The next goal is 20 percent.

How should this currency risk be managed? The answer is through a very advanced internal accounting management information system with intraday information. This is what the pension fund has asked.

Such requirements make the value-added solution totally different from what is necessary for formal regulatory reporting. American pension funds report to the Department of Labor and the Internal Revenue Service. But the accounting standards of these agencies are archaic. And what is more, the United States government takes two years to compile them. No major investor can afford to work that way.

---

8 Discussed in Part Two.

CHAPTER 6

American and British Regulators Look at Market Risk

1. INTRODUCTION

The motor behind the 1996 Market Risk Amendment has been, in my judgment, the huge exposure assumed by commercial banks and other financial institutions because of derivative financial instruments.[1] According to a statistic I heard during my meeting with the Federal Reserve of Boston, the big money-center banks today have a derivatives exposure between 80 and 150 percent of their capital.

If the 1988 Basle Capital Accord requirements by the Basle Committee stand at 8 percent of their assets, 150 percent of capital represents 12 percent of the balance sheet. This is more or less what the Swiss National Bank said about the current exposure in terms of off-balance sheet items in balance-sheet positions. We will talk of the new Swiss regulatory reporting in Chapter 8.

Commercial banks do appreciate that over the years, particularly since the late 1980s, they may have taken on an inordinate amount of exposure. Therefore, they are not adverse to new regulation. As a senior commercial banker said during our meeting in Boston in November 1996, he would welcome new regulations that streamline derivatives reporting. Today, he added, his people spend 20 percent of their time designing hedges and 80 percent arguing with accountants about how to present the results.

---

1 See D. N. Chorafas, *Managing Derivatives Risk* (Burr Ridge, IL: Irwin Professional Publishing, 1996).

Commercial bankers would also like to see settled the issue of what constitutes a trading book, what constitutes a banking book, and which of their elements should be marked-to-market or marked-to-model. I defined the trading book and banking book in Chapter 1, but also added that these definitions are not universal.

Differences of opinion regarding balance-sheet and off-balance sheet items also exist between countries and regulatory authorities. This creates both confusion and loopholes.

In a banking meeting in London, I was given as an example a case of supervisory authorities reproaching the chief executive officer about the large off-balance sheet exposure of his company. The CEO answered, "It is nonsense to look off balance sheet. You should only control the balance sheet." A few months down the line, the same CEO wrote to his shareholders: "Looking at the balance sheet is not enough. You have also to appreciate the positions your company has off-balance sheet."

Supervisory authorities and accounting standards boards are aware of the need to revamp and restructure current regulation, to close the loopholes, and to streamline reporting practices. This chapter looks at the position taken by the Federal Reserve, the Bank of England, and, correspondingly, the Financial Accounting Standards Board (FASB) in the United States and the Accounting Standards Board (ASB) in the United Kingdom.

2. FASB STATEMENT 119 AND THE NEW U.S. REGULATION

The first significant pieces of new regulation that addressed market risk, and most specifically derivatives, have been FASB Statements of Financial Accounting Standards 105 and 107 of the early 1990s. While they were criticized at their time by some commercial banks as being too tough on them, both FASB Statements were instrumental in giving the U.S. banking industry a lead over its competitors because they obliged U.S. banks to address some tough problems earlier than they otherwise would have.

These two pieces of regulation were followed by FASB Statement 119. Statement 119, which was made mandatory at the end of 1994, requires disclosures about derivative financial instruments and amends some of the requirements spelled out by Statements 105 and 107. The new disclosures concern amounts, nature, and terms of derivatives that are not subject to Statement 105 because they do not result in off-balance sheet risk. It also calls for a distinction to be made between financial instruments held or issued for *trading* purposes and those for *hedging,* which it more generally defines as "purposes other than trading."

Few people have noticed the impact of the FASB Risk Amendment by the Basle Committee. Yet there have been both direct and indirect effects, the latter induced by the Fed of New York and U.S. banks that were already well versed in marking-to-model.

In what regards derivative instruments for trading, Statement 119 requires disclosure of *average fair value* and of *net trading gains or losses.* Banks and other entities that hold or issue derivative financial instruments for nontrading reasons must disclose those purposes and follow guidelines on how the instruments are reported in their financial statements.

Banks and treasuries that hold or issue derivative financial instruments and account for them as hedges of anticipated transactions must disclose these anticipated transactions, the class of derivatives used for the hedge, and the amounts of hedging gains or losses being deferred. This means gains and losses recognized but not yet realized. They must also disclose the transactions or other events that result in recognition of the deferred gains or losses in earnings.

Another important characteristic of Statement 119 is that it encourages, but does not require, quantitative information about market risks of assets and liabilities—including derivatives—consistent with the way the bank manages or adjusts risks. Such a presentation must be made in a way that is useful for comparing the results of the bank's strategy in holding, buying, or writing derivatives.

In terms of changes from previous FASB Statements such as 105 and 107, Statement 119 calls for disaggregation of financial instruments with off-balance sheet risk by class, business activity, and exposure.

This must be done in a way that is consistent with the management of those instruments. Statement 119 amends Statement 107 by requiring that fair-value information is presented without combining, aggregating, or netting the fair value of derivatives with the fair value of nonderivative financial instruments. It also specifies that such information is presented together with the related carrying amounts

This can be done in the body of the financial statement, a single footnote, or a summary table of *comprehensive income,* addressing recognized gains and losses. This procedure is fairly similar to the British Statement of Total Recognized Gains and Losses (STRGL), which is discussed in Section 6.

Statement 119 specifies that *supplementary reporting* should make clear whether the amounts in reference represent assets or liabilities. In this connection, it is not dissimilar from the Swiss National Bank regulation about reporting gains and losses with derivatives, respectively, in assets and in liabilities, which became compulsory in 1996.

The common ground underpinning U.S., British, Swiss, and other regulations that came into effect in the mid-1990s is that more and more accurate disclosure is necessary about derivatives—and therefore about market risk. The following are some of the reasons for the change:

- Derivatives have become quite important in finance, business, and industry.
- Investors and creditors need information about the purposes for which derivative financial instruments are held or issued.
- Risk management cannot be effectively exercised without significantly improving current reporting practices.

Regulators consider quantitative disclosure about the risks of derivatives to be very useful and at the same time unlikely to be misunderstood or out of context. Hence the recent drive for the following:

- Disclosing more details about current positions and associated exposure.
- Experimenting on the most likely effects on equity and annual P&L (income statement).
- Calculating the value-at-risk, both day-to-day and at the end of the reporting period.

Stripped down to its fundamentals, these are the targets of the 1996 Market Risk Amendment by the Basle Committee. In this sense, U.S., British, and Continental European regulations regarding market risk tend to converge.

Supervisory authorities have capitalized on the fact that during the last seven years derivatives have been the subject of major studies by different government agencies as well as independent research organizations. All these studies cited the need for significant improvements in risk management and in regulatory reporting.

3. THE FED OF SAN FRANCISCO AND THE FED OF BOSTON LOOK INTO STATEMENT 119 AND NOTIONAL PRINCIPAL AMOUNTS

Statement of Financial Accounting Standards 119 by FASB states that some respondents objected to the requirement in Statement 105 to disclose the notional principal amount (contract amount) of financial instruments with off-balance sheet accounting risk. They suggested that notional principal amounts are not useful and could be misleading.

This point is made particularly in connection to leveraged instruments when the amount disclosed may not be representative of the risks involved in the trade. In its comments regarding this argument, the Financial Accounting Standards Board states that it understands that disclosure of notional amount is an imperfect measure of market risk or credit risk for some financial instruments. The face amount, however, is *contractual* and as such it provides an indication of the presence of risks and the volume of derivatives activity.

Therefore, the Financial Accounting Standards Board goes on record, in Statement 119, that it continues to believe the notional principal amount is useful information to investors and creditors as well as to the management of the bank.

FASB indeed accepts that if the instrument is geared and the information about the instrument is not provided, the face or contract amount might be misleading. But if the type of gearing is known, the notional principal can be a useful reference. Reporting entities anyway are required to disclose the effects of leverage features of the financial instruments they trade as specified by paragraph 8 of Statement 119 and paragraph 17 of Statement 105.

The Fed of Boston thinks that notional principal is not necessarily a good indicator of exposure, but it could constitute a useful reference. One of the reasons it is not always a good indicator of exposure is that leveraged swaps can make the notional principal look low and artificially reduce the level of exposure.

Therefore, each case has to be studied on its own merits, not as part of a larger number of transactions that are not particularly homogeneous. For instance, just tracking down the number of short swaps, long swaps, and offsets does not mean much except that someone is active in the market.

Another reason given during the meeting with the Fed of Boston for why the notional principal amount may not be a good indicator of exposure is the difference between swaps and structured notes, the latter being on-balance sheet according to U.S. reporting requirements. Yet structured notes have leveraged characteristics, with interest rates playing a key role.

Still another reason for downplaying the role of the notional principal amount as an indicator of exposure is *management intent,* a concept discussed in Section 4. As long as management intent is part of the picture, says the Fed of Boston, the system is unstable: A bank may be using derivatives for hedging, say, a 30-year contract, but tomorrow the market changes and management decides to sell, moving out of the hedge.

The Bank of England also thinks that the notional principal amount does not provide a good relation to risk exposure. But other central banks believe that, for *internal management accounting* purposes, the notional principal amount might be a useful indicator. A similar role is played by the internal interest-rate swap, which unloads interest-rate risk from the loans book and brings it to the trading book.

Personally, I believe that appropriately massaged through a demodulator,[2] the notional principal amount can be a good indicator of exposure in the context of IAMIS. In this sense, I side with the response given by FASB in Statement 119 to the notional principal's critics.

Let me give a brief example of how to compute the demodulator of the notional principal amount to bring it to a level that can be seen as corresponding to capital at risk with loans. Say that for an interest-rate swap (IRS) the notional principal of a contract is $100 million. You mine your IRS database and find that in the distribution of *absolute values* of gains and losses in connection to fixed/floating rates, the mean is 2.4, and the standard deviation is 1.

Then at a 99-percent level of confidence (two-tailed), the risk being taken is:

$$x + 2.6s = 2.4 + 2.6 \times 1 = 5$$

and the resulting demodulator is: $\dfrac{100}{5} = 20$.

Whether the notional principal amount is or is not used in connection with derivatives risk, the broader question remains: What is the impact of FASB Statement 119 on the U.S. banking industry? The answer is that beginning on December 15, 1997, U.S. banks will have to classify their derivative transactions into three types:

1. Fair market hedge.
2. Cash flow hedge.
3. Hedge of net investment in a foreign entity.

According to the Federal Reserve of San Francisco, this classification will create the need to predefine *management intent,* therefore clarifying the type of risk the bank takes in its derivatives transaction.

2 See D. N. Chorafas, *Managing Derivatives Risk* (Burr Ridge, IL: Irwin Professional Publishing, 1996).

Another effect of the foregoing classification of derivatives instruments for regulatory reporting reasons is the increased attention to cash flow by commercial banks. Such attention has much to do with reporting systems, and it first came in official regulation by the ruling issued by the German Bundesbank in September 1993.

"We feel that the more disclosure we have, the better it is for the financial system," said an executive of the Federal Reserve of San Francisco. Indeed, commercial bankers should appreciate that accurate and timely disclosure measures help to bring systemic risk under control.

But many quantitative milestones have yet to be crossed to be able to understand in a factual and documented manner how an expanding financial market really works. Parts of the puzzle are the metrics and measures necessary to reflect volatility in the markets. Current metrics are not precise. For instance, the Bank of America says there is a 10 percent increase in volatility for 50 basis points difference in interest rates.

Other bankers, however, think this statistic is exaggerated. The fact is that no one really has the measurement procedures that will prove or disprove such a statement and many others. There is still a great deal of work to be done in analytical finance.

4. THE TRANSFORMATION OF RISK THROUGH DERIVATIVES AND THE ISSUE OF MANAGEMENT INTENT

Because derivatives are geared financial instruments, the value of their positions can change very rapidly. This exposes the bank or the treasury of an industrial company and reduces the usefulness of the P&L picture portrayed in the annual statement. At the same time, the ease with which derivatives can be designed, sold, or acquired means they can readily be used to transform the risk profile. This transformation of risk is often done without the benefit of a rigorous analytical procedure.

For instance, a company with fixed-rate borrowing may take out a swap under which it pays floating rates and receives fixed rates. Such a deal leaves a net position of paying floating interest rates. Both interest-rate risk transformation and currency-exchange rate deals are not necessarily apparent by existing disclosure requirements.

There is another twist to this reference. With the new regulatory directives, a swaps agreement must be marked-to-market or marked-to-model. This is doable, and most major U.S. banks practice it. But they don't use the outcome as a natural hedge because this could lead to the wrong conclusions.

Basically, the disclosure problem starts with the fact that the classification of a derivative as a hedge rests on *management intent.* A lot of ambiguity is derived from the fact that accounting distinctions can change because of management intent. The British Accounting Standards Board is particularly critical of this issue.

Current disclosure requirements have been made for conventional financial instruments, such as shares and bonds. In this case, they more or less adequately cover the indicators of risk. But because derivatives quickly transform the risk profile, new disclosure rules are required. To appreciate the extent of leverage, it should be stressed that classical financial instruments, such as shares and bonds, involve a substantial initial cash inflow or outlay. This is recorded in the balance sheet as an asset or liability, and everyone receives notice as to its existence.

On the contrary, derivatives involve a low or zero initial inflow or outflow of cash. The result is that what is recorded in the balance sheet as an asset or liability is also at a very low level, but the exposure is high because the transaction is geared.

It is appropriate to point out that nonderivatives can also expose the company to large risks. In other words, through leveraging, banks and industrial companies experience embedded gains and losses, whether these result from derivatives or not. One example is leveraged buyouts; another is refinancing agreements.

The problem with leverage through derivatives is that it enables the assumption of a wide variety of risks, with relative ease but in large amounts of risk. Many of these transactions will mitigate preexisting risks, but this is not always the case. The new risks involved are not made readily apparent under existing disclosure requirements. Better disclosure can help assess real exposure, therefore helping both the company management and the regulators.

Dynamic accounting procedures can assist the management of the bank in controlling exposure, providing a good basis for reporting financial results to the authorities. But this must be done in an objective manner. Basing accounting distinctions on management intent presents two problems:

1. Management intent varies from one firm to the other and over time. Hence the results are heterogeneous and unstable.
2. Management intent is not based on external economic factors but on internal considerations that are often subjective.

Management intent may change, resulting in a different accounting treatment that does not reflect a change in the financial position of the bank. Management intent can result in losses reported as assets and gains reported as liabilities.

This happens when a realized loss on a hedge is deferred. Without appropriate guidelines in terms of reporting standards, a bank's accounts become less easy to understand if hedge accounting is used. The reason is that this practice gives rise to debits and credits in the balance sheet that are not assets and liabilities, but they are losses and gains.

As contrasted to P&L as classically represented in the income statement, gains and losses from hedge accounting are reflected in a different statement, as we will see in Section 6.

In order to interpret management intent, regulators and supervisors have to understand the policy of the directors and of the bank's executives. Without this understanding, it is not possible to say how risk averse a company is.

It should be added in this connection that the idea of asking a bank to explain its own objectives and policies, focusing on those instruments and risks that are of greatest significance, is not without merit. A description of the major financial risks faced by the bank, such as counterparty risk, interest-rate risk, currency risk, country risk, equity risk, legal risk, and settlement risk, can be illuminating.

Qualification, however, should be supported by quantified information included in the disclosure. Greater detail could be presented, for example, about how the bank approaches mismatch risk or the extent to which foreign currency debtors and creditors are hedged to the local currency of operations. A similar statement can be made about hedging of options, futures, and forwards in a way that can provide a quantifiable measure of intent.

5. CHANGING REGULATORY DIRECTIVES AT THE BANK OF ENGLAND

In a way that closely parallels the cultural change taking place at the U.S. Federal Reserve System and other central banks of the Group of Ten (G–10) countries, the way the Bank of England looks at regulation is in a process of major evolution. The Central Bank and the markets are no longer at arm's length; the Bank of England has become a market player—but also a partner of financial institutions, rather than being only a supervisor.

Says Ian Plenterleith of the Bank of England,

Ten years ago, I might have felt inhibited at meetings with fund managers; I might have feared I would say something that would have influenced their investment decisions—heaven forbid! Now every quarter I talk openly to them. We tell them exactly where we are with our gilt program and seek their advice as to what we should do in the forthcoming quarter. And it can all be done without comprising anybody.[3]

This change of attitude imposes an enormous obligation on the Bank of England, not only to *be* professionally competent, but also to be *seen as* professionally competent. The same is true of all reserve banks. Such competence must show both in their operations and in their understanding of how the markets work.

The change in culture is not only necessary because of the globalization and deregulation of the financial industry or because of fast product development and a rapidly advancing technology, but also because of practical reasons. The central bank's relationship to the commercial banks it supervises is not based on mystique, but on an analytical understanding of the markets and on thinking well ahead of time about what it wants and what it says.

Today, a regulatory policy can be successful only when the central banker's mind is genuinely open to new ideas and to new ways of doing things. This is, in a nutshell, the message I received from my meeting with senior executives of the Bank of England.

"The markets demand rigorous analysis and intellectual applications," the Bank of England executives said. "Not some sort of gut feeling." Therefore, many central bankers now appreciate that regulation and supervision must become a center of excellence in the way in which they conduct their operations.

One of the practical examples given during the meeting concerned the calculation of value-at-risk. This will be examined in detail in Part Two. Another case that was discussed was the impact of the Big Bang of 1986 on the Bank of England, its policies, and its procedures. The factors that resulted in the Big Bang have a great deal to do with regulation by central bankers:

- The huge advances in information technology.
- The globalization of the markets.

---

3 *The Old Lady,* September 1996, Bank of England, London.

- The determination to do away with too many regulatory barriers.
- The new-look, new-breed market players who came in with a different attitude.

In the past, the bank was at the center of financial intermediation. But as Ian Plenderleith points out,

> The old-established channels of communication were no longer appropriate (after the Big Bang). Institutions managed their investments more actively: They were more interested in the Bank's operations—and were more willing to criticize our performance and our actions.[4]

This has happened not only in England but in all G–10 countries, and in many others. Not only did the attitude of central bankers change, but it also became necessary to restructure the system of checks and balances in terms of accounting standards for regulatory reporting to the operations of the reserve banks themselves.

In Chapter 7, we will take as a case study the very thorough restructuring that currently takes place in the French system of financial accounting standards. Then in Chapter 8 we will examine, within a much broader framework, the evolving authority and responsibility of central bankers.

All this is very relevant to risk management because the incentives for money-center banks to hedge interest-rate risk and currency-exchange risk are significantly affected by the way the regulatory system works. In practically every country, large commercial banks, whether state-owned or not, have been (formally or informally) protected by the unwritten policy of reserve banks and of governments that they are too big to fail.

Under this policy, regulators extend deposit insurance at these banks to cover all liability holders, large or small—though not necessarily the stock markets. This serves as a subsidy to risk taking, and leads to the fact that big banks hold large interest-rate swaps with the compliments of the taxpayer.

The Bank of England has so far proved to be the only major central bank that did not follow such a policy. When in February 1995 Barings came knocking at the door for a salvage operation, the Bank of England's answer was No. This has not been the case of the Federal Reserve with Continental Illinois (in 1984), nor of the French government in connection to the on-and-off crises at Credit Lyonnais in the 1990s.[5]

---

4 "The Old Lady," September 1996, Bank of England, London.
5 See D. N. Chorafas, *Derivative Financial Instruments: Strategies for Managing Risk and Return in Banking* (London: Lafferty Publications, 1995).

6. THE BRITISH ACCOUNTING STANDARDS BOARD AND STRGL

In Britain, the Accounting Standards Board (ASB) is a new development, having been instituted in 1990. Its supervisory authority is the Accounting Standards Committee, and functionally it depends on the Financial Reporting Council. The higher-up authorities of the latter are the British government and the Bank of England.

There are several similarities between ASB and the Financial Accounting Standards Board (FASB) in the United States. Created in 1973, FASB followed in the steps of a previous organization that was the brainchild of certified public accountants. Today, the forces behind FASB are the Financial Accounting Foundation and the Securities and Exchange Commission (SEC).

The goal of both ASB and FASB, as well as of the French Commission Bancaire, which is discussed in Chapter 7, is the establishment of sound accounting standards that are universally applied within the country of their jurisdiction. Whether in manufacturing, banking, or other lines of business, large companies must disclose if they have followed such standards. This gives the financial accounting standards the force of law.

For example, in the United Kingdom, the Financial Reports Review Panel can challenge the accounts submitted by a company and bring its management to court. This is a civil case, not a criminal case, but the directors of the company are personally responsible.

To avoid an inordinate amount of personal responsibilty, any financial engineering solution—including the so-called creative accounting practice—must look at the substance of the accounts and follow the established rules. Reporting must examine and reflect the nature of the transactions. It should not be limited to the legal form.

While the "Derivatives and Other Financial Instruments" document issued by ASB in July 1996 is still a discussion paper, the Board encourages companies to adopt the outlined disclosures even before they are generally agreed upon and take the form of law. This helps establish a sound internal practice and get experience with the rules-to-be.

Some of the rules-to-be in the United Kingdom are already applied in the United States. There is indeed a significant similarity between the Comprehensive Income Statement specified by FASB and the Statement of Total Recognized Gains and Losses (STRGL) by ASB. Both address recognized but not yet realized gains and losses.

The concept underpinning STRGL is that if some gains and losses are not reported in the profit and loss account, they fall in time buckets outside the income statement. Yet they may represent significant exposure. There are only two other classical accounting places where these gains and losses might be put:

1. The balance sheet within assets and liabilities (as the Swiss are doing).
2. The balance sheet within shareholders' funds.

According to ASB, neither of these is an acceptable alternative. Positioning future gains and losses into assets and liabilities has the effect of losses being reported as assets and gains as liabilities. Manipulating the shareholders' funds account for reserve accounting reasons contradicts other established accounting practices.

To this is added the fact that the 1996 Market Risk Amendment has been instrumental in orienting regulatory and accounting standards authorities towards measuring all outstanding financial instruments at current value. This is computed either by marking-to-market or by marking-to-model through value-at-risk. This is discussed in Part Two.

STRGL (or comprehensive income in the United States) is a new concept being institutionalized in England. But it is not the first change to reporting standards taking place during the last few years. In 1993, new regulations in financial reporting required banks and other entities to include long-term debt and overseas accounts.

This has been done through a secondary statement. In the background of the new rules lies the fact that a sound accounting standard permits better appreciation of the effect of novel instruments such as derivatives; and for accounting purposes, it is rewarding to mark all instruments to market, whether these are in the trading book or the banking book.

This is the off-the-record opinion of ASB. British banks were horified by the banking-book reference. Their proposal has been that, rather than marking the loans to market, they should transfer the market risk of their banking book to their trading book by means of an internal swap. This concept has already been discussed.

ASB does not accept this alternative of an internal swap because it believes it will become a moving target. It also objects to having the two books valued in totally different ways: the trading book at market and the banking book at historical cost.

When I mentioned the subject of an internal interest-rate swap, the senior Bank of England executives answered that the reserve institution encourages (indeed promotes) such practice—but only for internal management accounting purposes, not for regulatory reporting by banks.

Practically all parties seem to agree that existing accounting rules and procedures have to fundamentally change through a comprehensive redefinition. The current difference of opinion is how this should be done.

New solutions will not be easy. While everyone aims to control exposure while generating a rate of return, there is more than one approach to disclosure. "Until you get actively involved, you don't meet detailed disclosure," said Allan Cook of ASB. "Solutions must be rigorous and generic." Hence, the new proposal by the Accounting Standards Board.

Personally, I like the STRGL concept that implies that realized profits and losses are reported in the income statement (P&L statement), while those recognized but not realized are reported in STRGL. For instance, STRGL would include gains and losses on interest-rate derivatives used to manage the interest basis of borrowings: fixed-rate loans and currency deals.

Another example of an STRGL item is currency derivatives where these are used to manage the currency risk because of, say, capital invested in overseas operations and any associated borrowings. This bypasses historical costs and leads to a distinction in reporting requirements depending on whether an item is *out-of-current-earnings,* hence to be reported in the STRGL, or *in-current-earnings,* to be reported in the income statement.

There is no contradiction in this practice because the profit and loss account continues to report an interest expense at an effective yield to maturity calculated on a historical cost basis. The STRGL/P&L bifurcation also has the effect that, provided a fixed-rate borrowing is held to maturity, any changes in its value arising from interest-rate movements that are initially recorded in STRGL would, in later years, continue in STRGL or come into P&L. Hence there is continuity.

7. EXISTING DIFFERENCES BETWEEN THE BRITISH AND U.S. REGULATORY POSITIONS

One of the preoccupations I saw in the course of the meeting with regulatory authorities in London is whether the Americans will come on board. While the new reporting practices currently being elaborated in the United Kingdom in the aftermath of the 1996 Market Risk Amendment are very close to those in the United States, there are also differences.

One of the differences brought into perspective during these meetings is that U.S. regulations make a distinction between realized and nonrealized profits. By contrast, the ASB discussion paper takes the position that, as far as financial instruments are concerned, there is not much difference between realized and unrealized profits, which leads to the need to mark the banking book to market.

My opinion is that while differences in reporting practices between countries are bound to exist (even within the same country there are differences in opinion regarding regulatory reporting), the basic guiding principles should be followed. Such principles have been clearly stated in the 1996 Market Risk Amendment. The rest is a matter of procedure.

But some procedures should be streamlined among the G–10 countries. For instance, FASB proposes using current values for derivatives only. By contrast, the concept of ASB is that current values should be used for all financial instruments, whether derivative or nonderivative, leading to the need to mark the banking book.

Being a more global view, the latter involves fewer hedge accounting problems and does not require distinguishing between derivatives and nonderivatives. By contrast, in terms of culture, the U.S. and U.K. viewpoints are not that far apart. A majority of FASB members have stated their belief that current value is the most relevant measure for financial instruments and the only relevant measure for derivatives.

One of the practical problems, however, is that measuring all financial instruments at current value would represent a major job. Therefore, FASB has somewhat constrained the scope by not addressing all financial instruments but, rather, determining the accounting for hedges while requiring all derivatives to be recognized and measured at current value in the balance sheet.

Another difference between British and American viewpoints concerns loans and related hedges through derivatives. FASB views floating-rate loans as a cash flow exposure. In this sense, a swap that converts a loan from a fixed to a floating rate may be considered a hedge of cash flow risk.

There is also a potential difference between British and American viewpoints that concerns hedges of future transactions. FASB proposes using hedge accounting for hedges of all kinds of future transactions, whether contracted or uncontracted.

ASB has not yet reached a conclusion on this issue but has advanced for discussion purposes three possible approaches that need to be further elaborated. Eventually one of them will be selected.

In regard to *comprehensive income,* FASB uses this notion as a temporary parking lot for gains and losses on hedges representing future transactions. In a later period, when realized, these gains and losses are transferred to earnings.

ASB recognizes that if hedge accounting is to be allowed for hedges of uncontracted future transactions, the resulting hedging gains and losses would need to be reported either in comprehensive income (the STRGL) or within liabilities and assets in the balance sheet. In either case, they will have to be recycled.

Let me add that in the not-to-distant future FAS by FASB will supersede Statements 105, 107, and 109. FAS is still in the discussion paper stage. It addresses derivatives and similar instruments. In an accounting sense, it permits the holder to participate in gains and losses without delivering the underlying.

Finally, with the Basle Committee setting up a subcommittee to study accounting issues, these mainly procedural differences should be brought into perspective and ironed out. Indeed, it will be a pity if they perpetuate themselves in the international regulatory system. The timing is right for a global agreement because most countries (and central banks) have not yet decided on procedures. Once they do, it will be too late to change the systems and procedures that have already been adopted.

In the 1980s, the International Accounting Standards Committee (IASC) accepted the challenge of developing principles of accounting for financial instruments. In response to this mission, in 1991 it presented an exposure draft E40; and in 1994 a reexposure draft IAS E48. This has advanced many new and controversial recommendations. Therefore, an accounting standard dealing only with disclosure was subsequently released: IAS 32.

There is as well an outstanding IASC position paper on "Accounting for Financial Assets and Financial Liabilities". Issued in March 1997, this document attempts to complete the work started by IAS 32. There are also four recent publications on derivatives and other financial instruments:

1. FASB's latest proposed statement of financial accounting standards (1996)[6]
2. FEE, a European perspective (1996)[7]
3. ASB's discussion paper (1996), and
4. BBA SORP[8] on derivatives (1996).

---

6 "Accounting for derivatives and similar financial instruments and for hedging activities," File reference 612–B.

7 Federation des Experts Comptables Europeens.

8 British Bankers Association, Statement of Recommended Accounting Practices. This statement was issued jointly by the BBA and the Irish Bankers Federation.

As far as the Financial Accounting Standards Board's proposed FAS is concerned, its area of impact will be in the United States not worldwide—just like new accounting standards proposed by FEE will have an impact only in the 15 countries of the European Union. This FEE document has been mandated by a resolution of the European Parliament on derivatives.

IAS 32 is more specific than both FASB and FEE, since it deals only with disclosure issues. During the First International Conference on Risk Management in the banking industry,[9] Martyn Taylor, Chairman, Banks Working Party of the European Federation of Public Accountants, described the expected content of the new IAS position paper. This is expected to be fairly similar to the Accounting Standards Board's position paper, but with hedge accounting largely unrecognized.

The FEE approach bases its valuation rules on whether the financial instrument contract (asset or liability) is held for trading or nontrading purposes, trading being broadly what one buys or sells for profit. Everything else is nontrading.

BBA SORP establishes a narrowier implementation horizon because it applies only to derivatives. It targets fair value in the trading book but defines trading in a way which contradicts the FEE proposal—starting with a statement of what is nontrading and then treating everything else as trading. Trading items must be reported at fair value.

What the reader should retain from the reference to all these complementary but also conflicting standardization efforts is that confusion rather than clarity leads the parade of new rules. Therefore, there are still a million miles of paperwork ahead of us.

---

9 London, March 17–19, 1997.

CHAPTER 7

Restructuring the Financial Accounting System of the French Republic

1. INTRODUCTION

At the end of August 1996, a rigorous plan for restructuring the French accounting system was presented to the Council of Ministers. The new accounting plan was based on three pillars:

1. The decree of August 27, 1996, concerning the new structure of the Conseil National de la Comptabilité (CNC). This decree enlarges the role of CNC and adds to its responsibilities. It also makes CNC a pivot point in the evolution of a new accounting structure.

2. The independence of Banque de France and the new mission given to the Commission Bancaire. While still part of the central bank, the Commission Bancaire gains some autonomy and a new role as bridge between the Ministry of the Economy and Finance and Banque de France.[1]

3. The new law to be submitted to the Parliament and to the Senate, leading to the creation of a new entity: the Comité de Règlementation Comptable (CRC).

---

1 The subject of how the Commission Bancaire works as a link between the Banque de France and the Ministry of the Economy and Finance is discussed in Section 7.

To appreciate where these structural changes lead in terms of new accounting rules and procedures, as well as their aftermaths, it is advisable to briefly review the history of evolution of accounting and reporting norms in France, particularly what has taken place since World War II.

2. THE PLAN COMPTABLE GÉNÉRAL (PCG)

The General Accounting Plan currently in use was adopted in 1947. It incorporated many elements from a 1942 accounting plan, known as Plan Delmas, after the name of the publisher. PCG targeted a solid industrial accounting system. It was decided that this new system was to be introduced softly, as the smaller and medium-size French companies were not ready for it.

Another key issue connected to 1947 is that since that time an autonomous status has characterized *industrial accounting* (management accounting) procedures, which were left outside the domain of normalization. This policy has been adopted by the Conseil Supérieur de la Normalisation, a government body established in the immediate post-World War II years. Emphasis on standardization was placed on general accounting—a practice similar to that followed in all other industrial countries.

The Plan Comptable Général evolved over time. From 1947 to the end of the 1960s, some 80 additions and modifications were made, with the goal both to embellish PCG and to embed the General Accounting Plan deep into French industrial practice.

This stream of new norms was sweetened by fiscal advantages to the companies that followed PCG. At the same time, it seems to have become general conscience that the evolution in accounting rules should be the result of a consultation between public authorities, industrial and other companies, and professional accountants.

Through this process of three-party collaboration (which is a policy followed in all major industrial countries) the Conseil Supérieur de la Normalisation Comptable—and its successor, the Conseil National de la Comptabilité (CNC)—have been able to introduce rules for the consolidation of accounts. Such rules help to provide adequate information for the following:

- Investors in the financial markets.
- The government, for reasons of taxation.
- The managements of the companies themselves.

While the first 20 years of PCG (1947–1967) were characterized by a process of apprenticeship in the new rules and of consultation, the high point of the next 20 years (1967–1987) was the effort of refinement through the experience gained by applications.

This second evolutionary phase was not without significant challenges. During the 1970s and 1980s accounting practices were changing worldwide. Even more important are the changes that took place since the late 1980s, characterized by globalization, deregulation, new technologies, and complex financial instruments, such as derivatives.

Each one of these factors and all of them together brought forward the need for restructuring not only PCG but the whole process of accounting normalization, including the creation of new rules for regulatory reporting. It is in this light that the new law now confronting the French Senate and the Parliament should be seen.

3. A RAPID EVOLUTION OF ACCOUNTING STANDARDS

The significant changes that took place in industry at large during the 1990s, most particularly in the financial markets, made an upgrade of the accounting system mandatory. This was true in all Group of Ten (G–10) countries, which are on the front line of rapid developments in financial instruments and economic issues.

Like many other countries, France found itself with a regulatory accounting system that consisted of a superposition of successive historical reporting structures. None of these structures had been revamped over the years. Therefore, France was ill-suited to confront the new requirements. To make matters worse each of the different layers of regulation and supervision was based on different juridical principles, and each corresponded, and still corresponds, to different accounting needs—which have to be integrated.

This dual scope of integration and modernization of accounting norms brings forward the requirement of developing and implementing new rules. Such rules must not only permit the presentation of assets and liabilities (A&L) in an efficient and accurate manner and proper recording of profit and loss (P&L), but must also reflect the risk embedded in the portfolio of a bank or a treasury department, and not only permit risk to be managed, but also make it a basic focus of company executives.

This focus on risk management was not a characteristic of old accounting systems. Feeling the need for a significant change in accounting norms, Americans and British confronted this problem somewhat earlier than most Continental Europeans.

In the United States, the Financial Accounting Standards Board (FASB) changed the reporting practice of U.S. companies through Statement 119 of 1994 by introducing the concept of *comprehensive income*. FASB also required an integration of balance-sheet and off-balance sheet assets and liabilities by integrating off-balance sheet liabilities into the company's equity.

The Swiss targeted the same results but took a different approach. In 1996, it became mandatory for banks to include into the balance sheet, at replacement value, their portfolio of derivatives. They are reported as "other assets" and "other liabilities," thereby integrating on-balance sheet and off-balance sheet A&L.

Neither the U.S. nor the Swiss solutions are considered the best approach by the British because they violate one of the 500-year old principles of the balance sheet: Items can move from assets to liabilities and vice versa depending on their market price. In the United Kingdom, the Accounting Standards Board (ASB) brought into being the *Statement of Total Recognized Profits and Losses* (STRGL). Comprehensive Income and STRGL represent gains and losses that are recognized but not yet realized. By contrast, the classical annual P&L account reflects profits and losses that are realized and therefore recognized.

The Statement of Total Recognized Gains and Losses and, alternatively, on-balance sheet reporting, are not officially accepted in France. The Banking Commission, however, can ask the banks it controls for reporting on gains and losses on a case-by-case basis.

Another practice by British banks that has not yet entered the French financial landscape is internal swaps. These are made by British banks to exchange the fixed interest rates of their loans portfolio with variable interest rates. Through internal swaps, financial institutions weed the mismatch risk out of their banking book, and bring interest-rate risk to their trading book, where it will be marked-to-market or marked-to-model.

The Bank of England accepts this practice, indeed promotes it, but only for management accounting reasons. Internal swaps are not admissible in terms of regulatory reporting. In France, internal interest-rate swaps are currently being debated. In a way similar to that of English law, under current regulatory rules financial institutions can make internal swaps for management accounting reasons, but this is not acceptable for reporting purposes by Banque de France. Both in the United Kingdom and in

France, commercial banks are in favor of internal interest-rate swaps, but accounting standards authorities are generally against them.

In France, there are also two opinions on the reporting of financial instruments worked out by MATIF. These have been taken over by the fiscal authorities. When adopted by law, one or the other of these opinions will constitute a significant accounting reform in the presentation of business and industrial financial results.

4. COMMISSION BANCAIRE, INTERNAL CONTROLS, AND INTRADAY DATA FLOWS

Many of the studies done by the French Banking Commission have followed the lines laid down by the Capital Adequacy Directive (CAD) of the European Union and the 1996 Market Risk Amendment by the Basle Committee. Such studies have focused on two issues:

1. A permanent system of measurement to permit a close follow-up of the trading book.
2. A way to evaluate on a daily basis the risks associated with trading book activities.

The guiding principle is that the same activities should obey the same rules in order to avoid distortions in the competitive environment. The necessary solutions, however, are not linear because they require departures from past practices as well as the proper authority to effect a cultural change.

The objective of this section is to describe the work done by the Commission Bancaire in terms of prudent reporting practices. Inevitability, this discussion has much to do with accounting standards. We will examine the relation that exists between the Conseil National de Comptabilité and the Commission Bancaire in Section 6.

The four main functions of Commission Bancaire are shown in Figure 7–1. General surveillance includes banking studies, juridical services, information technology, and international liaison to the Basle Committee and other bodies. The control of banking institutions is divided into two parts. One is of a general supervisory nature, with the bulk of the work done at headquarters. The other is hands-on control, exercised in the field at the financial institutions themselves.

Market risk is a new function. At the moment, it employes a handful of rocket scientists who work with models, and assists the French banks

F I G U R E   7-1

The Four Main Functions of Commission Bancaire

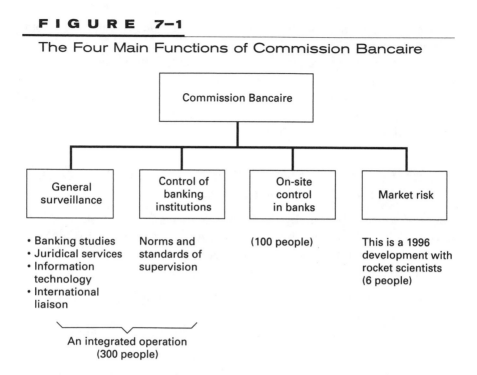

with *pretesting* their algorithms for marking-to-market—from conceptual design to the mathematics proper and database mining. The Banque de France rocket scientists verify:

- The concept underpinning the different models.
- The algorithms of the model itself.
- The market parameters used by the developers.
- Marking-to-model implementation in connection to the trading book.

The rocket sientists of the Comission Bancaire also do the *backtesting* procedures specified by the 1996 Market Risk Amendment by the Basle Committee. This pretesting/backtesting approach sees to it that the control of risk is done on two bases, one focusing on the fundamental notions, the other focusing on percentiles of correct projections of exposure.

Such duality can be of significant assistance in *stress testing*. The conceptual evaluation may present a bifurcation between normal market conditions and a hypothetical crisis situation in the financial market.

Both the Federal Reserve in the United States and the Bank of England have adopted a similar approach. At the bank of England, rocket scientists depend on the Division of Supervision and Surveillance, which is, in a way, the counterparty of the French Commission Bancaire.

Like the reserve banks in the Anglo-Saxon countries, the Commission Bancaire was right to institute a nucleus for the control of market risk through high-caliber skill, particularly people who are versatile in nontraditional financial studies. But the half-dozen rocket scientists at Banque de France are not enough to guide the hand of the French banking industry and to control the models at the same time. The Federal Reserve of Boston, for example, has 24 rocket scientists—and this is only one of the 12 federal districts.

Not only must the supervisory authorities be ready to assist in controlling the commercial banks under their jurisdiction, they must also be constantly developing their own systems and procedures for more efficient risk management. There are five examples provided by the transition:

- From *interday* financial time series, where information is provided daily, weekly, or monthly.
- To *intraday* time series, where financial transactions are registered and exploited tick-by-tick, at the minute or second level, as they happen.

If I am not mistaken, this orientation toward internal controls at the intraday level of financial data flows is not part of currently pending legislation. Yet it is very important because it constitutes the direction in which the financial industry is moving worldwide, at least among the G–10 countries.

Some central banks have taken steps to promote intraday thinking. For the last couple of years, the Federal Reserve of New York has been charging interest for intraday debit balances of commercial banks.

Commercial banks are also moving in this direction. Institutions such as J. P. Morgan are successfully using tick-by-tick time series to exploit market opportunities.

There are major risks involved in summary interday reporting. Just prior to its merger with Chemical Bank, Manufacturers Hanover found that, day in and day out, one client (General Motors) had a debit balance of $2 billion around 2:00 P.M. All three examples dramatize the interest that should be placed on *intraday data flows,* and to the work that needs to be done by rocket scientists.

5. ANTICIPATORY HEDGES AND PRUDENT RISK MANAGEMENT

Because of derivatives, deregulation, and globalization, competitive solutions make mandatory not only the need to record all operations on a tick-by-tick basis but the intraday computation of results as well. The trend among leading banks is towards an intraday evaluation of global positions and a detailed evaluation of exposure by instrument and counterparty.

Intraday volatility and tick-by-tick trades call for rigorous real-time approaches because they affect both the trading book and the banking book of a financial institution. The system to be adopted must flush out deviations from guidelines: therefore, it should go much further than it did in the past.

Another major point in the definitions to be provided by a new law is how to establish the sense of *management intent,* particularly in distinguishing between transactions done for hedging and those done for speculation. For instance, anticipatory hedges should be identified from the beginning of a commitment, not postmortem.

Anticipatory hedges are made in connection to future positions or cash flows that are not yet recognized in the balance sheet. An example is a hedge of interest-rate risk expected to occur on future lending or borrowing transactions.

Key to the use of anticipatory hedges is the assurance that the anticipated transactions will arise. This means that the transaction is part of an established business activity with a counterparty unrelated to the bank or treasury doing the anticipatory hedge.

Typically, realized and unrealized gains or losses of anticipatory hedges are deferred and included in the profit and loss account when they are realized. This is done in conformity with current practices, over the period when such gains and losses on anticipated transactions are taken to the income statement.

Other conditions are that the treasury of an industrial company or financial institution intends to create a hedge for anticipated exposure. The maturity, interest rate, and other factors of the hedged position and hedging instrument (in an anticipatory sense) are highly correlated, and there is internal evidence on the intent of the hedge.

That's what is said in theory, but the practice is not so simple. Not only in France, but all over the G–10 countries, the accounting methodology that will be necessary to distinguish between hedging and other reasons is being debated. Far from being an academic issue, this subject has a great deal to do with risk control. Prudent management cannot be exercised without a clear definition of what hedging is and what it is not.

It is interesting to notice that British legislation and regulation are at exactly the same crossroads on whether or not management intent can be taken as a basis of choice of the accounting method. This issue is new and challenging.

The traditional accounting rules are based on the notion of assets management and reporting. In practically all countries, such rules have aimed to protect the right of investors, associates, lenders, and other counterparties—including the public right to accurate information.

Based on long-held notions, the accountant knew how to present assets, liabilities, profits, and losses. But the expanding use of derivative financial instruments, and the aftermaths of a virtual economy, have radically changed the principles that past accounting practices rested on.

In a nutshell, this is the nature of the problem confronting the Commission Bancaire, the Conseil National de Comptabilité, the Senate, and the Parliament. From the budget to the balance sheet, noncommercial business has put into question existing notions. The distinction between P&L and STRGL calls for a redefinition of the concept of prudent management and puts at the front line the issue of cash flow to assure business continuity.

Nowhere is this change in concept, and in accounting practices, more evident than in banking—because banking represents the power behind the virtual economy. Therefore, regulators and legislators now focus on the financial industry and, as we will see in Section 6, there is also a structural change in the chain of command regarding new accounting principles.

The text of new legislation for the banking industry will be elaborated on by the Commission Bancaire. As with FASB and ASB, when approved, this text becomes a Recommendation Bancaire (CRB) and, therefore, the law of the land. Because of the globalization of business activity, much of the new legislation has a multinational perspective. The project of a new law currently under discussion in the Senate stipulates that French companies that take public deposits (in current accounts and savings accounts) in foreign markets are relieved from following the old accounting methods. But they must adopt the new ones.

A working group on new accounting norms was also instituted on the initiative of the European Parliament. This comes over and above the 1993 Captital Adequacy Directive (CAD) by ECDG XV of the European

Union (recently amended through an accord signed in Amsterdam). It may also go beyond the 1996 Market Risk Amendment by the Basle Committee of Banking Supervision, which stipulates new rules for financial reporting, integrating into them market risk.

6. A NEW STRUCTURE OF ACCOUNTING REGULATION IN FRANCE

The French Parliament and the Senate are currently examining the project of a new law that creates a Comité de la Règlementation Comptable (CRC). This will become a metalayer over the Conseil National de la Comptabilité (CNC) currently in the process of restructuring.

Figure 7–2 shows this dependence on the Commission Bancaire at the bottom of the food chain. This agency elaborates, and will continue elaborating, the texts of accounting regulation that affect the banking industry. As in all G–10 countries, the agency acting as an accounting standards board works on the text in consultation with the commercial and investment banks.

The CNC also changes. A great deal of what constitutes its renovation has to do with the inclusion of insurers and bankers in its ranks. Such an enrichment in professional skills has been found necessary in order to facilitate a harmonious application of new accounting directives. It is always rewarding to increase a standards body's sensitivity to the practical aspects of new regulations. It is also wise to include in the standards body professionals who can contribute to the complements or amendments to be made to standing accounting rules.

In its role, at the upper layer of Figure 7–2, CRC will cover all sectors of the French economy with the exception of government services. I personally believe that this exception is not wise. While the reasons for the exception are evident, there should be a sister organization that looks after accounting in the public sector.

In the United States, this takes place by distinguishing between the Financial Accounting Standards Board and the Government Accounting Standards Board (GASB). FASB and GASB are in the same location (Norwalk, Connecticut). They are sister organizations, though they operate as independent bodies.

In a way, the three-layered solution in Figure 7–2 corresponds to the FASB functions. CRC will confirm the accounting rules advanced by CNC, under the authority of a ministerial decision. The president of CRC is the Minister of the Economy and Finance (or his representative). Other members are as follows:

F I G U R E 7–2

The Three-Layered Structure for the Development,
Approval, and Management of French Accounting Rules

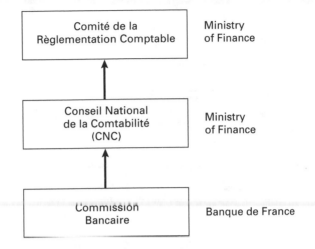

- The minister of justice (because of jurisdiction over commerce).
- The minister of the budget.
- The president of the securities commission.
- The president of CNC.
- The president of the Council of Public Accountants.
- The president of the order of auditors.
- Three members of CNC, representing the companies.

This representation is necessary in order to assure a polyvalent approach, given that the competence of CRC extends beyond industrial and commercial companies to include commercial banks, investment firms, insurance companies, and other financial institutions.

7. THE THREE BRIDGES CONNECTING THE BANQUE DE FRANCE TO THE MINISTRY OF THE ECONOMY AND FINANCE

The law that made Banque de France an institution independent from the Ministry of the Economy and Finance also provided for sharing authority over three agencies, which as we will see in this section, act as bridges. Figure 7–3 gives a visual snapshot of this statement, with the Commission Bancaire being on top.

F I G U R E 7–3

The Three Bridges That Followed the Autonomy of Banque de France

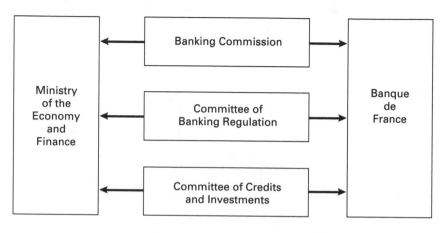

Several aspects of the role of Commission Bancaire have been already discussed in Section 4. Until the independence of Banque de France, the Commission Bancaire was an integral department of the reserve bank. Subsequently, the law established a permanent secretarial service to the Commission Bancaire and provided a new way of selecting the secretary general.

The secretary general is now nominated by the minister of the economy and finance on a proposition by the governor of the reserve bank. But the governor of Banque de France chairs the Commission Bancaire, in which the minister of the economy participates.

As Figure 7–3 shows, there are two other bridges between the Ministry of the Economy and Finance and the Banque de France: the Committee of Bank Regulation and the Committee of Credits and Investments. The Committee of Bank Regulation has minimal staff but significant authority. It is presided over by the minister of the Economy and Finance, with the governor of the Banque de France being a member. The Committee of Credits and Investments, however, is presided over by the governor of the reserve bank, with the minister being a member.

What I see as a missing link in these bridges is a Committee of the Currency. In all G–10 countries, protection of the currency is a duty of the reserve bank. But protection of the currency cannot be done without control of national debt and government deficits—which is the business of the

Ministry of the Economy and Finance. This statement is further strengthened today because of the *Stability Pact* currently being negotiated, which in all likelihood will be the successor to the Maastricht Treaty. The Stability Pact will submit national budgets to constraints. Therefore, it requires a very effective coordination between the Banque de France and the Ministry of the Economy and Finance.

This statement is not only true at the national level but also with respect to commercial banks supervised by Banque de France. The reason is *currency risk*—and the impact the Euro will have over a transition period on the old national currencies and the banks' own risk-management policies and practices.

Currency risk must be covered from the bank's own capital in case the net global position in foreign currencies is in excess of 2 percent of the total capital of the bank. This is implied by a French rule valid since February 1995, and it constitutes the following sound approach:

- The net global position in a currency-risk sense represents the larger of two positions: "net short" or "net long."
- It is calculated by adding the long and short positions in all other currencies converted in French francs.

Like the Swiss regulators, the French specify that gold held in a negotiable form is assimilated to currencies. Gold reserves and foreign currencies have to be coordinated by a blue ribbon committee throughout the Euro-transition period and for some time thereafter. I think there is a missing link in providing these connections within the French regulatory structure.

The controls to be put in place in terms of currency risk should be broad enough to also cover *interest-rate risk.* The two issues—currency risk and interest-rate risk are related—and they are both extremely important.

Not only are currency risk and interest-rate risk subjects that fall under the responsibility of both the Banque de France and the Ministry of the Economy and Finance, but they also are contrary to the Federal Reserve which controls only the commercial banks—the Commission Bancaire has responsibility over investment banks and brokers. The law of July 1996 extended its authority over all classes of banking.

As we have seen in Section 4, the 1996 Market Risk Amendment by the Basle Committee has been instrumental in bringing rocket scientists into the Commission Bancaire. Now the Stability Act, which is on the horizon, should provide the stimulus for developing the necessary infrastructure for currency-risk/interest-rate risk prognosis and coordination.

This new perspective of economic and financial regulation requires not only well-studied command and control solutions supported by legislation but steady attention by means of analytical studies and well-established procedures. Inevitably, these must involve high technology: intelligent networks, distributed deductive databases, high-performance computers—and rocket science.

I also think that the revamped CNC should be enriched with a few rocket scientists, who will surely be needed for analytical studies. The same is true about information technologists of a certain caliber. Any solution or law that does not take technology into account is half-baked.

After all, the first-ever normalization of accounting came in 1494 by Luca Paciolo, a mathematician and Franciscan monk. What Paciolo noted 500 years ago in his mathematical treatise, which led the accounting foundations, the "Summa de Aritmetica, Geometria, Proportioni et Proportionalità," is today not only the foundation of accounting, but of financial control. But financial control cannot be effectively exercised without networked databases and sophisticated software.

CHAPTER 8

The Group of Seven and the Group of Ten

1. INTRODUCTION

Privately, central bankers express acute concern over the explosive growth of derivative financial instruments and the exposure they create. They react in a similar manner in regard to the huge cross-border money flows. Until recently, money-center banks have been able to exploit a loophole in the 1988 Capital Adequacy accord, which in effect permits institutions to undertake almost unlimited derivatives risks without the required capital to back them up.

This happens because derivatives transactions since the mid-1980s have been off-balance sheet. Therefore, their risks do not appear on the banks' accounts. Financial institutions capitalize on the liberalization and globalization of financial market to increase the transborder mobility of capital.

While bending the curve of money flows between financial markets is an issue still waiting to be addressed, as we have seen in the preceding six chapters, the 1996 Market Risk Amendment advanced new rules to force the registration and reporting of off-balance sheet derivatives exposures.

The Basle Committee left the central banks to define the exact procedure on how to merge on-balance sheet and off-balance sheet acounts, and in most cases this procedure is still under study. What is certain, however, is that disclosure will necessarily convert to on-balance sheet obligations the off-balance sheet exposures requiring a bank's capital to be set aside to cover market risks and risk of default.

Some financial analysts suggest that, ironically, certain aspects of the unified action promoted by the Basle Committee on Banking Supervision, and agreed to by central banks, are being blocked by the Bank of England. The Bank of England is said to be worried that the huge volumes of trading flowing into the loosely regulated city from derivatives business might vanish. With it may go much of the influence of London as the world's leading financial center.

In private discussions, it is also suggested that BIS has let it be known that the market-risk disclosure plan might be instrumental in shrinking the $50 trillion[1] in off-balance sheet over-the-counter transactions to 10 or 15 percent of that amount. Such a small fraction is believed to be far less threatening to the global financial system. But many knowledgeable analysts believe that this sort of shrinkage is unrealistic.

What is feasible is a much closer collaboration between the members of the exclusive clubs that were created during the crises of the 1970s and are still going strong. One is the Group of Seven (G–7), whose members are the chiefs of state. The other is the Group of Ten (G–10), of which we have already spoken. It is the club of the central bankers. In this chapter, we will look into both G–7 and G–10 decisions.

2. CHALLENGES THAT LIE AHEAD OF THE ISSUE OF FINANCIAL SOVEREIGNTY

G–7 is mainly composed of heads of state and G–10 of heads of central banks. These are different groups of people who do not need to have the same objectives and viewpoints. However, many of their other concerns and efforts towards transactional coordination are very similar. At the top of the list of common objectives are:

- Preserving order in the system of global finance by avoiding disruptive action.
- Providing for an orderly transition so that business flourishes without taking inordinate risks.
- Seeing to it that the follow-the-sun overdraft characterizing the global financial market does not lead to systemic risk.[2]

Neither of these goals, which can be summed up as putting global risk under lock and key, is easy to attain because of the volume of trades taking place worldwide every 24 hours, their great diversity, and the

---

1 In notional principal amounts.
2 See Chapter 9.

amount of money they involve, including major swings in current assets.

Banks, particularly the 30 largest financial institutions of the G–10, are trying harder than ever to push into foreign markets; serve multinational enterprises through loans underwriting and other services; do interest-rate swaps with 10-, 20-, and 30-year horizons; and steadily develop personalized instruments, usually through derivative products.

As knowledgeable bankers know, with the increase in time horizon comes a growing level of risk. Figure 8–1 takes as an example four different financial instruments. These are among the workhorses of the financial industry as it races to expand its operations globally.

Propelled by technology, global financial systems virtually eliminate the boundaries of time and distance. There is always a next frontier to be conquered through innovation, while current products, which in the past have been highfliers, become commonplace.

Within this environment, the central banks not only look after money supply and try to regulate the commercial banking industry,[3] they also conduct official monetary operations in three markets:

F I G U R E   8–1

Growing Levels of Risk as the Time to Maturity of an Instrument Increases

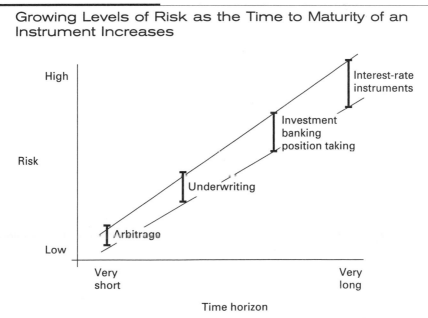

3 D. N. Chorafas, *The Money Magnet: Regulating International Finance and Analyzing Money Flows* (London: *Euromoney*, 1997).

- The money market.
- The Treasury bonds (gilts) market.
- The foreign-exchange market.

This obliges them to take great interest in the structural development of the forementioned markets, beyond what strict regulatory requirements might have suggested. This does not change the fact that the financial industry's next frontier has many unknowns.

Government leaders know that this is the case, but few care to ask for analytical studies that permit them first to clarify then to back up their judgment. Therefore, the best that can be obtained in these G–7 meetings is some agreement on principles that may sustain growth and control risk. This happens along a frame of reference shown in Figure 8–2. However, sustained economic growth with concomitant control of system risk does

F I G U R E   8–2

Government Heads and Central Bankers Are Searching for Compromises That Could Reasonably Sustain a Free Market

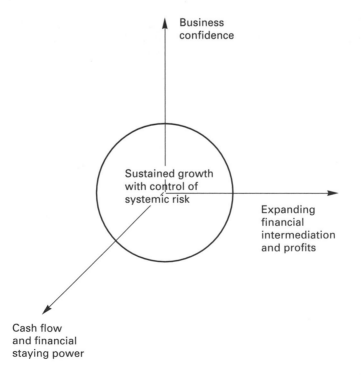

not come without a cost—or without global standards. The 1988 Capital Accord and the 1996 Market Risk Amendment are the first steps toward a new regulation of the financial industry, which is global.

Conservative bankers now suggest that had BIS taken the initiative on market risk, which we saw in Chapter 3, when it was first proposed in the late 1980s, a limit at the level of $4 trillion in off-balance sheet notional principal amount would have been feasible. Derivatives were then a relatively tiny part of the world's financial market and its trades.

Today, given the estimated $1.5 trillion in derivatives transactions worldwide every day, technical steps of a very restrictive nature are questionable. Though they may be able to control the booming derivatives trades, drastic steps can wreck market confidence. Loss of confidence would lead to a reverse-leverage blowout in the global speculative financial market.

Another critical aspect of the same issue is that nations also have to observe global rules of behavior. These are slowly elaborated by the G–7. In fact, the new rules-in-the-making pose the following query: Is there financial sovereignty?

In a globalized financial world, the sovereignty of governments is more hype than real. What the September/October 1992 events hitting the British pound and the Italian lira did was highlight the bogus nature of much monetary sovereignty.

Contrarians would say that there was little sovereignty in the gold standard and that the beggar-thy-neighbor period of the 1930s led to a worldwide depression. There has not been much more in terms of financial sovereignty in the Bretton Woods accord, but since it broke down early in the 1970s we first saw a good expression of monetary sovereignty—which was short-lived.

What has been the result of the free rise and fall of currencies with exchange rates set by the market? From 1972 to 1995, the British pound has been devalued by 40 percent against the dollar, 70 percent against the d-mark, and 80 percent against the yen. The market was the evaluator, but the aftermaths of financial sovereignty were not that good for sterling.

3. SOVEREIGN HEADS OF STATE, THE GANG OF FOUR, AND THE NEED FOR CONSTRAINTS

Because there is always a trend toward overshooting, governments feel there should be some limiting forces that tend to guide the market's hand. In the longer run, markets do appreciate limits. But no single nation can set all of the rules; hence the need for concerted action.

This was one of the top objectives of the June 27–29, 1996, G–7 meeting in Lyon, France; it was also a goal at the top of the agenda of the G–7 meeting that preceded it a year earlier in Halifax, Canada. Practically all of the participants were interested in *globalization* and *free trade.* But while the wish behind each of these two issues can be said to be universal, there were (and will continue to be) differences in interpretation and in procedures.

One of the issues that helps to differentiate June 1996 from earlier events of the same type is that this G–7 meeting was not attended only by the leaders of the United States, Britain, France, Germany, Japan, Italy, and Canada and their delegations. The roster featured Jacques Santer, president of the European Union Commission; Viktor Chernomyrdin, the Russian prime minister; and—a major "first" in G–7 meetings—the so-called *gang of four.*

The gang of four was made up of a diverse membership: International Monetary Fund (IMF) Managing Director Michel Camdessus, World Bank President James Wolfenshohn, World Trade Organization (WTO) General Secretary Renato Ruggiero, and Secretary General of the United Nations Organization (UNO) Butros Butros-Ghali.

The G–7 and the gang of four looked at the globalization of financial markets and of merchandising as the process underpinning the transfer of power and influence from the sovereign nation-states (and its national governments) to supranational bodies. At long last, it was appreciated that the transnationality of huge money flows, and of goods, is instrumental in establishing a new international order because of its momentum.

Forgotten somehow is the fact that such transnationality usually shows up in times of crisis and, therefore, has precedence. The best example is the Marshall Plan. In the late 1940s, however, there was one donor (who practically dictated the rules) and many recipients, while now every major nation is donor and recipient at the same time.

How much did the Marshall Plan cost and what were its aftermaths? The cost to the U.S. government of winning World War II was $341 billion. Then a loan of $3.25 billion was made to England to help it out of its financial straits, and $400 million was needed for the Truman Doctrine to help Greece and Turkey. Altogether, we are speaking of about $345 billion.

The initial guess was that the Marshall Plan would cost $6 to $7 billion. But this guestimate underrated the actual budget. The Marshall Plan cost more than $16 billion over a four-year period, which is still less than 5 percent of the cost of the war effort contributed by the American taxpayer.

But without this extra 5 percent, the peace would have been lost—to the Soviet Union.

Quite similarly, a common action by the G–7 would have costs. This would not be out-of-pocket money. A global effort to avoid systemic risk in spite of very rapid financial expansion will cost big money and therefore should imply constraints. Here again, the Marshall Plan can be a reference because it contained two conditions the Russians did not accept:

- Contribution of Soviet funds to rebuilt parts of Europe.
- An open accounting of how U.S. money was being spent.

Though it is spelled out in different terms, the first of these two conditions is already embedded in G–7 status. Every member state must contribute funds that, hopefully, are used for the common good. Make no mistake, this is *not* aid money. Such funds are recycled within the G–10 and only a few other nations because the First World's economy has been definitely decoupled from that of the Third World.

Satisfying the second condition is more problematic because it goes much more deeply into national sovereignty. Yet this constraint is just as fundamental as the first, if not more so. Here, we no longer talk about the American taxpayer's money but about the money of the taxpayers of every G–10 country.

Open accountability is the key. "Sunshine is the best disinfectant," Judge Louis Brandeis once said. First and foremost, the open accountability by market players should be of a nature that quiets the emerging market fears by regulators. "I have fears that we could see problems with some kinds of markets," said Barry Barbash, director of the Division of Investment Management at the U.S. Securities and Exchange Commission, at a meeting of the Society of American Business Editors and Writers in mid-November 1996.[4]

In search of higher returns, a growing number of mutual funds have poured money into small markets, such as emerging economies, as well as small-company and micro-cap stocks. This led the SEC to be concerned about potential liquidity problems involving the growing number of funds investing in emerging and other small markets.

Liquidity—that is, the ability to buy and sell securities on short notice under no fire-sales terms—can be hard to come by in markets with

---

4 *USA Today,* November 13, 1996.

limited numbers of buyers and sellers. "At some point there will be a test, and we'll see what happens," Barbash advised.

If institutional investors, banks, and other global players expect the taxpayers of G–10 to come up with cash in a salvage operation of the Mexico 1994–1995 type, there should be open books. This is an issue that has not yet been addressed—yet it is urgent.

Equally urgent is the question of supervision of cross-border banking, where on October 8, 1996, the Bank for International Settlements released a new international directive on *Supervision of Cross-Border Banking*. This document was prepared by the Basle Committee on Banking Supervision.

For the first time, central bankers have officially drawn their attention toward the administrative matters of the world's major offshore banking havens, including Cayman Islands, Gibraltar, Guernsey, Hong Kong, and Netherland Antilles. The new BIS rules are designed to close regulatory loopholes under which banks in one country are able to do prohibited banking activity through complex networks of affiliates in offshores.

Everyone should appreciate the importance of this step and its impact. The objective is to introduce at least a minimum of regulatory control of banks that are active in more than one country. Central banks want to prevent any future BCCI risk. They also want to control systemic dangers to the global financial system.

According to knowledgeable financial analysts, the BIS central bankers are perfectly aware of the growing number of de facto bankrupt banks across the Organization of Economic Cooperation and Development (OECD) countries[5] as well as several emerging market economies, including Brazil, Mexico, Russia, and numerous other countries in Asia and Latin America.

4. G–7, MARKET RISK AMENDMENT, AND NEW ECONOMIC POWERS

Some of the concepts that transpired through the June 29, 1996, G–7 meetings are worth retaining. One of them is that economic growth and industrial and social progress in today's interdependent world are closely linked to the process of globalization. This process provides great opportunities for the future for all countries—as well as risks.

---

5 The members of the Paris-based OECD are the original Marshall Plan countries plus Japan and some recent additions, such as South Korea.

The many "positive aspects of globalization," suggested the G–7 communiqué, "have led to a considerable expansion of wealth and prosperity in the world." Hence, the G–7 leaders and the gang of four "are convinced that the process of globalization is a source of hope for the future."

Drafted in significant part by the French government, the G–7 communique acknowledged that globalization has also produced "challenges to societies and economies." During the summit, French president Jacques Chirac profiled himself as "concerned" with those hurt by globalization as well as by the austerity programs necessary to right the balances in an increasingly unmanageable world.

In Lyons, the G–7 correctly underlined that the benefits of globalization "will not materialize unless countries adjust to increased competition." This, too, has a counterpart to the goals the Marshall Plan set itself to nearly 50 years ago. Practically all rich countries are now undergoing rigorous austerity programs to put their economies back on track.

In the late 1940s, the only "rich country" in the world was the United States. One of the objectives of the Marshall Plan was to recycle dollars out of the United States, through a simulated process of austerity, slowing their reentry into the United States. Had that money hit the U.S. market when the war industry was still recycling itself into civilian production, the result would have been unstoppable inflation.[6] In poorer countries, globalization may accentuate inequality, and certain parts of the world could become marginalized.

As in the late 1940s, the adjustments needed are imposing rapid and sometimes painful restructuring—both in rich and in poor countries. The added fact of 1997 is that globalization of financial markets generates new risks of instability, "which requires all countries to pursue sound economic policies and structural reform," according to the June 29, 1996, G–7 communiqué.

Though it was not stated in explicit terms, the sense of the meeting was that many of the participants in the G–7 meeting know that coming financial storms and political upheavals will radically transform the international situation in three basic ways:

- Social,
- Economic
- Financial

---

6 This happened in the mid- to late 1960s because of the combined effect of the Great Society and the Vietnam War.

Jacques Chirac said it would take "20 years before the benefits of globalization would become manifest"—but this cannot be said of the dangers. Therefore, I was quite surprised that in June 1996 the G–7 did not take the time and effort to analyze the January 1996 Market Risk Amendment and its aftermaths.

There was plenty of opportunity to do so. Otherwise, what was the sense of inviting the gang of four? The bankers who were present could explain to the chiefs of state what it means in economic and financial terms to calculate market risk in connection with a globalized trading of securities, commodities, currencies, interest-rate risk, and other derivatives.

My best guess is that some of the G–7 chiefs of state might be able to find the answer by themselves, but the majority will not. After all, it was president John Kennedy who once said that the only way he could remember that monetary policy is made by the Federal Reserve is that Martin, the (then) Fed chairman's name, started with "M."

Market risk should have been one of the items at the top of the G–7 1996 agenda. Since the different world leaders talked of globalization, they should have appreciated that the more risks the banking system takes, the more capital it will need as a cushion against possible trading losses.

The G–7 heads of state should have also considered that some of the proprietary risk-management models developed by some of the more sophisticated banks produce fairly accurate measures of market risk. And it should have been explained to them that the most dynamic of the globalized markets need high-frequency financial data to be managed. Figure 8–3 suggests that much.

Maybe it is not the job of national presidents and prime ministers to concern themselves with the technical ascpects of how banks measure potential trading losses or with the cost structure of individual banks as well as their reserves. But it is part of their responsibility to understand market risk, huge international money flows, and follow-the-sun overdrafts—and to make decisions about them.

The way huge financial institutions manage and account for market risks will determine how much capital must be set aside to cover those risks. The better the world's risk-management system operates, the more efficiently the world can deploy and use its capital.

Superior policies and advanced technological systems could be and would be a competitive advantage. But this brings into perspective other prerequisites, some of which greatly depend on policy issues that must be decided at the top. That's why the G–7 heads of state have to be personally involved.

Four Major Areas of Banking Activity Have a Common
Ground of Risk and Return to be Found in Databases
and Tick-by-Tick Data Streams

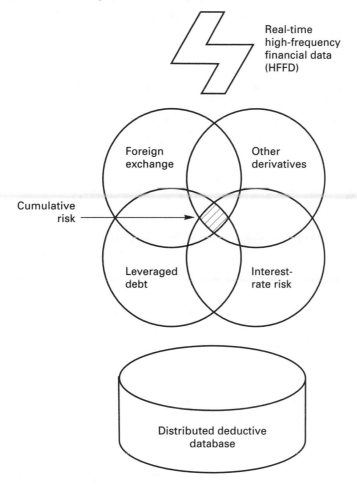

Finally, I cannot resist an afterthought on the future of the G–7, and
for that matter the G–10. Recently, the *Financial Times* published an article[7] that England, France, and Italy will be ousted from the seven biggest
world economies in the next 20 years as their weight in international organizations is reduced.

---

7 June 7, 1996.

This information is based on a leaked Treasury document. Its publication came ahead of a mid-June 1996 British government paper on competitiveness highlighting the skills gap between the United Kingdom and other advanced economies. The Treasury paper predicts that if recent growth trends continue, China will become the single largest nation in 2015, India will be in fourth place, Brazil in sixth, and Indonesia in seventh.

While the United States, Japan, and Germany would remain in the top seven. The Treasury paper says that the United Kingdom's role in international organizations—the G–7, the International Monetary Fund, OECD, EBRD, and the World Trade Organization—will change as the country moves down in rank. The same is true of France, Italy, and Canada—which means it's true of the majority of current G–7 members.

5. THE RISKS FROM REFLECTION AND MARKET BUBBLES: EXAMPLES FROM THE UNITED STATES AND JAPAN

Here is more food for thought by the G–7. Over three years, between December 1990 and December 1993, M-1, the money supply metric followed by the Federal Reserve, expanded by almost 50 percent. During that period, short-term Fed funds interest rates were pushed down to a low of 3 percent and kept there for months until early 1994, while the Fed permitted major banks to lower Fed reserves to zero. This freed up more bank funds to buy no-risk U.S. Treasury bonds and bills. By borrowing at 3 percent from the Fed and investing in Treasuries at 6 percent, banks were able to make big risk-free profits.

That policy helped U.S. banks write off tens of billions of dollars worth of bad real estate loans, corporate loans, and sovereign loans. They needed that breathing space to rid themselves of what was left from the excesses of the 1980s.

But there was also a problem. While the banks appeared to return to profitability, the cheap money reflation generated by the Fed also created a great speculative bubble.

Hedge funds joined in the party, borrowing from banks at the low interest rates to speculate on U.S. government bonds. Using derivative financial instruments, they leveraged their loans as much as 50 times. Then, on February 2, 1994, in an effort to gradually deflate that dangerous bubble, the Fed raised its funds rate for the first time since December 1990, by a mere 0.25 percent.

Because of the high gearing by hedge funds done on borrowed money, that tiny rise and those that subsequently followed it set off a great run on the world bond market, leading to its collapse. By the time the Fed put an end to its round of rate rises in 1994, a number of leveraged funds had failed, and bond valuations had sunk into the abyss.

This is the classic cause and effect. The cause, cheap Fed funds, had a rational base. What went wrong was the high gearing. But no one seems to have learned the lesson from the troubles eventually associated with that loophole.

Within a year, financial history repeated itself. By early 1995, with a major crisis hitting the big Japanese banks, the focus of the world's financial system shifted to Japan. The new weak link in the chain came as a sequel to the collapse of Japan's stock market and real estate market in 1990.

"Tragedy and comedy," Socrates once said, "are essentially the same thing and they should be written by the same authors." The tragedy was the collapsing Japanese financial system. The comedy has been that, by April 1995, the yen hit a postwar high of 79.75 to the dollar—in spite of the fragility of the Japanese banking industry. This was a rise of 45 percent from January 1990, when the Japanese economy had reached and passed its peak.

The Japanese banking crisis threatened a deflationary implosion of the country's (and the world's) financial system and a collapse of Tokyo's stock market below the 15,000 mark. Then, on July 6, 1995, the Japanese Ministry of Finance and the Bank of Japan decided to act in concert with Washington to prevent the meltdown.

Not only because the international economy is tightly woven, but also to save their skin, Japanese banks were on the verge of liquidating tens of billions of dollars' worth of their U.S. Treasuries to cover their losses. This threatened the U.S. financial system and might have led to global systemic risk if the U.S. government had not worked out the Washington-Tokyo agreement.

The Fed announced that it had agreed to make an emergency credit line available, up to $500 billion (if necessary), to aid any large Japanese bank in a payments crisis. This calmed interbank lenders, who were then blacklisting Japanese banks on the credit markets for fear of bank failures—by instituting "Japan's premium."

Part of the strategy of reflating and averting a banking meltdown was the removal of key restrictions on foreign investments. Emulating the

Federal Reserve, the Bank of Japan lowered its lending rate to a very low 0.5 percent and began injecting liquidity into the banking system.

Like American banks a few years earlier, Japanese banks were able to borrow for almost nothing, sell the borrowed yen for dollars, go abroad and buy U.S. Treasuries, and earn as much as 7 percent, all risk-free. The outflow from yen to dollar was part of the planned lowering of the yen but also had all the aspects of a new bonds bubble.

With this background, my question is very simple. Have the G–7 heads of state learned any lesson from the American and Japanese experience of the 1990s? Or are the major governments too bureaucratic, hierarchical, inflexible, and alienated from the economies they manage?

6. A CLOSER COLLABORATION AMONG G–10 REGULATORS: THE MAY 1996 ACCORD

Without a close collaboration among governments, central banks, securities and exchange commissions, and other regulatory bodies, the January 1996 Market Risk Amendment or any other top-level decision regarding the financial industry would be welcome but ineffectual. When new rules are set, particularly supervisory rules and procedures with far-reaching consequences, supervisory authorities have to collaborate and assist one another in the execution of their self-imposed duties.

Cooperation among supervisory authorities regarding market risk was not explicitly specified by the Basle Committee. This was settled a few months later by an agreement reached among the G–10 central banks and the securities regulators of the G–10 countries—in a conference that coinvolved the Bank for International Settlements (BIS) and the International Monetary Fund (IMF).

In the annual meeting of the G–10 central bankers that took place on May 20, 1996, in Frankfurt, Germany, banking and securities regulators from the world's most important industrial countries agreed to work more closely together in supervising financial institutions. This was prompted by the collapse of some banks and other mishaps in financial markets. New regulations, such as the Market Risk Amendment, also played a role in this decision, which was further motivated by a request by the heads of governments at the G–7 Halifax summit of mid-1995.

In May 1996 in Frankfurt, two main bodies from the G–10 countries, representing commercial banking and investment banking regulators, issued a joint statement of principles for improved cooperation but carefully underlined that the agreement in no way impairs the special turf of any one of the signatories.

The overall initiative has been promoted by the Basle Committee on Banking Supervision and its counterpart, the International Organization of Securities Commissions (IOSC). However, as it currently stands, this accord does not commit supervisory authorities in any one country to specific ways of working with each other. The most likely aftermath is that this decision will reinforce a move towards groups that combine banking and securities operations and will tend to bring institutions under joint scrutiny of regulators from the two financial industries.

Even if limited, the decision about cross-country collaboration in commercial banking and investment banking is important because so far regulators have failed to share information among countries regarding financial industries. Examples are BCCI, the Barings bankruptcy and the £90 million ($144 million) by Nat West Markets revealed in March 1997.

Worse still, in the past there had been tension between regulators in the banking and securities sectors. Tension between supervisory authorities usually arises because of overlapping duties, and they came to a head in 1992 with the breakdown of talks intended to provide a common standard for capital to cover trading risks.

Tensions surfaced again in the 1993 to 1995 time frame with the delays experienced in regard to the approval of the Market Risk Amendment by BIS and the changes the original script went through. On the other hand, the need for better cooperation has been spurred by the consolidation of financial industries in recent years and the increasing takeovers of securities firms by commercial banks.

The irony is that in the late 1980s, investment banks had been the motor behind takeovers in other industries, from which they gained hefty profits. Then, in the early 1990s, as shown in Figure 8–4, the takeover fever slackened. When it started again in 1993, investment banks and brokers found themselves a main target of mergers and acquisitions.

This takeover business of investment banks and brokers was particularly intense in Europe. Examples of takeovers from the 1980s are Phillips and Drew by UBS, and Morgan Grenfell by Deutsche Bank. Examples from the 1990s are CSFB by Credit Swiss; Warburg by Société des Banques Suisses; Kleinwort, Benson by Dresdner Bank; and Barings by ING Bank.

A close cooperation between regulators of the commercial banking and investment banking institutions not only makes sense in and of itself,

F I G U R E   8–4

The Ups and Downs of Business: Mergers and Acquisitions Fees Paid to Investment Bankers in the 1988 to 1995 Time Frame

(Wall Street Data)

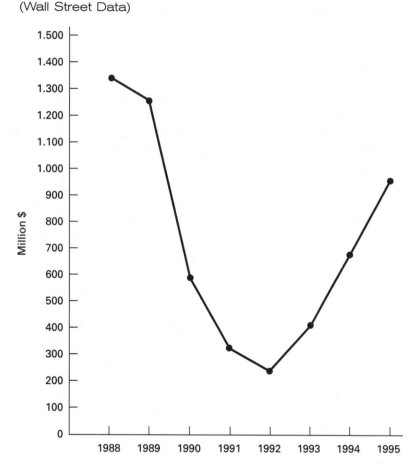

it also creates the infrastructure of a supervisory activity that should definitely be extended towards *nonbank banks* in regard to capital adequacy for credit risk and new norms for reserves regarding market risk and other exposures.

It is indeed a curious feat that, in spite of their size and their risks, nonbank banks and some other parties, such as hedge funds, pension funds, and postal banks, are regulated by no one and there is no authority supervising them.

There is plenty to do in terms of nonbank banks' supervision. Not only does the treasury of major corporations operate like a bank, it is also the strategic plan of some companies to transform themselves into mighty financial institutions. To document this reference, Figure 8–5 shows General Electric's current and projected transformation within 10 short years.

Hedge funds, pension funds, mutual funds, and the morphing of the manufacturing industry into financial players—by means of treasury operations and pension funds—demonstrate that even the collaboration between central banks and securities commissions only covers part of the financial market in terms of supervisory requirements.

At present, this cooperation rests on the following basic principles:

- All banks and securities firms should be subject to effective supervision, and regulatory rules should see to it that the capital base is adequate.

- Special supervisory arrangements will be projected for geographically and functionally diversified financial groups, but their provision poses problems.

- In the longer run, supervision will be more homogeneous and as free as possible from different national impediments, probably using the Basle Committee as a pivot point.

F I G U R E   8–5

General Electric's Transformation in 10 Years

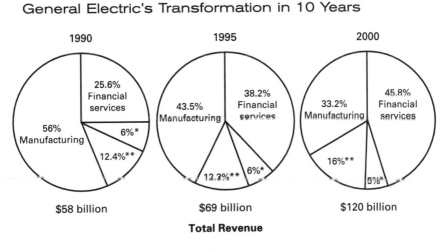

Total Revenue

* Broadcasting   ** After-sales services

Practically everyone agrees that regulatory arrangements should account for globalization. The problem is how to do it without curtailing national jurisdictions. International agreements are necessary because global controls can only then become effective if all banks and securities firms have proper *risk-management* systems at least at the state-of-the-art suggested by the Market Risk Amendment.

A further principle of the accord reached on May 20, 1996, in Frankfurt concerns adequate reporting and disclosure to ensure the transparency and integrity of markets. Still another is that markets must be able to survive the failure of individual firms, which goes beyond current systems and procedures, implying that the supervisory process has to be constantly improved.

Some reservations have been expressed in connection to the agreement advanced at the May 1996 meeting. An example is the statement that arrangements to improve coordination and cooperation "will not in any way reduce the powers and responsibilities" of individual national supervisors.[8]

As long as this sort of parochial spirit prevails, it means that a global view leading to an integrated process of supervision will remain a chimera. But things may change in the years to come toward a truly international regulatory and supervisory landscape, particularly if some major bank or nonbank failures bring home the urgency of global rules for financial operations.

7. THE INTERNET, THE REGULATION OF CYBERMONEY, AND IMF'S ELECTRONIC BULLETIN BOARD

In an age where telecommunication and the media bring the news instantaneously around the globe and people have grown accustomed to thinking with their eyes, it is not enough to reach the right decisions. It is also very important to communicate them, explaining the reasons for tough choices and making sure that the spirit of each decision is well understood.

It is equally important to study the further-out effect of new technologies at a time when the world's main financial markets work in synergy. For instance, what will be the effect of the Internet on financial regulation? On money supply?[9]

---

8 *Financial Times,* May 21, 1996.
9 D. N. Chorafas, *The Money Magnet: Regulating International Finance and Analyzing Money Flows* (London: *Euromoney,* 1997).

Financial regulators in the United States have set up a task force to examine how emerging electronic transactions, and most particularly transactions on the Internet, will affect current rules for payment systems. As Robert Rubin, the U.S. Treasury secretary, stated, while central banks and governments want to avoid inappropriate regulation, electronic money posed "difficult issues in consumer protection."

Likening the development of electronic money to other major changes that took place in the past, Rubin said the Federal Deposit Insurance Corporation and the Treasury have put together a task force to look at the necessary regulatory measures.[10]

The ongoing study may lead to a change in current position, where the prevailing legal advice from the government is that money held on smart cards offered by banks does not technically qualify as a deposit. Therefore, it does not count in the money supply, but it also does not have state insurance.

In the United States, the Smart Card Forum, a grouping of the largest card offerers, was broadly supportive of the government's stance. But it cautioned that it would be premature to introduce detailed regulations now as they might be rendered technologically obsolete within a year or so.

This problem of rapid obsolescence is not going to disappear with time. If anything, it will become more acute. During the working meeting I had at the Bank of England in September 1996, central bankers expressed concern about the Internet and cybermoney because there are still too many problems with unknowns, from security connected to network access and databases to the effects of cybermoney on money supply if and when electronic purses become big game.

In the background was the issue that in both cases one can get a lot of exposure. Therefore, the whole question of electronic money (E-money) is now elaborated in the United Kingdom by the Bank of England and internationally by the Bank for International Settlements.

Many subjects are being debated. Who should be allowed to issue cybermoney and who should not? Is E-money like deposit taking or not? How should cybermoney be regulated? To whom does this responsibility fall in a globalized financial market? And what will be the most likely effect on the money supply of each country?

Don't worry, said the Federal Reserve of San Francisco, "Cyber-money and smart cards will not expand the U.S. money supply by more

---

10 *Financial Times,* September 20, 1996.

than $50 billion." While this still remains to be seen—depending on consumer acceptance, the real number may range from a fraction of $50 billion to a high multiple of it—the larger issue is that cybermoney is global money. It obeys no reserve bank's national jurisdiction.

If the Internet presents central bankers with a problem regarding cybermoney, it also provides a solution. An example is the recent IMF Electronic Bulletin Board for economic statistics. The International Monetary Fund has drawn up standards for categories of data that it believes should be met eventually by the 60 to 70 countries that have access to international financial markets. Such standards cover the scope, frequency, and timeliness of financial series and help improve the integrity, quality, and availability of public information.

IMF's data standards are essentially *quality standards* for economic statistics and are supported on a special site on the Internet. However, of the 34 countries supposed to constitute the first nucleus, only 18 are able to supply the economic information that would be displayed on the Internet site maintained by the IMF. This quality-data initiative was taken at the 1995 Group of Seven summit in Canada.

The following 18 countries, in alphabetical order, are among the first subscribers: Argentina, Canada, Denmark, Finland, Ireland, Italy, Malaysia, Mexico, Netherlands, Norway, Peru, the Philippines, Singapore, Slovenia, Switzerland, Thailand, the United Kingdom and the United States. The remaining 16 economies to be posted on the IMF site are Austria, Belgium, Chile, Colombia, Croatia, France, Germany, Hungary, Iceland, Israel, Japan, Lithuania, Poland, South Africa, Sweden, and Turkey.

The Internet site carries only *metadata,* that is, descriptions of the statistics provided by subscribers, rather than the statistics themselves with the globalization of finance and trade. Such statistics are expected to reflect accurate and timely information about trade, debt, and foreign-exchange reserves by country, permitting national authorities and international financial institutions to act quickly enough to avert a crisis.

CHAPTER 9

Policies and Procedures Against Systemic Risk

1. INTRODUCTION

A *systemic crisis* is a disturbance that severely impairs the working of the financial system and may eventually cause a complete breakdown in its functioning. *Systemic risks* are risks with the potential to cause such a crisis. Though systematic crises may originate in a variety of ways, ultimately they impair at least one of the key functions of the financial system:

- Market confidence.
- Credit allocation.
- Pricing of financial assets.
- Payment methods.

When financial activity reaches the edge of chaos and tends to get out of control, a disturbance can grow into a systemic crisis, depending on the economic circumstances prevailing when the shock occurs and the degree of confidence that exists in the market.

Because of globalization and deregulation of financial markets, there is a definite need for a supranational authority that is able to influence economic policy in all countries that are financially strong, providing conditional support to insolvent countries and managing the international response to systemic emergencies, for instance, debt crises of the type that occurred in the 1980s and 1990 and the coming derivatives crisis of the 1990s or early 21st century.

Since the first Mexican crisis of 1983, the role of the the fire brigade for systemic risk has been increasingly played by IMF. Private capital markets cannot deal well with challenges that happen on a global scale. A supranational institution has a major role to play in managing systemic risk—provided it has been endowed with the necessary authority.

Down to the fundamentals, an important element in any financial system is systemic risk management. Central banks and securities regulators must decide what could be the overall leverage the markets might afford—and how much of the financial resources at their disposition could be committed to salvage operations, if and when a panic hits.

There are no simple rules for making these decisions. A prudent regulatory mechanism should reflect the credit quality of counterparties, and this requires that banks integrate counterparty dependability into their reporting of on-balance sheet and off-balance sheet risks.

In this chapter, we will see an example with the new directives by the Swiss National Bank concerning the integration of balance sheet and off-balance sheet items. Chapter 13 will explain the difference between credit risk and counterparty risk, particularly in connection to important derivatives contracts.

Understanding both the explicit and implicit functioning of products and markets is most vital—including volatility, liquidity, money flows, and reciprocal obligations. This means studying, analyzing, and appreciating all *risk dimensions*. It is not only the financial institutions originating the transactions that face exposure. Very often, the clients too may also find themselves vulnerable in the case of systemic risk.

2. ONE OF THE MAJOR PREOCCUPATIONS OF CENTRAL BANKERS: AVOIDING SYSTEMIC RISK

Managing systemic risk in a proactive manner is a new task, made more urgent as the exposure of the banking system mounts into nearly $100 trillion in notional principal amount, largely because of over-the-counter trades in derivative financial instruments. We will talk more on this issue in Section 4, but first we should address a more basic question: Do governments and central bankers have a clear idea about what should be done on a global scale to avoid potential systemic risk?

Among regulators, in the financial industry itself and in other sectors of the economy, there is plenty of misconception about dealing with global financial crises. One of the most basic regards the ability to somehow micromanage market volatility.

Controls put in place after the stock market crash of 1987 are thought to decrease the likelihood of wild market swings. This assumption is false. The circuit breakers concern the gyrations of the stocks' market price—not of derivative financial instruments. Yet today there is more trade in equity derivatives than in equities themselves.

There are, of course, plenty of good intentions, but some of the measures being taken are paper tigers. Both in terms of capital requirements for banks and in overall market performance, regulators have been working to strengthen the financial system. In 1988, central bankers established risk-weighted capital requirements that gave banks incentives to stick to low-risk investments and businesses. In 1996, the Market Risk Amendment provided the background necessary for some control over derivatives and suggested marking-to-model as the better tool.

In terms of naked numbers, things look as if they are going in the right direction. In the United States, the Treasury says capital levels at U.S. banks are at a 30-year high. This is not surprising since the capital requirements mandated by the Basel agreement are also at a 30-year high. But in other countries, the banks are agonizing with compliance; hence, the dangers remain.

For this reason, financial institutions must not only be able to provide regulators with evidence that they have a first-class risk-management system in place, they should also see to it that it is used effectively. Managers and traders, for example, must be able to assess exposure information on many different levels of reference. Ideally, pricing, tracking, and risk control should be at both the macro and micro level.

The macro level is *stress analysis.* The micro level is *detail.* At the same time, for internal control purposes, senior management at every bank must be able to look at risk on the trader, instrument, and counterparty level, as well as firmwide.

Globalization and the speed with which transactions move today because of real-time networks mean that problems can spread more quickly than ever before. The failure of a major money-center bank could cause losses for lenders ranging from New York to London, Zurich, Frankfurt, Paris, Tokyo, and Singapore. Adding to these risks are the fast development of synthetic securities and derivatives, as well as the potentially destabilizing market dynamics that are not yet so well understood.

Another wrong message regards transaction clearing. While there are improvements in settlement and netting procedures aimed at reducing the number of transactions outstanding across the system, this regards mainly commodities and equities traded in exchanges, not-over-the counter instruments. Yet, the OTC market is colossal.

Table 9–1 and Table 9–2 provide statistics to substantiate this argument. These percentages represent a real-life situation. They are based on actual numbers on the 1994 annual report by the Union Bank of Switzerland. Gross volume of buy and sell contracts is combined. The percentages include unsettled spot transactions. In notional principal amount, OTC trades are 335 percent more important than exchange-traded instruments.

When two derivatives dealers—Bank of New England and Drexel Burnham—failed, the damage was successfully walled off. But in notional principal amounts, the exposure of these companies was relatively trivial. Each had only about $30 billion of contracts outstanding when the crash came.

So far, the derivatives industry has not been tested by a giant failure. This would have been the case if serious problems affected one of the banks with an estimated $4 trillion or more in notional principal derivatives exposure. The Chase Manhattan, which resulted from the merger with Chemical Bank, and J. P. Morgan are at that level.

T A B L E   9–1

Notional Principal Amounts in Derivatives OTC versus Exchange-Traded

1.	OTC	77.1%
1.1	Currency products	41%
1.2	Interest-rate products	30%
1.3	Equity derivatives	5.0%
1.4	Precious metals/commodities	1.1%
2.	Exchange-Traded	22.9%
2.1	Currency products	1%
2.2	Interest-rate products	21%
2.3	Equity derivatives	0.5%
2.4	Precious metals/commodities	0.4%

T A B L E   9–2

Notional Principal Amounts by Taxonomy of Derivative Instruments

1.	**Currency Products**	**42%**
1.1	Over-the-counter (OTC)	41%
1.2	Exchange-traded	1%
2.	**Interest-Rate Products**	**51%**
2.1	OTC	30%
2.2	Exchange-traded	21%
3.	**Equity Derivatives**	**5.5%**
3.1	OTC	5.0%
3.2	Exchange-traded	0.5%
4.	**Precious Metals and Other Commodities**	**1.5%**
4.1	OTC	1.1%
4.2	Exchange-traded	0.4%

A close call might have been the case of liquidity problems that affected Salomon Brothers at the time of its Treasury bond scandal in 1991. Salomon had more than $600 billion in derivative contracts on its books— still small fry compared to today's amounts, but a big number at that time.

As knowledgeable bankers appreciate, a great deal of the systemic risk comes from the fact that no one really knows how this quickly expanding interlocked business of off-balance sheet and on-balance sheet financing would come through a severe crisis. Some hypotheses talk of failures of cataclysmic proportions. There is also the opinion that when confronted with the option, central banks will choose inflation rather than let the financial fabric tear itself apart.

According to a 1996 survey by the Bank for International Settlements, the central bank of the central banks, the top twenty American commercial and investment banks had $23.1 trillion in derivatives (expressed in notional principal amounts). That's one third of the overall 1996 total exposure characterizing the global banking system. In terms of size, it is followed by:

- A $11.5 trillion exposure by nine Japanese banks, and
- A $9.4 trillion exposure by a handful of French banks

The derivatives holdings of Chase Manhattan were $4.8 trillion in notional principal amount, at the end of 1995. Nine months later this amount rose by 18 percent. As shown in Tables 9–3a and 9–3b:

- On September 30, 1996, Chase's derivatives holdings stood at $5.66 trillion, against $21 billion in stockholders' equity, and $323 billion in assets.
- Even after demodulation by a factor of 30, which is a conservative approach, in loans equivalent terms Chase's derivatives portfolio was 9 times its net worth.
- A loss equivalent to just 11 percent of this derivatives portfolio would wipe out Chase's entire equity.

That relatively small margin between existence and deep trouble is a dominant feature of today's international financial system. The problem

T A B L E   9–3a

Derivatives Holdings of Major U.S. Banks in $ Billions
(As of September 30, 1996)

Bank	Assets	Equity	Derivatives
1. Chase Manhattan	323	21	5,660
2. J. P. Morgan	212	11	4,509
3. Citicorp	272	20	2,557
4. Bankers Trust	121	5	1,906
5. BankAmerica	243	21	1,808
6. NationsBank	188	13	1,325
7. First Chicago	107	9	1,024
8. Republic NY	51	3	289
9. First Union	134	9	147
10. Bank of New York	52	5	119
Top Ten Banks	1,703	117	19,344
All U.S. Banks	4,458	370	20,385
% of Top Ten on All U.S. Banks	31.2	31.9	94.9

*Sources: Comptroller of the currency and company reports.

T A B L E   9–3b

Derivatives Holdings of Major U.S. Banks in $ Billions
(As of September 30, 1996)*

Bank	Derivatives Demodulated by 30	Demodulated Derivatives as Multiples of Equity	Demodulated Derivatives as Percent of Assets
1. Chase Manhattan	188.7	8.98	0.58
2. J. P. Morgan	150.3	13.56	0.70
3. Citicorp	85.23	4.17	0.30
4. Bankers Trust	63.53	11.93	0.53
5. BankAmerica	62.26	2.93	0.23
6. NationsBank	44.17	3.33	0.23
7. First Chicago	34.13	3.77	0.33
8. Republic NY	9.00	0.00	0.20
9. First Union	4.90	0.56	0.03
10. Bank of New York	3.97	0.77	0.06
Top Ten Banks	646.82	5.53	0.38
All U.S. Banks	679.50	1.83	0.17

*The percent of exposure of top ten on all U.S. banks is: <u>94.9</u>

is that it could lead to a global *systemic crisis,* starting with one money center bank and leading to a snowball effect.

In absolute terms, next to Chase the most exposed American bank in regard to derivatives is J. P. Morgan. This, however, changes if exposure is measured not in absolute terms but relative to *assets* and *equity.* Demodulated derivatives exposure as a multiple of the bank's equity is 13.56 times for Morgan; 11.93 times for Bankers Trust; and 8.98 times for Chase Manhattan—but only 0.77 for the Bank of New York, compared to a 1.83 average for all American banks.

- Even when examined in a conservative way, the U.S. banks have, on the average, an exposure in derivatives which is almost twice their equity.
- This compares to the crisis of the early 1980s when the 5 largest American banks had lent to Mexico, Argentina, and Brazil an amount of money greater than their equity.

Regarding derivatives exposure in terms of assets, J. P. Morgan is again at the top of the list with a ratio of 0.70, this time followed by Chase with 0.58 and Bankers Trust with 0.53. The Bank of New York has in derivatives exposure only 0.06 of its assets, against an average of 0.17 for all American banks.

Notice that whether or not the notional principal amounts are demodulated, it changes little in this classification because the high exposure in derivatives is there, no matter how one measures it. After all, whether one likes to use the notional principal as frame of reference, or prefers not to do so, the fact remains that such amounts represent *contractual agreements* from which the banks cannot walk away.

3. THE 1996 INTEGRATION OF ON-BALANCE SHEET AND OFF-BALANCE SHEET EXPOSURE IN SWITZERLAND

Chapter 2 explained in a fair amount of detail how the French system of regulation and supervision works. By way of introducing the integration of balance-sheet and off-balance sheet reporting that became mandatory in Switzerland in 1996, it is proper to say a few words about the Swiss regulatory system.

The Swiss National Bank (SNB) does not do bank supervision. This is the responsibility of the Swiss Federal Banking Commission (SFBC). The mission established by the Swiss National Bank's charter prescribes two main functions: monetary policy and lender of last resort.

SNB participates the Basle Committee for Bank Supervision since Switzerland is one of the G–10 countries. It is also the government agency directly responsible for systemic risk.

SFBC exercises bank supervision through its Secretariat, which employs about 50 people. This is done through a two-step approach, as shown in Figure 9–1. The Swiss Federal Banking Commission gets involved in direct inspection if it is not happy with the auditor's report.

As trading in derivative financial instruments reached trillions of dollars in notional principal amounts,[1] like so many central banks and other regulatory agencies, the Swiss National Bank felt the need for an integration of on-balance sheet and off-balance sheet exposure. According to the new regulation:

---

1 See also in Chapter 14 the statistics that underpin counterparty risk.

F I G U R E   9–1

A Two-Step Approach to Bank Supervision by the
Swiss Federal Banking Commission

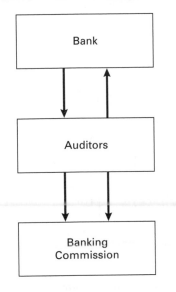

■ Off-balance sheet assets are integrated into the balance sheet as
  other assets.
■ Off-balance sheet liabilities are integrated as *other liabilities.*

The approach that has been effectively practiced in Switzerland since
1996 is shown in Figure 9–2 and Figure 9–3. Respectively, these two figures
represent assets and liabilities on-balance sheet and off-balance sheet, and
are based on the annual report of one of the largest Swiss banks.

This interactive solution permits market risk to be reflected in the
traditional balance sheet. The careful reader will remember from Chapter
5 that this is one of the alternatives examined by the Accounting Standards
Board in the United Kingdom.

The solution chosen by the Swiss National Bank constitutes a
change to the classical use of the balance sheet. Since its invention by
Luca Paciolo in 1494,[2] the balance sheet reflects *positions,* not risk.

Conceptually, however, all positions, whether in assets or in liabilities, have embedded into them an element of risk. It is inescapable that

2 See D. N. Chorafas, *Financial Models and Simulation* (London: Macmillan, 1995).

F I G U R E   9–2

Assets in the Balance Sheet and Off-Balance Sheet of a Major Financial Institution
(Up to $300 billion)

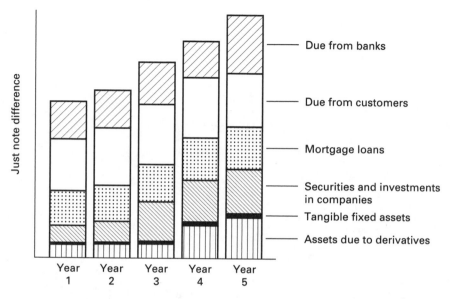

every position shown in A&L has an exposure associated with it. This is the sense of *position risk* that was defined in Chapter 1. Therefore, the 1996 Swiss rule of reporting market value in derivatives transactions can be shown as a refinement of current methods rather than a contradiction.

The downside, as the U.K. Accounting Standards Board pointed out in its July 1996 discussion paper,[3] is that with this solution, the same derivatives instrument will find itself sometimes among the assets, and at other times among the liabilities. Where exactly it will be written depends on the prevailing market price. If the present value of a derivative in the bank's portfolio is positive, this instrument will show in the assets. If, however, the present value of that same instrument is negative, it will land in the liabilities.

In Chapter 6, we have seen that to get around this duality in financial reporting, which fundamentally alters what classically goes in the assets and what goes in the liabilities side, the U.K. Accounting Standards Board introduced the Statement of Total Recognized Gains and Losses

---

3 *Derivatives and Other Financial Instruments* (London: ABS, 1996).

FIGURE   9–3

Liabilities in the Balance Sheet and Off-Balance Sheet
of a Major Financial Institution
(Up to $300 billion)

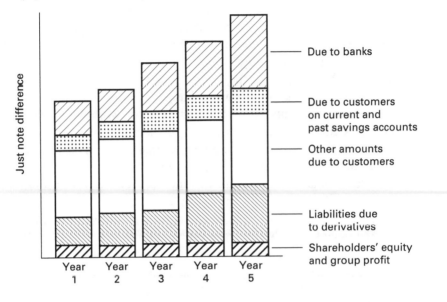

(STRGL). As has already been explained, STRGL supplements the well-established profit and loss (P&L) statement (income statement). It does so by showing gains and losses recognized but not yet realized.

The point has also been made that in the United States the Financial Accounting Standards Board has introduced a fairly similar solution into American regulatory practice. As with STRGL, items that show in its comprehensive income statement will eventually be recycled into P&L. In the Swiss case, derivative contracts will be in the assets or the liabilities, but they may also move in successive balance sheets from assets to liabilities and vice versa.

4. MARKET RISK AMENDMENT AND DYNAMIC ADJUSTMENTS IN CONTROLLING SYSTEMIC RISK

The growing activity in derivatives may not per se result in increased threats to the stability of the world's financial system, but this statement is not valid in regard to possible aftermaths compounded by a panic. A great deal of systemic risk comes from the exponential growth in trades with novel instruments whose exposure has not yet been properly analyzed. Because of leveraging, the next crash might hold many surprises. A similar statement could be made regarding the possible crash of financial institutions.

A faster-moving payments and settlements system might reduce Herstatt risk. Following the demise of Drexel Burnham Lambert in 1990, the mortgage market found itself obliged to modernize its practices to speed settlement. Because of the Securities and Exchange Commission rule adopted in 1993, by the middle of 1995 equity and corporate bond trades started being settled in three days, down from the classical five.

One of the bright spots of the early 1990s was improvement in disclosure requirements, but this mainly happened in the United States thanks to FASB Statements 105, 107, and 119, not worldwide,[4] though this situation is changing. Better disclosure is needed universally on risk posed by derivatives, investments in emerging markets, and other volatile financial deals.[5] The same is true about cross-market risk.

Improved global market linkages would help reduce risk in foreign-exchange transactions and from moves in interest rates. Hence, IMF's Internet initiative is a good idea (see Chapter 7). Supported through knowledge-enriched models, the recommendations of the Market Risk Amendment can aid in establishing dynamic bank capital levels according to prevailing economic activity.

The dynamic adjustment of capital requirements and reserves can play a capital role because systemic risk may come as a result of a *domino effect*. The interdependence of banks and dealers in derivatives is tighter than that of participants in the more classical capital markets and other traditional market sectors. On the surface, the off-balance sheet credit risk is no more than that present with other instruments: One market participant won't make payments that others expect. But the bottom line is that derivatives tie markets together so effectively that shocks in one place can have severe global aftermaths.

The shock wave from a major bank failure can spread to other markets with such speed that regulators do not have time to manage the situation, particularly since few checks and balances are in place worldwide in connection to derivative instruments.

One key factor making the salvage difficult is globality. Global markets have become more closely linked, primarily because of the rise of cross-border capital flows and efforts by governments to open national

---

4 See Chapter 6.

5 See D. N. Chorafas, *Managing Derivatives Risk* (Burr Ridge, IL: Irwin Professional Publishing, 1996).

borders in the hope of attracting mobile capital. Derivatives are part of this larger phenomenon, and there is reason to believe that they can transmit shocks that would otherwise be contained, as the February/March 1994 earthquake in the leveraged bond market helps document.

The theory that dynamic hedging could produce overwhelming pressures in the cash market and the exchange-traded derivatives market is also based on the assumption that those who write options do not quite understand options pricing (as the March 1997 Nat West Market losses demonstrated) and do not prudently limit their short options positions.

Unfortunately, the hypothesis behind this theory is true, as the near bankruptcy that hit Germany's Metallgesellschaft as a result of huge exposure in its U.S operations helps demonstrate. Because they are not thoroughly analyzed and understood, some derivatives deals can significantly increase systemic risk. This means that commercial banks and investment banks must follow the 1996 Market Risk Amendment, strengthen their risk-management practices, and essentially create a first line of defense against systemic problems.

This leads to a question about the adequacy of internal controls and risk-management systems of players in derivatives—not just the 30 major players in Table 9–3, but every player. Control of exposure simply cannot be done through legacy software, mainframes, and the batch-type operations most banks still use. Control of exposure requires rigorous internal controls, knowledge engineering, real-time systems, and advanced techniques for managing risk.

Figure 9–4 gives a snapshot of the solution banks should be after: powerful networked workstations (WS) with fast-track development of software, integration of competitive and legacy computer programs, and a virtual network that permits integration of all nodes in a seamless manner to the end user.

Networks, computers, and software that made derivatives possible also help disseminate news, rumors, and misunderstandings at speeds that leave market participants and central banks very little time to react in the event of a crisis. In turn, this can affect liquidity in markets where trust is an important ingredient. Effective risk control also calls for a top management policy able to guarantee that each bank is steadily improving its risk-control practices, hence, top management involvement.

Analytical risk-control systems operating in real time are essential to conducting business in the financial markets—in all domains, not just in derivatives. Solutions must address credit risk, market risk, and liquidity risk as well as operations and legal risks.

FIGURE 9-4

Organizational Reengineering of Communications, Computers, and Software Resources

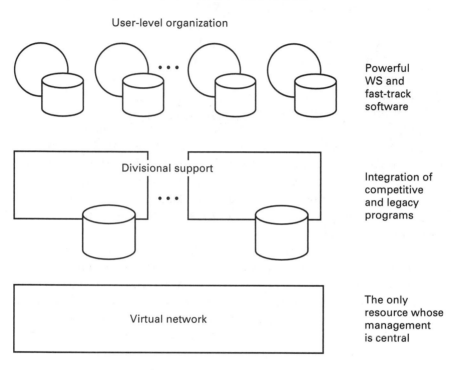

During the 1990s, some market players exploited what they said was modest risk correlation across national market segments. In interest-rate products, for instance, certain banks could find significant offsets of the risks embedded in their book in different currencies. Including both traditional and new products, the aggregate forex book contains a growing amount of diversification gains and losses across currencies. Institutions also exploited risk offsets arising from relationships between exposures in foreign-exchange, interest-rate, and equity markets.

For these reasons, some commercial and investment bankers think that systemic risk has decreased somewhat. But central bankers and clearers believe that systemic risk has increased. The most commonly cited events capable of triggering systemic problems are the defaults of financial institutions and settlements failures, to which has recently been added the year 2000 problem.[6]

---

6 D. N. Chorafas, *Agent Technology Handbook* (New York: McGraw Hill, 1997).

Individually and in unison, these factors are instrumental in shaking the classical degree of complacency with respect to systemic risk. Also, the Barings bankruptcy has knocked down the more or less firmly held belief that central banks or public authorities will act to prevent a well-known institution from collapsing or that they will always do whatever is needed to stabilize markets, the way the French government treated the crisis of Crédit Lyonnais.

5. LENDERS OF LAST RESORT AND RISK MANAGEMENT BY SOVEREIGN STATES

Classically, one of the basic functions of central banks has been lender of last resort for financial institutions under their jurisdiction. Both the government and the reserve bank have discretionary powers on this issue. As we have seen in Section 4, some authorities take action (as in the case of Crédit Lyonnais), but others adopt a hands-off attitude (as with Barings).

Much more complex is the role of lender of last resort at a global level. In the 18th and 19th centuries, municipalities and governments that mismanaged their finances went bankrupt, carrying down with them the banks that had given them loans. But after World War II, the fear of systemic risk led to last-minute efforts to save the day. In the 1970s, New York City was saved from bankruptcy five minutes before the 12th hour. This was also the case with Mexico in 1983 and, once again, in 1994–95.

Who is supposed to act as lender of last resort in international financing when companies and governments are at the limits of bankruptcy? Even more to the point, is it wise or unwise to save governments from the results of their own greed? To bail out banks that willingly got overexposed? What about the risk of making a practice out of bailouts?

The massive rescue effort for Mexico, with $52 billion put on the table by the United States, the International Monetary Fund, the Bank for International Settlements, and a few money-center banks (as junior partners), should not be repeated. Other "emerging markets" with financial problems should not expect such a remarkable rescue as a matter of course.

Neither the United States nor the supranational institutions should be a lender of last resort for mismanaged countries. Congress had a hard time digesting Mexico's rescue even though it had little authority to change it. What would Congress think about rescuing Pakistan, Venezuela, Kenya, Turkey, or Bulgaria?

No emerging markets should be getting themselves into Mexico's shoes. When governments understand that *caveat emptor* applies, they will be more prudent. For their part, individual and institutional investors will do well to weigh the potential risks in emerging markets and require increased transparency and surveillance to help them scrutinize economic performance.

Even with enhanced resources, the IMF and BIS do not have enough money to play Santa Claus. Nor do they have the information beforehand to judge which national governments and major municipalities are out of tune with good financial sense. Yet, tomorrow's megacities of 15 and 20 million people will be quite prone to creating systemic risk by pulling major banks down with them. Look at Sao Paulo's Banesto.

In 1994–95 Mexico taught the world several difficult lessons, which should not be lost on governments in other emerging markets. The next country to misbehave must be made an example of in terms of how world markets and the IMF will deal with unsound policies. The European Union's *Stability Pact,* signed in December 1996 in Dublin and reconfirmed in June 1997 in Amsterdam, is a fair model, and it should constitute a precedent:

- There must be quantitative objectives in budget deficits and government debt for all countries eventually aspiring to a rescue.
- Penalities should be applied when these objectives are not met— in the understanding that a safety net is useful, but only for real accidents.
- If catastrophic events are the result of government incompetence or greed, the country should not expect much help.

Though gauging the financial health of governments and major municipalities might not have been its intention, the Market Risk Amendment by the Basle Committee could contribute a lot in terms of providing early signals of financial poor health at the government level. If banks can mark-to-model their trading book, governments can also do so in regard to their cash flow, their budget, their current account, their assets, and their liabilities.

Marking-to-market and marking-to-model can apply to sovereign borrowers just as they apply to banks. This valuation procedure is helped by the fact that the IMF is almost steadily inspecting the economic realities of countries that come hat-in-hand for loans, and its norms are stiff. But the recipes are standard—which is wrong because no two countries have the same problems.

Provided that parametric, flexible, knowledge-enriched models are developed and used in connection to the finances of sovereign states, marking-to-model can provide a factual and documented way, making a material difference in the way systemic risk is managed. As I mentioned in Chapter 7, IMF's Internet initiative is a good start.

As with banks, the objective of marking-to-model a country's trading book and portfolio is to produce a reliable estimate about how much value it has at risk. Such methodology should be universal, and the algorithms should be verifiable. This is the only way that permits transnational regulators to apply their judgment in estimating a country's economic health and capital adequacy. With banks, *intraday* data flows should be the rule, with governments, *interday* statistics will be sufficient, provided they are properly databased.

There is, of course, a fair amount of subjective judgment in any process, including modeling. Also present is the fact of which we have already spoken: For a good part of assets and liabilities belonging to a bank or to a government, there may be no active market.

Therefore, it is not unusual that critics of marking to market include many bankers who have loans backgrounds, as well as many accountants. Among the advocates of marking-to-market are some academics, the risk managers at major financial institutions, and those bankers who have a trading background.

As for the alternative of marking-to-model, proponents are the academics, risk managers, and traders. Accountants are skeptical about the method; the same is true of classical bankers. Regulators are divided, mainly because the majority of them are not trained in rocket science.

6. DEVELOPING AND USING A METHODOLOGY FOR THE CONTROL OF MARKET RISK

Whether the concept is used in regard to financial institutions, the treasuries of major corporations, or the treasuries of sovereign states, risk management breaks down into a number of component parts, with the principal areas being credit risk and market risk. As we have already seen throughout the eight chapters of Part One, credit risk is the more classical in terms of attention paid to it by bankers, regulators, and sovereign lenders. The importance of market risk has only recently been appreciated, yet it has been a key factor in banking and finance for many years.

I have also stressed on several occasions that not only has market risk been institutionalized by the 1996 Market Risk Amendment of the Basle Committee, but also a significant innovation in risk management has been presented because of using risk models as a means of relating the price of an asset or liability to market conditions.

Valuation models for financial instruments can be simple or complex, with some freedom of choice given to user organizations in terms of their development. The freedom to choose the model started in the United States with an agreement between six major Wall Street securities firms, the U.S. Securities and Exchange Commission (SEC), and the Commodity Futures Trading Commission (CFTC). This stipulated that in managing derivatives risks the firms can use their own internal systems, which rest on a value-at-risk methodology, which is explained in Chapter 10.

Risk management, however, is more than just a model. It is an aggregate of policies and limits. Whether we talk of commercial banks and investment banks or of sovereign states, *internal controls* are key to its success.

The control of risk boils down to a three-dimensional frame of reference. In order of priority this involves top management decisions, rigorous internal controls, and mathematical models. A complete system of mathematical models should include at least three main components:

- Value-at-risk.
- Pricing.
- Tracking

The 1996 Market Risk Amendment does not say so, but knowledgeable bankers appreciate that this is what should be done. I have also mentioned in Chapter 1 that top-tier banks today develop even more sophisticated approaches than VAR: stress analysis, net present value divided by a demodulator, intrinsic value based on cash flow, capital at risk (CAR), and earnings at risk (EAR). They also integrate credit risk and market risk to get an integrative view of the exposure assumed with each important counterparty.

In a way, market risk is a philosophy underlying the business strategy of a financial institution or of a government. With private companies, like banks, part of the business philosophy is to *manage to regulation.* In this manner, the approach changes as regulators become more demanding.

The philosophical touch is important because, both conceptually and pragmatically, any organization, be it a bank or a government, makes its money from taking risks. Therefore, it is fundamental to understand and control the risks in the business at the individual transaction level, in each division, and across the organization.

Analytical tools have been developed to this effect, examples being value-at-risk (VAR), daily earnings at risk (DEAR), risk-adjusted return on capital (RAROC), RiskMetrics, and return on risk capital (RORC).[7]

---

7 See D. N. Chorafas, *Managing Derivatives Risk* (Burr Ridge, IL: Irwin, 1996).

Models allow for correlation between asset classes and operate across an entire balance sheet or portfolio as well as by single instrument. A crucial approach is to simulate the impact of specific rate and price scenarios, particularly on options, futures, forwards, swaps, and generally instruments with significant market risk. But note that:

- A model is only as good as its assumptions and the rules it employs—these need to be checked constantly for validity.
- The same applies to internal controls, systems and procedures, and the methodology to be adopted.

It is beyond any doubt that no amount of modeling will replace experience and professional judgment in managing risk. This is why the role of the chief risk-management officer (CRMO) has grown substantially in importance. Nor is there doubt that without an appropriate methodology a new organizational position will not deliver the desired results.

The right methodology and rigorous models for valuation purposes are particularly important for those assets and liabilities that are more difficult to value. An example is real estate. Depreciated original cost and book value adjusted for market changes are alternative solutions. If there is no market for a given asset at a particular moment, then an algorithmic approach is the only alternative.

Many banks hold assets like bad loans and sour securities, which represent very little in terms of assets. Other banks have liabilities that mushroomed, as often happens with derivatives characterized by unlimited risks.

There is a certain parallel between the IMF denying a loan, therefore letting a government go bankrupt, and a central bank closing down a bank, which in terms of financial value is an empty shell or has negative assets. Both moves avoid having good money run after bad money if the rotten conditions continue to deteriorate. This statement is synonymous to saying that the G-7 governments and the G 10 central banks must clearly define the following:

- *Risk parameters,* which should be set systemwide, guiding the way in which money-center banks and institutional investors operate.
- *Confidence intervals,* to delimit the risk parameters and assure that their meaning is unambiguously identified.
- *Investment horizons,* to help evaluate the assets and liabilities holding period.

As Figure 9–5 illustrates, risk tends to change in relation to counterparties, instruments, term of commitment, and investment horizon. There is also the need to properly define conversion factors to provide a common denominator for risk measurement.

Also important is the degree of accuracy with which risks are characterized: whether a risk yield curve tips, its curvature changes, or possible variations exist over different intervals. It is necessary to complement the mathematics of the model by establishing the most crucial decision criteria. This brings into perspective another obligation in risk management: *validation criteria* developed by banks (and governments) and used in marking-to-model. We will examine these issues in Part Two.

FIGURE   9–5

Risk Tends to Change in Relation to Counterparties, Term of Commitment, and Investment Horizon

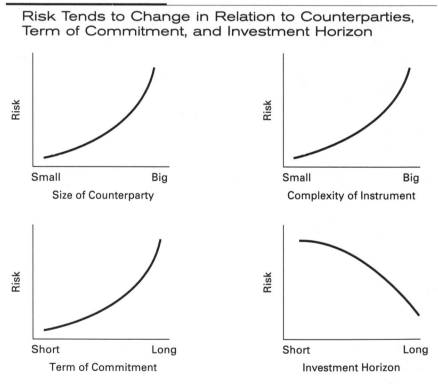

PART TWO

Understanding Marking-to-Model

CHAPTER 10

The Calculation of Value-at-Risk (VAR) with Parametric Models

1. INTRODUCTION

Part One has documented that with derivatives, and securities trading at large, during the last few years there has been a significant change in the measurement of risk. The development of the derivatives market has given banks the incentive to focus on trading—but also underlined the need to control their risk profile more closely. The 1996 Market Risk Amendment made this focus compulsory.

The dual requirement for pricing financial instruments and for controlling exposure led to fairly sophisticated in-house systems to measure the risk inherent in the trading book. This effort has been helped with cross-fertilization from physics, engineering, and mathematics, through the employment of rocket scientists.[1]

It is not easy to develop a model that accurately represents market movements, but it is doable. However, though necessary, the development of models is not enough. Risk measurement requires thoroughly studied procedures. In an operational sense, the development of models is an attempt to forecast future market actions. This is what traders, bankers, investors, and speculators are continually trying to do through guts. If one can predict the future, one holds the high ground in bringing exposure under control.

---

1 See D. N. Chorafas, *Rocket Scientists in Banking* (London: Lafferty, 1995).

The irony is that a serious approach to modeling starts by accepting that we cannot accurately predict the future. What we usually do is put historical data under stress in an attempt to reveal a pattern of market movements.

As knowledgeable bankers appreciate, it is incorrect to assume that future market behavior will follow the same pattern as the past. The reason we gather and analyze historical data is to make an informed and objective estimate of future risks. The aim is to *quantify uncertainty,* which is what risk-management models such as *value-at-risk* (VAR) try to do.

Value-at-risk is the expected loss from an adverse market movement, with a specific probability over a period of time. What we measure is the worst case in a change in portfolio value that over one day, at a given level of confidence, will not exceed a computed amount: the VAR. It is proper to remember that modeling is not perfect, nor does perfection character- ize the financial industry at large or, more specifically, risk control. Modeling is approximate, and the use of risk-management systems and procedures is not an exact science.

If one had to choose between precision in modeling and precision in the implementation of risk management, the better solution by far would be an approximate model applied by people with dediction, intuition, and experience. This is far superior to a perfect model in the hands of people who don't understand it or don't pay attention to its application.

2. UNDERSTANDING THE CONCEPT OF VALUE-AT-RISK

Value-at-risk is one of the models for risk management currently very popular in the banking industry. Its implementation is changing past prac- tices where banks have traditionally measured the risks in individual parts of their trading book separately, without appropriate coordination and through different metrics.

By moving toward a whole trading-book approach through value-at- risk, bankers and treasurers aim to calculate on a more consistent basis the *likely loss* they might experience on their transactions. As with all models, this approach is not exact, but it reveals the exposure that exists between and within different markets.

VAR models are being used to assess likely price changes of finan- cial instruments within individual markets. They are also applied in com- puting the extent to which prices in one market vary relative to those in other markets. Even if the results are approximate, under a rigorous risk-management methodology they serve a purpose.

The problem is not the approximation. As FASB Statement 119 aptly states, value-at-risk has the disadvantage of being little known among investors, creditors, bankers, treasurers, and generally, financial entities that are not derivatives dealers. Most banks and other parties do not yet have the measurement or reporting system to report the disclosure. There is also a fair amount of illiteracy about models and the notion of a specific probability over a period of time.

The concept underpinning any model, and this reference includes Black–Scholes (which we will study in Chapter 12) and many others, is the usefulness of having a prognosticator. Figure 10–1 suggests a pattern to follow in evaluating our trading book. A similar approach can be applied with loans and investments in our banking book. First comes the overall view presented by economic assessment. The model to be used for value-at-risk is the second box in the top row. The balance of the block diagram is the procedural solution we should establish in order to control risk.

The crucial question targeted through VAR is: What can I lose under certain assumptions of market behavior, given the current exposure in my trading book? The answer varies in functions of the outstanding forward interest-rate contracts, currency and other swaps, options purchased and written, equity/index derivatives, other over-the-counter deals as well as

F I G U R E   10–1

Sound Practices Require a Sense of Balance in Risk Management

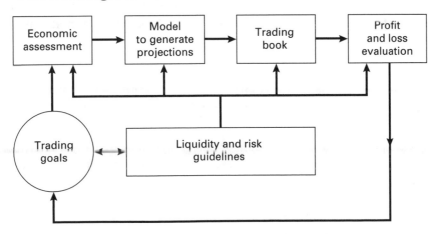

futures and options traded in the exchanges. Typically, VAR models developed by banks for their internal risk management try to measure the loss on a portfolio over a specified period of time, often the next 24-hour holding period.

Banks use value-at-risk techniques to measure the possible losses arising from the effect of movements in interest rates, exchange rates, equities, bonds, and commodity prices on the trading book. The resulting figure, whose derivation we will follow in the following sections, gives a measure of aggregate risk. In essence, it is providing a measure of theoretical losses characterized by a high degree of probability: the confidence level that we apply. This means that the VAR figure will only be exceeded on a given fraction of occasions, for instance, in 1 percent or 5 percent of cases, as we will see in subsequent sections.

This approach to the quantification of probable exposure came of age because, as we have seen in Chapter 2, the 1996 Market Risk Amendment by the Basle Committee promoted the use of models. Tier-1 banks look at this event as a major advance in the implementation of both quantitative and qualitative techniques. The *qualitative criteria* stress policies and procedures promoting checks and balances through an independent risk-management operation run by the bank. The *quantitative criteria* include modeling and backtesting the system, converting prognostication results into internal and supervisory capital requirements.

For reasons of steady follow-up on exposure, VAR should be calculated daily, using a 99 percent confidence level, a minimum holding period of 10 days, and a historical observation period of at least one year. As Chapters 2, 3, and 4 explained, according to the Basle Committee the capital charge should be the higher of the latest VAR and the average daily VAR for the past 60 days. Depending on the fitness of the model, these will be multiplied by a factor assessed by national regulators (x3 for models in the green zone).

3. DIFFERENT LEVELS OF SOPHISTICATION IN MEASURING PROBABLE LOSSES

As explained in the chapter introduction, a bank's or treasury's value-at-risk is the expected loss from an adverse market movement, with a specified probability over a period of time. Based on a simulation of a large number of possible scenarios, we can determine with 99 percent probability that any adverse change in the portfolio value over 24 hours will not exceed a calculated amount: the value-at-risk.

Value at risk is used by dealers in managing risk associated with derivative financial instruments and other assets because it is a convenient method. Some financial analysts think that value-at-risk is a helpful indicator of the minimum safe level of capital. Even if the model is approximate, it can be useful, provided the methodology is right. This methodology involves the following:

- The definition of value-at-risk.
- The model of computation.
- The financial time series to be used for marking-to-model.
- The calculation of confidence intervals.

With this background, we can compute value-at-risk for interest-rate instruments and fixed-income securities, foreign-currency options, call and put options, and common shares.

Provided we know how to apply and how to control value-at-risk measures, we can calculate the positions in our trading book or in any other portfolio. Figure 10–2 however, suggests that there are alternative ways for reaching the goal of measuring probable losses.

The graduation shown in Figure 10–2 places value-at-risk as a more sophisticated approach than the simpler *sensitivity* models, but somewhat less rigorous than what I call the capital-at-risk (CAR) solution.[2] With CAR, the capital-at-risk is allocated to different trading classes. With VAR, we estimate the exposure that is there.

At the bottom of the pyramid in Figure 10–2 are the now standard option-pricing models, for example, Black–Scholes. Above options pricing is the sensitivity analysis approach, which is commonly used by banks and may include higher-order metrics such as delta, gamma, theta, kappa, and rho.[3]

The lower of the two layers of the VAR reference is a parametric model based on the assumption that returns are normally distributed. Call it VAR/P. The more complex (and more accurate) approach to VAR is based on a nonparametric simulation (call it VAR/S), where no assumptions are made about the underlying distribution.

Stress analysis[4] is also a simulation procedure, which permits looking at the effects of extreme market movements (but not necessarily panics) on the contents of a portfolio under scrutiny. The use of capital-at-risk

---

2 See Chapter 11.
3 See Chapter 13 and D. N. Chorafas, *Advanced Financial Analysis* (London: *Euromoney,* 1994).
4 Discussed in Chapter 11.

F I G U R E   10–2

Six Levels of Sophistication in Risk Management
Models and Procedures

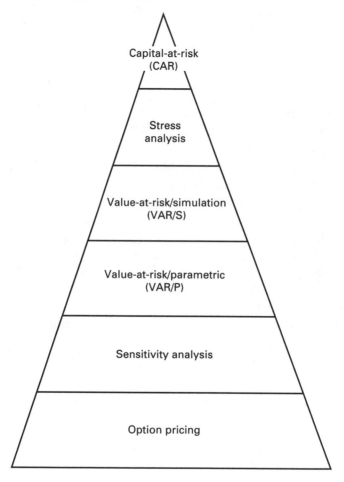

rather than value-at-risk requires a much greater awareness of the allocation of capital and a major focus on the control of risk.

Only a handful of banks worldwide have the knowledge necessary
for using CAR. A few more, but not too many, have the rocket scientists
to develop and employ VAR/S models. A somewhat greater number of
banks use VAR/P, but the majority of banks using models are still at the
level of Black–Scholes and sensitivity analysis—or not yet even there.

Let me recapitulate the message in this section. There are two types of value-at-risk solutions. They share common statistical tools such as confidence intervals, but some of the basic mathematical notions underpinning them are quite different. The same is true of the methodology being used as well as of the results.

Because the mathematical tools for these value-at-risk methods are not necessarily common knowledge, prior to looking into the mechanics, I will briefly review the necessary statistical notions. This will help provide a common background and will also answer the comment indirectly made in FASB Statement 119 that the concept of a specific probability over a period of time eludes many bankers and investors.

4. THE BELL-SHAPED PROBABILITY DISTRIBUTION

Let's start with an example from personal loans. Scores are often applied to indicate the quality of the counterparty. The way to bet is that the good score system represents the likelihood that the person with the best score can prove more dependable in paying the interest and repaying the capital. The opposite is true regarding the person with the lowest score.

Not everyone would get the highest or lowest score. Whether with loan seekers or with students in a classroom, a grading system typically ends up in a *rank*. This indicates where each individual stands with respect to the others.

Many statistical procedures can be applied to manipulate numbers that are measurements in order to get a pattern out of them. Typically, these measurements form a distribution, with the extremes having a lower *probability* of showing up than the middle values.

In our example, this probability is a measure of the likelihood of occurrence of a score. If we consider events that can occur in N mutually exclusive and equally likely ways, and if n of these outcomes have an attribute A (a specific score in the measurement scale), then the probability of A is n/N—a number between zero and one.

The statistical basis used in connection to the distribution of measurements and their study is, most often, the *normal distribution,* if for no other reason than because we have tables available that assist in computation and experimentation. The normal distribution is bell-shaped, like the one shown in Figure 10–3.

X, the abscissa, is the horizontal axis with the measurement or score. Y, the ordinate, presents the *frequency* of observations of an assigned value

F I G U R E   10-3

Expected Value and Worst Case in the Evaluation of
Risk from a Financial Transaction

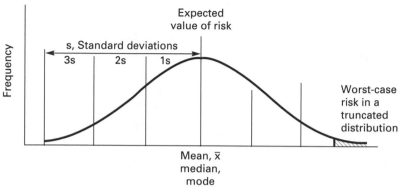

of X. The *mode* of a distribution is the point of highest frequency, the *mean* is the arithmetic average, and the *median* is the midrange. In a normal distribution, the mode, mean, and median coincide. In real life, this bell-shaped distribution is an approximation, but it is widely used for describing random events. In a sample, it is characterized by the *mean* $\overline{x}$, or central tendency, and the *variance* s^2, which indicates the spread.

In Section 6, we will contrast the statistics of the sample to the parameters of the distribution. Analysts would have liked to work with the parameters, but typically this is not feasible. With the parametric method, we make some hypotheses about these parameters, which is the weakness of the method.

The square root of the variance is the standard deviation, s, and it is the statistic that will interest us the most in this discussion. In the distribution under study, the probability of a random event falling within given standard deviations around the mean, also known as *two-tailed probability,* is given in Table 10–1.

The example with a score system for loans can be extended to other domains, for instance, market values of a financial instrument or the risk that we are taking with a given investment. The distribution of these events may not be normal but skew or leptokyrtotic.[5] However, in this text

---

5 D. N. Chorafas, *How to Understand and Use Mathematics for Derivatives,* Volume 2 (London: *Euromoney,* 1995).

T A B L E   10–1

Two-Tailed Probablities of an Event Falling within
One, Two, or Three Standard Deviations in a Normal
Distribution Curve

Probability	Standard Deviations
68.27%	±1s
95.45%	±2s
99.73%	+3s

we will not concern ourselves with these distributions because they don't
enter the computation of value-at-risk as it currently stands.

   If the mean is the expected value of the risk, which is the way to bet,
and we take one standard deviation on either side of the mean, then 68.27
percent of all occurrences will be expected to fall within $\bar{x}$ ± 1s. The balance of normally distributed risk values will fall outside the range of one
standard deviation.

   This is not satisfactory. By contrast, an outcome more than three
standard deviations away from the mean would have a very low probability of occurrence: 0.27 percent. Though an outlier beyond $\bar{x}$ ± 3s would
not be impossible, three standard deviations over (or under) the mean represent a *significant level of confidence:* The large majority of events will
fall within 3s. (The concept of a level of confidence will be explained
more fully in the next section.)

   With three standard deviations, the confidence that in a normal distribution a risk event will fall within the established limits is 99.73 percent. Whether in engineering, applied experimental psychology, or analytical finance, we tend to work with three different levels of confidence.
For a two-tailed distribution:

- The high level is 99 percent.
- The middle level is 95 percent.
- The lowest level is 90 percent.

   Notice that 90 percent is a pretty low level because it means that, in
a two-tailed distribution, 10 percent of the time the value of risk will fall
outside the limit we have established. Table 10–2 gives the number of
standard deviations for the 90 percent, 95 percent, and 99 percent levels
of confidence in two-tailed and one-tailed distributions.

T A B L E   10–2

Levels of Confidence and Standard Deviations

With a Two-Tailed Normal Distribution	
Level of Confidence	**Standard Deviations**
90.0%	1.65s
95.0%	1.96s
99.0%	2.60s
With a One-Tailed Distribution	
Level of Confidence	**Standard Deviations**
95.0%	1.65s
99.0%	2.34s
99.5%	2.60s

The sense of a one-tailed, or truncated, normal distribution is also shown in Figure 10–3. If, as the 1996 Market Risk Amendment implies, we should be interested in not exceeding the expected loss from an adverse market movement with a specific probability over a period of time, then the one-tailed distribution fits our purpose.

We will talk more about this concept in Section 5. But already with the definitions and algorithms this section has presented, it is possible to better appreciate the goals we are after with value-at-risk. The method makes feasible calculating a worst-case scenario with a *specific probability* that is valid as long as our hypothesis of a bell-shaped distribution of risk outcomes can be sustained.

5. LEVELS OF CONFIDENCE AND VALUE-AT-RISK

Because the concept of *level of confidence* (or level of significance) is indivisible from the process we study, before entering into the specific aspects of the value-at-risk models it is wise to consider in more detail what level of confidence means. As we have seen in Section 4, this is a statistical measure aimed at providing a reference on the confidence with which a statement about risk is made.

The sense of a level of confidence is the assurance it gives that the real risk will not be higher than the estimated value except in very rare cases. In statistical tests, the levels of reference typically used are 0.1,

0.05, and 0.01—which respectively mean no more than a 10 percent, 5 percent, or 1 percent error—or *percentiles*. In Section 4, we wrote this reference through the complements of 90 percent, 95 percent, and 99 percent. 10 percent, 5 percent, and 1 percent represent the probability that the worst-case risk we compute will be exceeded. 90 percent, 95 percent, and 99 percent are the probabilities that the worst-case risk will be contained within the limits.

The choice of the percentile level as well as the notions of one-tailed and two-tailed distributions have been standard statistical tools since the 1930s. One of their first implementations was in applied experimental psychology.[6] These tools entered finance in the 1970s and 1980s, and as we have seen among other implementations, they are used in connection to the Market Risk Amendment of the Basle Committee.

The theoretical background of the level of confidence can be found in the operating characteristics curves (OCC) developed during World War II for the Manhattan Project. As shown in Figure 10–4, this concept is based on limits: an acceptable quality level (AQL) and a lot tolerance percent defective (LTPD). When statistical sampling is used, the producer takes a risk that a good lot would be rejected.

This is known as α (alpha), Type I error, or producer's risk. It represents the probability that an outgoing lot may be of acceptable quality, yet with $\alpha = 0.01$ it has a 1 percent probability of being rejected. In the preceding paragraphs this $\alpha = 0.01$ corresponded to the 1 percent error—and its complement the 99 percent level of confidence.

- The consumer also takes the risk of receiving a percent defective β (beta) beyond the lot tolerance he or she bargained for.

A balancing act between the producer's and the consumer's risk is necessary because both the producer's and the consumer's interests should be protected. Beta is known as Type II error. Note, however, that this β has nothing to do with the same symbol used for volatility, which represents the standard deviation of a price distribution assumed to be normal.

For a given sampling, plan α and β correlate. They can both be reduced if we make the OCC steeper by increasing the sample size. This particular quality of the operating characteristics curve makes it very suitable for judging, among other things, the quality of loans along the line of

---

6 See D. N. Chorafas, *Statistical Processes and Reliability Engineering* (Princeton, NJ: D. Van Nostrand, 1960).

F I G U R E   10–4

An Operating Characteristics Curve with Identification
of Type I and Type II Errors

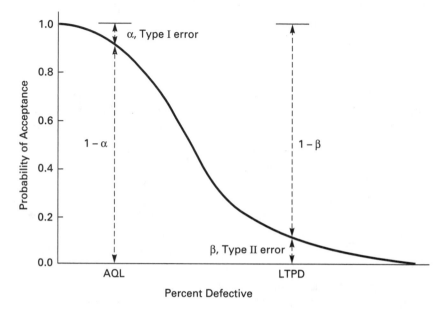

Percent Defective

the example at the beginning of Section 4. This statement is correct provided we have a scoring system and a database that can be mined for pertinent information elements.

The different values of α and the confidence levels we use in risk
management relate to one another in the way shown in Table 10–3. Notice
that both α and β are important, but once more, in financial analysis, confidence levels use only α, which I think is a shortcoming.

What the preceding paragraphs have explained through the use of Type
I error is that in risk management we can apply statistical levels of confidence by choosing in advance a daily change in either direction that is not
expected to happen more than 1 percent, 5 percent, or 10 percent of the time.

The 1996 Market Risk Amendment implies the 99 percent level of
confidence (hence $\alpha = 0.01$) for one-tailed distribution. This will correspond to x ± 2.33s. Because, however, as we have seen in Part One, there
are penalties for mismatch between model results and real-life risk, I pre-
fer to take x ± 2.60s, which effectively protects 99.5 percent of the time.

In either case, the basic assumption behind this statistical approach
is that the projection of future movements in market prices—interest rates,

T A B L E   10–3

Producer's Risk and Confidence Levels

Level of Confidence	Type I Error
90.0%	$\alpha = 0.1$
95.0%	$\alpha = 0.05$
99.0%	$\alpha = 0.01$

currency rates, equities, bonds, or derivatives—is based on the hypothesis of a normal distribution of historical market movements. As already stated, this is not absolutely correct, but it is in line with current practice.

6. LOOKING AT VALUE-AT-RISK AS A PARAMETRIC MODEL

The value-at-risk parametric model, VAR/P, is also known as the *whole book* approach, or *variance/covariance analysis.* As explained in Section 3, it uses statistics calculated from historical data on price volatility. It also employs correlations within and between markets to estimate likely potential losses.

The concept of a distribution of data characterizing a parametric VAR analysis arises from the fact that statistics are estimated from historical financial time series under the assumption that the sample of data comes from a population with parametric characteristics, such as mean μ and variance.

The mean μ and variance of the unknown population of values are *parameters,* and when we base our hypothesis on these parameters, the procedure we use is *parametric.* Since we don't know μ and σ^2, we estimate them through a sample. Our computation, which is *sample-based,* uses the *statistics* $\bar{x}$ and s^2.

The hypothesis we make about the normal distribution concerns price changes. As we have seen in Section 5, even if approximate, the assumption of a normal distribution enables the bank to calculate a *confidence level* for the value-at-risk over the next 24 hours.

This confidence level is calculated by reference to the standard deviation of past price changes multiplied by a scaling factor. The smaller the α, the greater the confidence that the calculated value-at-risk is the worst case.

The matter of confidence intervals is not to be taken lightly. The higher the degree of confidence we choose, expressed in standard deviations from the mean, the greater the exposure computed through value-at-risk. Based on a recent project on interest rates at different maturities, Figure 10–5 presents a family of curves that dramatize the level of market risk at 99 percent, 95 percent, and 90 percent confidence.

Because historical data is critical to the computation of the confidence level, as well as to any other modeling solution, a crucial issue is the ability to proceed with database mining. Under the variance/covariance approach, the database we exploit consists of statistics on the magnitude of past price movements and correlations between price movements.

The goal we are after is to estimate likely potential losses in a specified instrument in the trading book. However, many banks make the mistake of believing that the algorithm will do miracles, without paying a great deal of attention to the database.

Not only is the richness of database contents in connection to the parametric VAR model critical, but a very important reference to the risk profile of a trading book is *short-term* rather than longer-term correlations. If we pursue *intraday* time series or daily marking-to-market of positions, then hedges must be effective over days or weeks rather than months or quarters.

F I G U R E   10–5

Market-Risk Factor at Three Levels of
Confidence Intervals

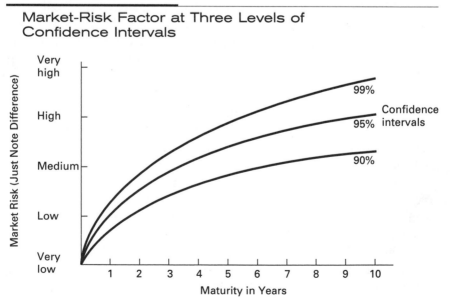

Using estimates of the mean variance and covariance of returns, we aim to calculate the daily loss that will be exceeded with a given probability, as has been explained in the preceding sections. By contrast, the simulation approach to VAR consists of establishing out of a long run of historical time series the loss exceeded on a given percentage of the days in the sample. In this connection, no distributional assumptions are made.

Speaking in statistical terms, the parametric and nonparametric approaches are not only different but also, theoretically, opposed to one another. With both, we aim at estimating return volatility for rather well-diversified portfolios, but this is about where the similarity ends.

Nonparametric assumptions are more accurate because they avoid making statements about the population that may prove wrong. Another important factor in terms of accuracy is the technique we use to calculate volatility. The approach we choose can affect forecasting, whether the object of our study is interest-rate swaps (IRS), foreign-exchange rate agreements (FRA), government bond prices (whether gilts or 30-year Treasuries), or any other financial instrument.

In terms of methodology, to calculate value-at-risk of, say, interest-rate exposure in a particular market, the portfolio must be broken down into a number of *maturity bands*. Part of the method is a rule enabling nearly identical risks to be netted against one another within each maturity band, as specified by the 1996 Market Risk Amendment. Alternatively, with eigenmodels, a bank may choose its own time bands, which it has classically practiced, for example:

- Up to six months.
- From six months to one year.
- From over one year to two years.
- From over two years to four years.
- From over four years to eight years.
- Over eight years.

Apart from the time buckets, a valid methodology will look into other crucial issues, such as the sensitivity attached to the exposure. By means of sensitivity models an exposure due, for instance, to swaps can be reduced to a smaller number of bond positions. These bond positions have sensitivity to interest rates similar to the cash flows from the swaps. Placed in the maturity bands, the bond positions can be used as a proxy for the swap positions.

Finally, a basic issue with VAR models is the way to treat intermarket correlations. This is one of their weaknesses, in the sense that a variance/covariance approach does not reflect the variation in correlations between markets—which may be significant—because it is based on average correlations calculated for the whole period of the time series. This contrasts to the solution provided by the simulation method (VAR/S), which we will study in Chapter 11.

7. PROBLEMS PRESENTED WITH CORRELATIONS AND WITH SENSITIVITIES

Section 6 made reference to intermarket correlations. If we look at the exposure of our total bond portfolio across all bond markets, we must compute the correlations between price changes at each point in the yield curve in the different markets. If we examine value-at-risk in connection to the bank's equity positions in each market, we should compute the likely volatility of the index and the likely correlation between movements in the indexes in different markets.

There are problems, however, with this correlation approach, and they have to do with market dynamics. There used to be a time when Western equity markets were not that highly correlated. But during the October 1987 crash in equity markets, the correlation between major markets was close to one. Stock markets in the North Atlantic nations moved downward in unison.

Since then, equity markets in the G–10 countries have remained highly correlated, with the possible exception of Japan because of severe problems in that market. As a result, for risk-diversification purposes, financial analysts, investment advisors, and traders discovered the emerging markets[7] to which a great deal of reference has been made in Part One. For the time being, G–10 equity markets and emerging markets have a low correlation. In some cases and at some time, this correlation can even be negative.

It is a self-evident truth that there is little benefit from diversification between highly correlated markets. But there could be considerable benefit from having long and short positions in different markets that are not correlated, leading to a diversification of risk.

---

7 See D. N. Chorafas, *Managing Derivatives Risk* (Burr Ridge, IL: Irwin Professional Publishing, 1996).

The study of differences (and changes) in the degree of correlation between markets is important because there are benefits from diversification in terms of hedging. Correlation analysis can also be done within a market, targeting specific groups of securities that do not move exactly in line among themselves or with the index.

A similar statement can be made about the study of covariance. Statistically, both correlations and covariance are very well known, but applying them in financial analysis is another matter. We have seen the uncertainty connected to correlations. Dr. Alan Greenspan says that its usage in finance is still in its infancy.[8]

If we use VAR, sensitivity analysis, stress analysis, or any other model for estimating and (if possible) prognosticating our exposure, we do so in order to take measures that permit us to bring risk under control. This is the objective of *hedging,* even if, in several cases, hedging has become an excuse for assuming risky positions.

The hedging of interest rates is a good example because it interests both the trading book and the banking book. Another aim in connection to hedging a diversified portfolio is to compute currency position risk by calculating the volatility of each currency and the correlations between currencies.

Depending on how comprehensive the VAR model is, equity/index and foreign-exchange exposures may be found to correlate. This will provide a more complex pattern of likely losses because it involves correlations between price movements in different risk groups.

Obtaining results significant in terms of risk management requires, so to speak, financial models that are higher up the food chain. For instance, in the case of the value-at-risk approach, we can use simulation models that themselves can be of different levels of complexity. The more complex nonparametric and nonlinear models are generally classified as nontraditional.[9] We will speak about them in Chapter 11.

But, as cannot be repeated too often, though they are necessary, models alone like numbers alone—are a bare-bone approach to management. If we are not able to interactively visualize, and in many cases qualify, the results of quantification, we will be at a disadvantage.

Qualification requires understanding the counterparty, the instrument, and the market. For instance, a challenge with options is that an

---

8 Alan Greenspan, "Optimal Bank Supervision in a Changing World," *World Statesman,* New York, Winter 1994.

9 D. N. Chorafas, *How to Understand and Use Mathematics for Derivatives,* Volume 2 (London: *Euromoney,* 1995).

instantaneous sensitivity measure does not provide an accurate picture of potential gains and losses in a portfolio. This happens because option pay-offs are asymmetrical and can be highly leveraged. As a result, sensitivities can change sharply under different scenarios.

Other problems exist because of the hypotheses we make. While analysts think of normal distributions, options sensitivities do not display normally distributed returns. This exposes the flanks of a bank or investor because a sharp move into-the-money of out-of-the-money options may cause a sudden need to rehedge, and such a move can potentially cause losses.

CHAPTER 11

The Calculation
of Value-at-Risk
through Simulation

1. INTRODUCTION

Value-at-risk (VAR) is the expected *minimum loss* over a time interval for a level of confidence selected by the reserve bank. The calculation of VAR through modeling is intended to give the bank, treasury department, or investor an estimate of exposure, as it affects the trading book or portfolio. But while VAR is an important metric of financial health, the model can only quantify about two-thirds of the risk. Other models are necessary to handle the remaining third. These include fuzzy engineering and Monte Carlo simulation.

Simulation is essentially a working analogy based on similarity of properties without identity.[1] When analoguous systems are found to exist and can be mapped into the computer, the study of one of them may lead to the investigation of the other. This provides the means for better comprehension of how the more complex of the two systems works.

We can visualize the behavior of an unfamiliar system through prior knowledge of the behavior of a familiar system. This is basically what we have done in Chapter 10 with value-at-risk, the difference being that this was accomplished under the assumption of parametric characteristics that may or may not be fulfilled.[2]

---

1 See D. N. Chorafas, *Systems and Simulation* (New York City: Academic Press, 1965). Also, an introductory discussion in Chapter 4, Section 3, of this book.
2 See also the discussion on the shortcomings of CAR's parametric approach in Chapter 14.

Both with a parametric and with a nonparametric solution, we aim to develop equations that govern the phenomena under observation. In this chapter, we will focus on how the nonparametric approach to VAR helps to increase accuracy and therefore constitutes the better way to proceed with the computation of value-at-risk.

Simulation done through analog means, for instance, scale models, has been practiced since the early 1930s in regard to aeronautical studies and water dams. The use of digital differential analyzers (DDAs) was prominent in the study of electrical networks and in other domains in the late 1940s. Computer-processed simulators first began in engineering and physics in the late 1950s, and they entered finance 20 years later.

In connection to value-at-risk, the whole process of backtesting can be seen as a simulation approach. It reflects the actual correlations that are detected between computer-generated data and market-generated financial time series. One objective we are after as far as this simulation is concerned is to establish whether on particular days extreme changes in correlation coincide with periods of high or low volatility or how many outliers are likely to fall outside the chosen confidence interval—therefore outside the exposure identified by VAR.

This distinction in operating characteristics of a financial system, such as particularly high or low volatility as contrasted to average values, has a parallel in the distinction in the physical sciences that leads to equations describing the behavior of a system. As we will see through practical examples, whether in engineering or in finance, the method of solution often depends on the type of problem.

2. CALCULATING VALUE-AT-RISK BY MEANS OF SIMULATION MODELS

As the chapter introduction has explained, to simulate a process under study we develop analogies,[3] expressing them in algorithmic form. Rocket scientists know how to proceed in this domain because in physics and in engineering there are already numerous applications of simulation procedures.

As required by the 1996 Market Risk Amendment, we can effectively employ algorithms and heuristics to emulate the behavior of a financial system, just as we have done with scale models in technology. This is becoming increasingly important within the context of modern

---

3 See also the discussion about case-based reasoning in Chapter 15.

finance, geared around the notion of research, development, and implementation (R, D, & I), an interactive process shown in Figure 11–1.

On these basic concepts about the role of simulation in an interactive R, D, & I and in experimentation, lies the value-at-risk/simulation (VAR/S) approach, which is also also known as *historical simulation.* Say, for example, that the trading book is reduced to its essential elements using maturity bands for the interest-rate exposures, as in the case of VAR/P. The database is mined for historical data to calculate the changes in the value of the trading book that would have been experienced if it had been held throughout the period or to revalue the current portfolio without the parametric approximation implied by the use of a normal distribution.

Some financial institutions tend to misinterpret the simulation as being the way that permits their not having to reduce the trading book to its essential elements. This might be one approach to simulation, for

F I G U R E   11–1

The Key Words in Modern Finance Are *Research, Development,* and *Implementation* (R, D, & I)

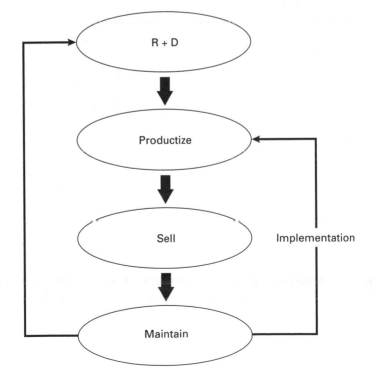

instance, in the case of *stress analysis.* An example is the use of a demodulator to reduce notional principal amounts to real money.[4]

But in general, the absence of detail is not the frame of reference that should be used in simulation or in contrasting VAR/S to VAR/P (see Section 3). The knowledgeable reader will appreciate that the lack of detail is also an approximation sometimes necessary because many banks still use mainframes and other low technology.

The mathematical way of looking at the difference between the two types of models is that parametric statistics make use of the standard statistical distribution and its tools. That much has been explained in Chapter 10. With nonparametric statistics, value-at-risk is computed through either a discrete distribution or a continuous distribution:

- A *discrete distribution* uses ordinary differential equations and algebraic equations.

- A *continuous distribution* employs partial differential equations.

In Chapter 13, we will see examples with partial differential equations in connection to delta hedging. In this section, the theme is the methodology necessary for a simulation procedure, including the greater or lesser detail needed as well as database support.

Historical simulation requires a significant amount of database support. The problem is that in many banks information elements on all individual currencies, bonds, equities, or derivative instruments are not stored over long periods of time, as should have been the case.

A steady reason for faults in analysis and simulation is not the algorithms or heuristics but the way the bank manages its data resources. If we don't have a rich database, we will gain little from simulation because 80 percent of the problem is data.

The good news with simulation is that it is possible to calculate the confidence intervals without assuming that the price changes are normally distributed. We do so by computing the loss that has not been exceeded on, say, 1 percent of occasions, where 1 percent represents the chosen confidence level $\alpha = 0.01$.

What can be gained through a simulation approach that is not available through VAR/P? The answer is that it is closer to the way the mind of the banker, treasurer, or investor works. They base their expectations

---

4 See D. N. Chorafas, *Derivative Financial Instruments. Strategies for Managing Risk and Return in Banking* (London: Lafferty, 1995).

and, at times, their calculations on potential future gains and losses. This is done by means of a prognostication that uses data of past price movements in the instrument in reference and estimates the losses that would have been sustained on *that* portfolio in the *past.*

One of the rather promising experimental approaches is to use VAR/S with information elements on daily profits and losses, which would have been made *if* the portfolio were held over, say, the past three years. This permits one to look at spike periods that took place in the three-year time frame,

The next step is to estimate how likely are movements of that type over the next 24 or 48 hours. As with weather prediction, this involves certain hypotheses. The approach is useful because it makes feasible hedging the possible adverse results of the prognostication. This methodology can be used in connection to interest rates, equity positions, and commodities risk.

If the obtained results need to be combined, adding them arithmetically would be the wrong solution. A better method to reach the total value-at-risk is fuzzy engineering,[5] which permits combining distributions in a more elegant manner.

3. A COMPARISON BETWEEN VAR/P AND VAR/S RESULTS

It is intellectually rewarding to compare the performance of parametric VAR and simulation VAR methods. As the description in Section 2 about different levels of VAR/S complexity helps to document, there is a significant difference between VAR/P and VAR/S. Let's start by identifying the differences between the two approaches in terms of confidence levels:

- With VAR/P, the confidence level is calculated.
- With VAR/S, the confidence interval is observed.

A variance/covariance method typically uses the assumption that price changes are normally distributed and it proceeds by means of standard deviations computed on that distribution. But as has already been underlined, this assumption of normality is not that realistic since prices tend to exhibit more extreme movements than represented in a normal distribution.

---

5 See D. N. Chorafas, *Chaos Theory in the Financial Markets* (Chicago: Probus, 1994).

An improvement can be made through Hurst's exponent, which reflects the fact that the statistical distribution has fat tails. This partly does away with the assumption of normality, and it permits accounting for outliers. Figure 11–2 compares a leptokyrtotic distribution to a normal distribution.

A second difference between VAR/P and VAR/S is that the simulation method can encompass the spread and basis risk existing between instruments. A sophisticated financial analyst would expand this approach to nonlinear modeling. For instance, he or she will integrate delta and gamma risks in options. We will discuss delta hedging in Chapter 13.

In terms of a quantitative evaluation, a good way to compare the results of VAR/S and VAR/P is to proceed through an asset breakdown consisting of maturity buckets, or intervals along the yield curve. The level of detail varies between banks, but the standard method of the Market Risk Amendment specifies the time brackets to be used.

Another issue to keep in mind with parametric and nonparametric value-at-risk models is tail probabilities. Because VAR/S does not yield a time series of volatility forecast errors, in calcualting the one-day cutoff points, analysts tend to restrict their comparison to the tail probabilities.

At the 99 percent level of confidence, losses exceeding the 1 percent cutoff much more than 1 percent of the time tend to demonstrate the

F I G U R E   11–2

Normal and Leptokyrtotic Distributions

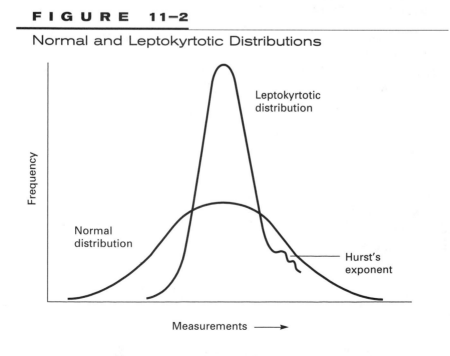

inaccuracy of tail probability measurements implied by parametric VAR. This can be explained by the existence of leptokyrtotic distributions of interest rates and stock returns. In a study done at the Bank of England,[6] the nonparametric approach outperformed VAR/P because the tail probabilities were matched more accurately. The tail probabilities for the parametric approach consistently exceeded the 1 percent level of confidence, reflecting a nonnormality of financial returns.

Patricia Jackson, however, comments that this observation does not seem to be valid with 10-day returns because, with some portfolios, there is a reversal in accuracy in applying VAR/S. The reversal with 10-day returns underlines the statistical problems present in attempting to extrapolate 10-day volatilities from estimates on 1-day volatilities prevailing in the market.

The careful reader will recall that in Part One we spoke of the approximation inherent in 10-day volatilities based on one-day estimates. The experimental findings at the Bank of England should be kept in mind both in 10-day extrapolations and in the larger context of implementing value-at-risk.[7]

Another research project, by Jackson, Maude, and Perraudin, also came to the conclusion that VAR simulation yields more accurate measures of statistical tail probabilities than parametric VAR.[8] The researchers credited this outcome to the nonnormality of financial returns, which is a plausible hypothesis.

The Bank of England researchers make the point that they are not convinced by the common argument that mismeasurement of the level of tail probabilities by a parametric VAR does not matter because the model correctly ranks different portfolios. Looking at the same issue from a theoretical viewpoint, I concur to the Jackson, Maude, and Parraudin argument.

However, not everything about parametric VAR models is negative. VAR/P tracks the time series behavior of volatility in an acceptable way and also appears to yield somewhat better volatility forecasts compared to VAR/S models. But the Bank of England team found that this difference is not statistically significant. Parametric VARs poorly fit the tails of return distributions, and capital requirements based on them tend to be too low.

One of the significant findings by Jackson, Maude, and Perraudin is that the parametric models mean absolute forecast error is relatively

---

6 Patricia Jackson, "Risk Measurement and Capital Requirements for Banks," *Bank of England Quarterly Bulletin,* May 1995, London; and from a personal meeting with Patricia Jackson.
7 See also the references made in Section 5.
8 Patricia Jackson, David J. Maude, and William Perraudin, "Bank Capital and Value at Risk," a not-yet-published paper.

insensitive to the length of the *time window* over which the time series has been taken. However, a shorter window tends to yield a little more accurate forecast. This contrasts to other assertions, like that of the Morgan Bank in regard to RiskMetrics,[9] which suggests that different window lengths do make a difference.

Let me add this thought. In spite of some theoretical shortcomings because of being based on assumptions of normality in the price or risk distribution, the parametric value-at-risk approach is gaining acceptance. The fact is that VAR/P is relatively easy to understand and, therefore, to implement compared to the more demanding simulation and stress testing.

In conclusion, differences in terms of accuracy should not hide the similarities existing between the two VAR methods. With both parametric and nonparametric experimentation, it is statistically possible to compute the degree to which capital requirements are covered. For instance, in connection to VAR/P, hence normally distributed returns, at the 99 percent level of confidence we can estimate 1 percent cutoff points as milestones in risk taking. These indicate the loss that will be exceeded in the long run 1 percent of the time.

Note that this is precisely what the 1996 Market Risk Amendment demands. It is also what will eventually be tested by regulators in order to classify the results of marking-to-model in the green, yellow, or red zones, which were explained in Chapter 5.

4. PRACTICAL EXAMPLES WITH THE CALCULATION OF VALUE-AT-RISK

Say that a trader holds an overnight £/$ position. He is £50 million short on sterling, equivalent to $78 million at the prevailing spot rate of 1.56 when this example was written. Here are the important statistics to bring into perspective, including the confidence level of historical £/$ daily price changes:

- Mean $\bar{x}$ = £/$ 1.5245.
- Standard deviation s = 0.035, which is the daily volatility.
- $\bar{x}$ + 2.60s = £/$ 1.6155, at 99 percent level of confidence, two-tailed distribution.
- $\bar{x}$ + 1.96s = £/$ 1.5910, at 95 percent level of confidence, two-tailed distribution.

---

9 See Chapter 15. Also the discussion on CreditMetrics in Chapter 1.

If the bank assumes that historical volatility will hold over the next 24 hours, it can be estimated at the 99 percent level of confidence that the value of the position will not deteriorate by more than $2,775,000, which the trader will need to pay on the bank's behalf to cover his short sterling position.

In other words, the bank does not expect this position to lose more than $2,775,000 with $\alpha = 0.01$, this amount being the *value-at-risk*. However, 1 percent of the time—a little less than three days in the year—the bank should expect the loss to exceed that level.

Notice that if the 95 percent level of confidence were chosen, then in the estimated worst case the loss would have been considerably less, equal to $1,550,000. But in the longer run, in 5 percent of all cases (or 13 days per year), this loss would have been exceeded. We gain nothing by reducing the level of confidence, as some banks tend to do for internal management accounting reasons.

In fact, as I suggested in Chapter 9, my advice is that for IAMIS the bank stick to the levels of confidence of a two-tailed distribution with $\alpha = 0.01$, even if the Market Risk Amendment speaks of a one-tailed distribution. The reason is in the difference between *tolerance limits* and *quality control limits*.

Figure 11–3 shows the confidence intervals with one-tailed and two-tailed distributions. The former is what the Basle Committee asks. The latter is what I am advising. As can be appreciated, in the two-tailed case the limits are tougher, corresponding to engineering tolerances. One can exceed the tolerance and still the process is in control, as long as it remains within the quality-control limits, precisely those implied by the Market Risk Amendment. Figure 11–4 presents this engineering practice, which is nicely portable to finance. The $\bar{\bar{x}}$ is the mean of the means.[10]

Let's examine the dynamics of the value-at-risk computation. In this example, the trader was short on sterling because he expected the dollar to rise in the currency-exchange market. The value-at-risk regards the possibility that, contrary to expectations, the dollar will fall against the sterling. Say, as an alternative, that the trade was long rather than short on sterling.

In this case, if everything else in the preceding example is kept the same, the trader will make a profit.

But we should also consider the case where the dollar rises against sterling, which essentially means the other end of the distribution. If the

---

10 See D. N. Chorafas, *Statistical Processes and Reliability Engineering* (Princeton, NJ: D. Van Nostrand, 1960).

F I G U R E   11–3

Confidence Intervals with One-Tailed and Two-Tailed
Tests of Significance

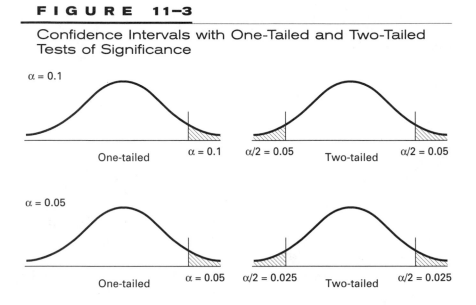

trader is long on sterling and sterling falls against the dollar, the values-
at-risk at 99 percent and 95 percent intervals will be those we have already
examined, but for the opposite reasons. In other words, we will still be
dealing with a one-tailed distribution, but our concern will be the left tail
rather than the right.

The actual gain or loss to be realized will depend not only on
whether the £/$ movement is up or down but on the nature of the bet:
going long or short. In either case, the higher the confidence level we
choose, the greater the VAR that results—but also the better our chance
that our estimate really represents the worst case.

5. TAKING THE HOLDING PERIOD INTO ACCOUNT

The focus so far has been a snapshot evaluation of risk. A more complete
approach would consider the *holding period,* which impacts upon the calculation we have just seen in two ways. First, to find how the holding period affects the VAR estimate, it is necessary to choose the standard deviation appropriate to the time window.

If we consider a holding period of one day and liquid assets, then we
are justified in estimating the daily standard deviation. Notice, however,
that the Market Risk Amendment asks for a 10-day holding period, as has
already been discussed in Part One. Because of this, the current practice

F I G U R E   11–4

A Statistical Quality-Control Chart with Tolerance Limits and Control Limits

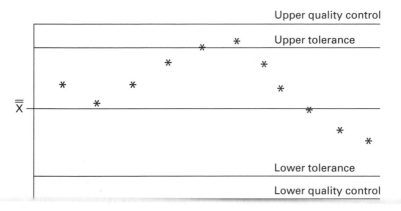

is to multiply the daily standard deviation by the square root of 10. This is an unwelcome approximation; we will see why.

Just thinking aloud for the sake of an example, for a longer-term investment in illiquid assets a holding period of at least a month will be appropriate—or even a year. The 1996 Market Risk Amendment does not say so. This is my opinion—for the time being a hypothesis that leads to an example I find instructive.

If the holding period is taken to be a month (or a year), volatility calculations should be done on monthly (or yearly) price data because adjusting daily volatility data does not necessarily give dependable results. This is no news to the reader. We spoke of this fact in Chapter 4, in relation to the 10-day holding period, and in this chapter, in connection to the research by Patricia Jackson.

Other things being equal, the longer the time window, the further the asset prices may move. If the assumption of a normal distribution holds, then a longer holding period must use a multiplication factor. The previous paragraphs explained that this multiplication factor is usually taken as equal to the square root of the number of trading days.

Say the holding period we choose is one week, hence *five* days. Taking as a basis daily volatility (standard deviation), we compute:

$$\text{Weekly volatility} = 0.035 \times \sqrt{5} = 0.035 \times 2.24 = 0.0784$$

Never forget, however, that this is not a very dependable estimate even if it is generally used by financial analysts. The absurdity of taking the daily volatility and multiplying it by the square root of trading days can be shown if we calculate the annual volatility by the same method. In this case, there is a very significant amplification effect:

$$\text{Annual volatility} = 0.035 \times \sqrt{260} = 0.035 \times 16.124 = 0.56434$$

There is still another limitation to be brought to the reader's attention. The solution space we have examined is appropriate for single assets and portfolios whose content does not significantly change over a certain period of time. This consistency in assets makes it feasible to compute the historical volatility.

In practice, however, banks always hold more than one risky asset at a time. Furthermore, the composition of the portfolio changes rather rapidly. Therefore, the compound exposure is beyond the risks computed on individual assets or asset classes. Another way of looking at this subject is that we need a methodology to aggregate individual risks into a *compound risk measure* for the whole bank—and also study their correlation.

This brings into perspective the *coefficient of correlation,* ρ, which helps express how prices move in relation to each other. Correlation statistics, and therefore the value of ρ, vary from -1 to $+1$. A correlation of:

- $+1$ means that the two assets move in concert: when one rises the other rises, too.
- 0 means that there is no statistically defined relationship between the two assets.
- -1 means that the two assets move in opposite directions: when one rises the other falls.

In Figure 11–5, Asset A and Asset B have a negative correlation. The coefficient however is not -1 but roughly -0.5. Investors actively look for assets with negative correlation to reduce the risks embedded in their portfolio.

If all assets move in concert, the risk of a portfolio is additive. This is the concept that underpins some of the clauses of the European Union's Capital Adequacy Directive (CAD). But in real life, whether positively or negatively, no assets are perfectly correlated all the time. This is the reason there are benefits from diversification.

If the assets in a portfolio move together, the risks are added together. If they move in opposite directions, the risks can be netted. In the spectrum between these two cases, risk is progressively diversified. The

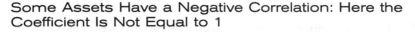

FIGURE   11–5

Some Assets Have a Negative Correlation: Here the Coefficient Is Not Equal to 1

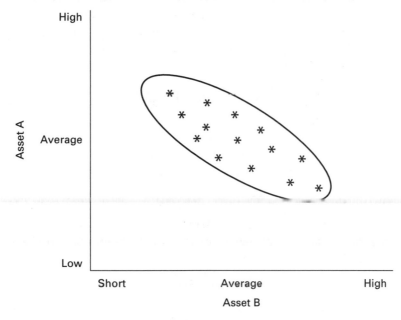

statistical formula for estimating the risk of a two-asset portfolio with assets K and L is

$$\rho_{KL} = \sqrt{k^2 s_K^2 + (1-k)^2 s_L^2 + 2k(1-k)_{KL} s_K s_L}$$

where:

s_K, s_L = standard deviation of asset prices for each asset K, L

ρ_{KL} = correlation coefficient between assets K and L

k = proportion invested in asset K

For risk-control purposes, a portfolio with many assets must include cross-correlations between each asset class. The problem is that with an increase in the number of assets, the number of correlations that need to be calculated goes up rapidly. Doubts also exist as to whether risk management through correlations is conservative enough. Correlations are not stable over time and can be subject to sudden changes.

6. WHAT CAN BE OBTAINED FROM STRESS ANALYSIS?

Models and procedures for *stress analysis* can be seen as a more sophisticated level of reference than value-at-risk. At the same time, the two methods complement one another rather than directly compete. Stress tests are used to look at the effects of extraordinary market movements in a trading book or banking book. The objective of stress tests is to compute the extent of exposure under extreme assumptions. This is quite different than the VAR hypothesis of the most likely loss under more or less normal market conditions.

With stress analysis, the portfolio is revalued according to imposed parameters. This contrasts to the statistics calculated from historical data, as in the simulation solution, and to the normal distribution hypothesis, as in the variance/covariance approach with value-at-risk.

The scenarios developed for stress analysis are essentially of a sophisticated what-if type. Tier-1 banks develop plausible scenarios regarding risk outcomes at the edge of market conditions. Others use more standard tests, such as a shift of 1 to 10 basis points in interest rates along the yield curve. Some banks combine numerical results with assumptions about shifts in the yield curve, such as short rates moving more than long rates or shifts in bonds' yield curve and concomitant rise or fall in equity markets.

Like sensitivity analysis, stress analysis is less well structured than value-at-risk. Practically everyone has his or her own method. Mine is to take the *notional principal amount* and torture it until it confesses the secrets it holds in terms of risk. As I have explained in Part One, this is done by means of demultipliers (demodulator or decompiler)[11] of the notional principal, which give an instant exposure by order of magnitude. Such a demodulator changes the function of market conditions, calling for a different level of inspection from reduced to tightened.

What is essentially done with the use of demodulators in connection to notional amounts in swaps and, by extension, other derivatives products is to put the notional principal exposure under stress. The level of stress varies with the prevailing conditions in the market, which can be characterized in the way the military standards MIL-STD-105A treat the following:

---

11 See Chapter 6.

- Normal inspection,
- Reduced inspection, and
- Tightened inspection.[12]

This approach has been very successfully used in quality-control and reliability studies with the Manhattan Project and in nuclear engineering as well as with missiles and other weapons systems. It is an integral part of rocket science, and it can be quite useful in finance.[13]

If volatility in the market is at a historical average level, normal inspection is acceptable with a demodulator equal to 25 or 30, depending on how conservative the management of the bank is. If volatility sharply increases, the demodulator should be reduced to 20, which corresponds to tightened inspection. Reduced inspection is the case of very low volatility. The demodulator could then be equal to 35.

The way a senior executive of the Federal Reserve of San Francisco looks at the use of notional principal as a means for risk control is through a bifurcation of concepts. On the one side, it means very little; it is a kind of smoke and mirrors. But on the other, the notional amount can be a handy method for:

- Ranking banks in terms of the risks they take since the notional principal reflects contractual exposure by derivative instrument.
- Bringing attention to the relative weights of different derivative instruments in the trading book.

This means that notional principal is not only a tool for stress analysis but also an interesting metric for surveying of the type of risk exposure. Its variation over time and from bank to bank can, for instance, show a sharp increase or decrease in exposure, which can be better appreciated in a macro sense.

Another method of stress analysis, which combines rigorous mathematical analysis of a system under stress with the visualization of results, is the Weibull distribution.[14] It was developed in connection to reliability studies for ballistic missiles, but I find it an excellent tool for risk management in the financial industry.

---

12 U.S. Government Printing Office, Washington, DC, September 11, 1950.

13 See D. N. Chorafas, *Derivative Financial Instruments. Strategies for Managing Risk and Return in Banking* (London: Lafferty Publications, 1995).

14 D. N. Chorafas, *How to Understand and Use Mathematics for Derivatives,* Volume 2 (London: Euromoney, 1995).

In terms of overall methodology, the following main differences distinguish stress analysis from VAR. First, with VAR/P, correlations between markets are statistically calculated. With stress analysis, they are imposed. The same is valid in regard to intramarket volatility by maturity band.

Two other issues that are statistically calculated with VAR/P but handled differently with stress tests are correlations between maturity brackets and risk spread between bonds by governments and companies. In the case of maturity-band correlations, the stress test revolves around a yield curve. The risk spread between bonds may be statistically computed with stress analysis, but this is not necessarily the case.

For instance, attention may be paid to the volatilities of government bond prices in a large number of maturity bands, converted to the chosen level of confidence, preferably $\alpha = 0.01$ of a two-tailed distribution. Along the yield curve, correlations in price movements between maturity brackets must also be examined.

The outlined method should be used for each market, along with the analysis of the relationship between price changes in corporate and government bonds. A valid methodology would pay particular interest to separating the risk due to corporate exposures into pure interest-rate risk on government bonds and the spread between government and corporate bonds. The latter also has a credit risk.

Another significant difference between stress analysis and value-at-risk is the attention paid to outliers. Stress tests explicitly focus on the effects of extreme movements in financial markets, which are not a characteristic of VAR.

Several scenarios may be developed to map the aftermaths of stress. Some or all of them will show a step function or a spike period. Nearly all scenarios will address the hypothetical loss on, say, the trading book under given circumstances. Let's keep in mind, however, that the art of scenario building differs much more from one company to another than from one method to another. Also, value-at-risk and stress analysis can complement one another. Some banks study changes in *volatility* and *liquidity* separately from the viewpoint of different models. Then they compare obtained results in order to detect differences leading to better predictions.

This can be stated in conclusion: Both stress analysis and the VAR models can be helpful in studying exposure in connection to market risk rather than credit risk. One reason for this is that the necessary data is more readily available and more homogeneous in regard to, say, interest-rate risk and currency-exchange risk than in regard the credit behavior of counterparties.

7. APPLYING THE CONCEPT OF CAPITAL-AT-RISK

As we have seen in Sections 2 and 3, the nonparametric approach is more flexible than the parametric value-at-risk approach, and it also offers greater accuracy. Another example of a flexible method is stress analysis, which was discussed in Section 6. But stress testing and VAR/S are not the only examples of a better approach than parametric solutions.

Based on findings from simulation and experimentation, management can allocate capital between various operations, which means that VAR/S can lead to *capital-at-risk* (CAR).[15] Through the same method, management, and the analysts, can evaluate how a particular exposure changes the value-at-risk. This can be found experimentally by exploiting the contents of a rich database.

The concept of capital-at-risk is more complex than value-at-risk because it must integrate the allocation of capital by product line or, depending on bank policy, all the way down to the instrument and desk level. This solution has the advantage of integrating well with *limits* placed by top management because in its foundation is *current exposure.*

Current exposure is the net replacement cost for a financial instrument contracted with a given counterparty.[16] It can be computed through historic default probabilities in conjunction with a credit score assigned to the counterparty or through replacement value, as explained in Chapter 2. Either one of these methods provides an estimate of current credit capital-at-risk. The same is true about the method of allocating limits for interest rate, currency exchanges, and other trades.

Many banks use this approach, though they may give it a different name than capital-at-risk. Some banks adopt it because it allows for collateral offsets and bilateral netting, when and where netting is legally permissible.

I don't particularly like netting because it leads to wishful thinking. Rather, I would use capital-at-risk with potential exposure determined through a market-risk process by computing the value-at-risk through simulation and comparing it with capital allocated through limits.

With this method, credit risk can also be taken into account. Default probabilities can be applied based on credit scores, thereby generating a potential capital-at-risk projection. If we wish to go into detail on capital estimation and risk control, CAR can be allocated by any of the following:

---

15 The concept is also known as *economic capital.*
16 See also the definitions of *credit equivalence, replacement value,* and *net present value* in
   Chapter 2.

- Counterparty.
- Instrument.
- Specific transaction.

In all this, however, should be remembered the very important role played by a rich database, to which I have made frequent reference. Real-time data feeds and distributed deductive databases are very important in simulation.[17] One way to significantly enrich the database contents is by using *intraday* time series, rather than *interday*. Current technology easily permits handling five-minute intervals, and tier-1 banks take advantage of it.

On an eight-hour basis, five-minute intraday information provides two orders of magnitude more data than interday statistics. Technology also permits subminute intervals, leading to three orders of magnitude improvement in database contents, as well as to much better insight for risk management.

Figure 11–6 dramatizes the importance of intraday information by comparing interday quotes to intraday 15-minute intervals—which are coarse grain when contrasted to 5-minute intervals. With opening/closing quotes, only prices A and C are databased. If the maximum and minimum

F I G U R E   11–6

The Difference in Precision between Opening/Closing Interday Quotes and Intraday 15-Minute Intervals

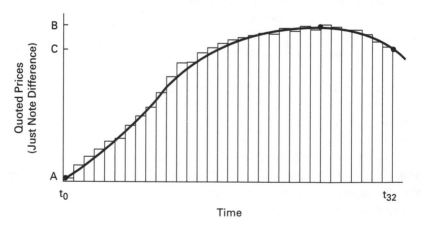

---

17 See D. N. Chorafas, *Intelligent Multimedia Databases* (Upper Saddle River, NJ: Prentice-Hall, 1994).

quotes are also recorded (as some banks do), then prices A, B, and C are stored. But with 15-minute intervals, the database will be much richer, containing 32 quotes; this will be 96 quotes with 5-minute intervals.

Rich databases make feasible a more accurate simulation approach because typically a portfolio's value varies nonlinearly with changes in the market. The problem becomes more complex when there are:

- Large market movements that should be reflected into the model and
- Discontinuities that exist in market behavior and have to be accounted for.

The more complex the model we develop, the more we need in terms of databases and rocket science. This is not yet generally understood in the banking industry. Nor is it truly appreciated that the larger the number of people we put on a VAR project, the worse the results will be.

CHAPTER 12

The Black–Scholes Model, Sharpe Index, and Olsen Formula

1. INTRODUCTION

There is no copyright on financial products. Once an instrument is launched, it can be copied by everyone, improved upon, combined with other underlying assets, or used to generate new options and relaunched. Therefore, the best strategy is to introduce new financial instruments that other banks cannot immediately compete with because of the complex analytics and the high technology supporting them.

Another strategy that tends to preserve some ownership of the financial instrument is personalization. From manufacturing to banking, tier-1 companies today tend to customize their products. Auto manufacturers, for instance, are doing so, and the financial industry is no exception to the new rules of competition. Personalizing means doing the following:

- Focusing on the customer and his or her profile.
- Patterning the customer's investment behavior into trading on her or his behalf.
- Accounting for the customer's investment horizon.
- Estimating and emulating the way the customer looks at gains and losses.
- Evaluating the customer's policies in the control of risk.

Our aim should be not only to develop new financial instruments and provide metrics and tools for the control of exposure, but to price and cost these products. This means dynamically evaluating their content, market appeal, and return to the investor.

Risk and return are always key issues in banking, and skilled management will look for a delicate balance. We don't want to take an inordinate amount of exposure, but neither do we wish to make the bank risk-averse. As Sir Hugh Walpole said, "Don't play for safety. It's the most dangerous game in the world."

The Black–Scholes model, which occupies the better part of this chapter, is already a quarter century old. It exists in many versions, and it has finally become fairly popular among financial institutions. Black–Scholes is better known than value-at-risk and, in its way, it helps explain the role of algorithms in risk management.

However, sound risk-management policies don't only rest on algorithms but on a rigorous system of internal controls as well as a real-time solution for interactive computational finance. The Group of Thirty (G–30) did a study involving 300 derivatives operators and 600 derivatives users worldwide. Of these, 274 responded. However, while 53 percent of derivatives operators said they perform mathematical worst-case scenarios, only 43 percent indicated they have a value-at-risk concept in connection to their trades.

Worse yet, my research indicates that fewer than 10 percent of derivatives operators are organized to perform real-time simulation for risk-management purposes. While many banks and treasuries are using the Black–Scholes model for pricing, few understand how it works, and even fewer appreciate that its results are approximate. We will look more closely into this issue in Sections 2, 3, and 4.

2. THE BLACK–SCHOLES ALGORITHM FOR OPTIONS PRICING

A basic question in the science of evolution as well as in finance, in connection to prediction theory, is *how to determine* the macroscopic variables that characterize the behavior of a complex system. Processes of modeling that project on future events have many similarities with the quest to quantify unpredictability in the study of chaos,[1] whether the undergoing system is the behavior of financial markets, astronomical observations in the cosmos, or patterns connected to weather prediction.

A system targeting pattern recognition helps to make understandable the results of prognosis connected to these cases. The typical formulation

---

1 See D. N. Chorafas, *Chaos Theory in the Financial Markets* (Chicago: Probus, 1994).

of the problem is to classify spatial information in a manner amenable to interpretation. This requires identifying and then handling in a skilled manner both *independent* and *dependent* variables.

Usually the independent variables provide the *inputs* from which, given the *model* we have made of the real world, we aim to obtain *outputs*. This is what we did in Chapters 10 and 11 in connection to value-at-risk. The output that tells us about the behavior of the dependable variables may, for instance, be:

- A yield curve,
- A volatility curve, or
- A cap curve.

For each maturity, the cap curve gives the price of an at-the-money differential cap, which pays at a rate equal to the positive difference between the short rate and the strike price. For any maturity, an at-the-money cap has a strike equal to the forward rate for that maturity.[2]

This perception of an algorithmic representation of inputs and out-puts in connection to financial systems is rather recent. It comes from a steadily evolving experience with financial modeling and options pricing mechanisms, which for all practical purposes started with the 1972 seminal paper by Fisher Black and Myron Scholes.[3]

Because the Black–Scholes paper created a significant historical precedent, it is rewarding to turn back 25 years and examine the very structure of the algorithm that has been so instrumental in opening new horizons in securities pricing. Two and a half decades of implementation of the Black–Scholes model demonstrates that market prices of stock options and warrants on a stock exhibit a very interesting agreement with the formula:

$$F(x,y,T,r) = xN(d_1) - ye^{-rT} N(d_2) \qquad (1)$$

where:

x = stock price

y = strike price

$T = t^* - t =$ time to maturity

$t^* =$ maturity date

$t =$ today's date

$r =$ interest rate

$N =$ cumulative normal density function

2 Fisher Black and Piotr Karasinki, "Bond and Option Pricing when Short Rates are Lognormal," *Financial Analyst Journal,* July–August 1991.

3 The paper by Dr. Fisher Black and Dr. Myron Scholes was submitted for publication in 1970.

The cumulative normal density function is tabulated in most statistical texts. It can also be approximated using a simple algebraic expression.

In the options pricing algorithm in Equation (1), $F(x,y,T,r)$ estimates the value of an option (or warrant) on the stock. The quantities d_1 and d_2 are given by the following formulae:

$$d_1 = \frac{\ln(x/c) + (r + 1/2\ s^2)T}{s\sqrt{T}}$$

$$d_2 = \frac{\ln(x/c) + (r - 1/2\ s^2)T}{s\sqrt{T}}$$

which can also be written

$$d_2 = d_1 - s\sqrt{T}$$

where:

    s = standard deviation of the stock's return

    s^2 = variance of the stock's return

    c = strike price

$N(d_1)$ and $N(d_2)$ are *lognormal* distributions, discussed in Section 3. The logarithm is not on base 10 but on base e, where e is Euler's number:

$$e = 2.7182818 = 1 + \frac{1}{1!} + \frac{1}{2!} + \frac{1}{3!} + \cdots + \frac{1}{n!} + \cdots$$

Logarithms to the base e ($\log^e$ or ln) are called natural, or Naperian, logarithms. Their usage leads to a significantly simple formula:

$$\frac{d}{dx}\ln\ x = \frac{1}{x}$$

$$d\ \ln\ x = \frac{dx}{x}$$

The reasons the Black–Scholes option-pricing model uses the lognormal distribution will be explained in the following section. What the reader should retain from this discussion is the relative simplicity of the model.

An algorithm does not need to be complex in order to be useful, but it had better be understandable. The Black–Scholes model is also a good example of the aftermaths of *backtesting*. No other factor has been more instrumental in the model's acceptance than the fact that it has been able to hold its own against repeated comparisons with historical data.

3. PREDICTABILITY AND THE LOGNORMAL DISTRIBUTION

A model written for option pricing can use a lognormal process, a square-root approach, or another process. The Black–Scholes model uses the lognormal distribution, which is more general than others because it allows the local process to change over time.

A lognormal distribution is that of a random variable whose logarithm follows an approximation of a normal distribution.[4] But while, with the normal distribution, the three metrics of central tendency of the measurement—mean, mode, and median—coincide, this is not the case with the lognormal distribution, as Figure 12–1 demonstrates.

Like any other distribution, the lognormal has a mean and a variance. As long as the process of ln r, where r is the local interest rate, is linear at each time, there is a lognormal distribution for the possible values of the short rate at a given future time.

Assuming a different lognormal short-rate distribution for each future time allows both mean and variance to depend on time. Notice, however, that the underlying asset's expected return does not appear in the formula. If the investor is bullish on an asset, she may buy shares or call options. This will not necessarily alter her estimate of the option's returns.

F I G U R E   12–1

Example of a Lognormal Distribution for Option Pricing

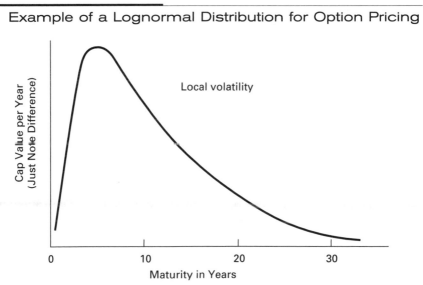

4 See Chapter 10.

In a mathematical sense, the process of taking the logarithms of the random variable x sees to it that the frequency distribution F(x) arises from massaging the random observations by a transformation process:

- If $y = \ln x$,
- Then the population of the y distribution has the mean μ_y and variance σ_y^2.

This transformation has become increasingly popular in physics and engineering as well as in the life sciences, social sciences, and finance. Notice that the lognormal distribution tends to be skewed with a long tail to the right and that it is also leptokyrtotic, a process explained in Chapter 10.

One of the basic reasons economic and financial modeling uses the lognormal distribution is its *multiplicative* reproduction properties. By contrast, the normal distribution has *additive* properties.

The multiplicative properties of the lognormal distribution have proven very important in engineering studies—for instance, in connection to *reliability* in estimating the mean time to failure and mean time to repair. For x > 0, the algorithm of the density function of x is:

$$f(x) = \frac{1}{\sqrt{2\pi}\,x\,\sigma_y}\,e^{-\left[(\ln x - \mu_y)/\sigma_y\right]^2 \bullet \frac{1}{2}}$$

where:

μ_y = population mean
σ_y = population standard deviation
$\ln x = y$ = natural logarithm of x

For $x \leq 0$, $f(x) = 0$. For x > 0, the mean and variance of the lognormal distribution are calculated by:

$$\mu_x = e^{\mu_y + \sigma_y^2/2}$$

$$\sigma_x = e^{2\mu_y + \sigma_y^2}\left(e^{\sigma_y^2} - 1\right)$$

This is of interest in financial analysis because recently reliability metrics and algorithms have been used in connection to risk measurements—and have proven very useful in this connection.[5] The following formulas help to calculate the median and the mode:

$$\text{Median} = \tilde{x} = e^{\mu_y}$$

$$\text{Mode} = \hat{x} = e^{\mu_y - \sigma_y^2}$$

5 D. N. Chorafas, *How to Understand and Use Mathematics for Derivatives*, Volume 2 (London: Euromoney, 1995).

Higher moments of the lognormal distribution are given by the algorithm:

$$\mu_k = e^{k\mu y + k^2 \sigma_y^2 / 2}$$

where k indicates the higher moment. Skewness is computed by:

$$\mu_3 = \left(\mu_x\right)^3 \left(g^6 - 3g^4\right)$$

and kyrtosis by:

$$\mu_4 = \left(\mu_x\right)^4 \left(g^{12} + 6g^{10} + 15g^8 + 3g^4\right)$$

where:

$$g = \left(e^{\sigma_y^2} - 1\right)$$

Other metrics and transformations of the lognormal distribution that can be of interest to analytical studies are the coefficient of skewness, which measures departure from symmetry, and the coefficient of kyrtosis, which measures departure from peak conditions displayed by the normal frequency.

Some studies have used the lognormal distribution in connection to two variables. If x_1 and x_2 are *independent* lognormal variables with parameters (μ_1, σ_1) and (μ_2, σ_2), respectively, then the product $X = x_1 \cdot x_2$ has a lognormal distribution with parameters $(\mu_1 + \mu_2)$, $(\sigma_1 + \sigma_2)$—in application of the multiplicative reproduction property.

Projects that employ the lognormal distribution demonstrate that predictability is enhanced through the use of multiplicative reproduction properties. We should always make use of the best mathematical tools available in reaching the modeling goals we have set for our project.

4. BLACK–SCHOLES, VOLATILITY, AND BACKTESTING

A concept underpinning the Black–Scholes algorithm is that the value of the option changes as a function of the stock price, interest rate, and time remaining until the option expires. In real life, the price of an option is also affected by the volatility of the underlier.

Accounting for volatility would be an improvement of the original form of the model. Let's never forget that, as stated in Section 2, the Black–Scholes option-pricing formula is approximate. Therefore, many financial analysts tend to develop and use modified versions, some of which are proprietary. The downside is that improved versions are incompatible with one another. Therefore, the results in terms of fair-value calculations are not comparable either.

The improved version we examine in this section was developed in Zurich. What it tries to correct is the fact that with imperfect markets the Black–Scholes model provides unreliable results. The pricing outcome could be improved through an optimization procedure aimed at more reliable estimators of volatility.

Developed in conjunction with a project by SMI, the Swiss Index, this approach has benefitted from extensive simulation. The researchers subjected to a simulation process some 29,000 complex derivatives strategies. One of the results of this experimentation was that accounting for volatility positively impacts the Black–Scholes output.[6] Another finding was that more than volatility affects the outcome. There is a decrease in efficiency of derivatives trades because of tariff structures.

The concept behind this SMI research came from a computer program originally written to serve in the evaluation and behavioral analysis of market response to derivatives positions. The algorithms used by Baechler and his colleagues were based on statistical movements examined by both the Wiener Process[7] and Black–Scholes.

It is interesting to note that this research was based on high-frequency financial data (HFFD). The time series concerned European-type options on the SMI. The time frame of these statistics starts January 3, 1994, and ends July 7, 1995. The set includes 107,000 data elements on options, 92,000 underlying data elements, and 298,000 data elements on SMI futures.

Expressed in a nutshell, the basic finding of this research has been that the central factor influencing the results of Black–Scholes is volatility, hence the need for measuring volatility in an accurate manner and for accounting for its effects. Basically, volatility arises through historical and projected price movements. However, projected price movements include information asymmetries, news, and psychological factors.

The SMI researchers have focused on two basic kinds of volatility estimation: historical volatility as *ex-post* evaluation, and the *ex-ante* evaluation of volatility with an exponential moving weighted average (EMWA) model. EMWA is used in the Morgan Bank's RiskMetrics, which is discussed in Chapter 15.

One of the tests done by the SMI study applied the EMWA volatility model. Another used historical volatility. All tests considered real dividend

6 Konrad Baechler, "Black & Scholes–Analyse Optimieren," Schweizer Bank, Zurich, September 1996, pp. 24–25.
7 See D. N. Chorafas, *How to Understand and Use Mathematics for Derivatives,* Volume 2 (London: *Euromoney,* 1995).

payments based on market data. Volatility results were plotted after weeding out anomalies. The root-mean-squared-error method was used to measure how the model's results fit real market behavior. The chosen methodology reflects the differences between market price and model price. This is a good example of backtesting, the procedure that was established as a requirement to continuing marking-to-model by the Basle Committee's 1996 Market Risk Amendment.

Plotting the differences between model price and market price, when real-life data becomes available, is a good way to control the fitness of the model—beyond regulatory compliance requirements.

With the modified Black–Scholes algorithm it has employed, the SMI project provides a good example of backtesting. As the examples we have seen demonstrate, it is rewarding to evaluate the fit of time series computed through modeling to the data streams generated by the financial market.

There are two rules I have used in my practice, and I find them rewarding. One is that the systems we develop and use should produce results that cover their costs and leave a profit. When this is the case, there is no problem getting financing for new projects.

The second rule is that no system and no model are good forever. Other events, such as treaties, are subject to the same law of wear and tear. Therefore, whatever we do should have a steady stream of feedback for its evaluation and calibration. The feedback concept shown in Figure 12–2 underpins backtesting.

5. USING ANOMALIES AS A WAY TO IMPROVE MODEL RESULTS

Another priority the SMI project set for itself is the handling of anomalies. Many financial analysts, including the late Dr. Fisher Black, loath weeding out anomalies because they consider them important pieces of reference. In essence they are *outliers,* not anomalies in the classical sense of the term.

The exception proves the rule, says an old proverb. But the SMI researchers had a different view of this subject. Improvements observed by the handling of anomalies were set to range from a minimum of 64 percent to a maximum of 89 percent. In the opinion of the researchers, this tuning-up of the model opened substantial application perspectives.

One implementation made possible after tuning is the evaluation of risk in a derivatives portfolio as a function of time to maturity. Another application domain, projected by the researchers, regards accruing transaction cost, brokerage charges, and so on.

F I G U R E   12–2

A Feedback Mechanism Characterized both
Engineering Constructs and the Financial Markets,
but Many Bankers Lack This Sensitivity

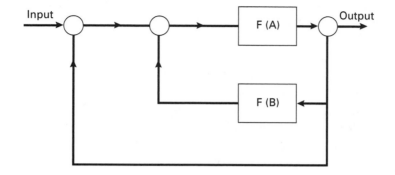

A total of 29.109 investment possibilities were simulated 10,000
times. Because each option strategy consists of two contracts, the computing environment included some 582,120,000 option prices. This
roughly corresponds to the contract volume of SOFFEX—the Swiss
options and futures exchange—for the next decade, a projection based on
current volumes.

To keep the estimation close to real life, the project emulated the
market organization of SOFFEX. In every case, the simulation concerned 50 contracts, but liquidity problems that may exist because of
contract size were ignored. Costs for margin calls were not taken into
account either.

These simulation processes produced a three-dimensional graphics
output that helped to visualize the risk strategy. An example is the profit
and loss structure of a long butterfly over a 21-day period, taking into
account the tariff structure of the market.

The SMI simulation demonstrated that the payout of a long butterfly
is negative throughout. Therefore, with the financial time series that were
used, an investment based on a long butterfly would have been irrational,
even if such a strategy is generally considered low risk.

Another test concerned a vertical spread. Here P&L results proved
to be better than in the preceding case. The main message, however, is that
such applications help demonstrate the wisdom of using experimentation
for the evaluation of positive or negative behavior of different scenarios
concerning derivative financial instruments.

Other projects capitalized on the existence of outliers to produce better estimates of volatility. One of the most interesting applications to which the Black–Scholes formula has been put is its usage *in reverse* to find a volatility level that makes a given option worth a certain price, for example, the current market price. Option-pricing models were originally designed to produce a theoretical value or price for an option, but over the years, their greatest worth has proven to be in computing *implied volatility*.

Because fairly precise models for the calculation of implied volatility are intense in terms of computer resources, the way most financial analysts go about options pricing is by trial and error or, more precisely, through heuristics. An initial guess is made, and the resulting value is compared to the actual option price. If the theoretical value is too low, the volatility guesstimate is too low. If the theoretical value is too high, the volatility guess is too high.

By means of high-performance computers, this process is repeated time and again, until the computed value equals the current market price for the option. When this approach is taken, it is proper to keep in mind that every different price that an option trades at in the market has a unique implied volatility value. When it changes, option positions can change in value even though the underlying instrument does not.

Anomalies detected by the model are not the only reason for differences in results. Both outliers and outright errors may result from the approximations involved in the algorithm itself. Another factor influencing the choice of one solution versus another is computer time.

Figure 12–3 presents a semilogarithmic scale of needed computer time versus average absolute errors detected in the valuation of options. The test was done with puts and calls. Both scales are just note difference (JND). It is interesting that in the case of Black–Scholes, the model produces twice as many average absolute errors with put options than with call options.

In the opinion of many financial analysts today, though universally accepted as a valid tool—which is its main strength—the Black–Scholes options pricing model is a rudimentary approximation of what really happens in the market. It does not measure risk, and it underestimates maximum volatility.

In intraday trading, as well as within any other time frame, the price of the derivative vehicle itself may move away from what Black–Scholes says, and the model provides no way for the necessary real-time adjustment, which becomes more and more important.

F I G U R E   12–3

Average Absolute Error versus Computer Time with Black–Scholes and Other Option-Pricing Models

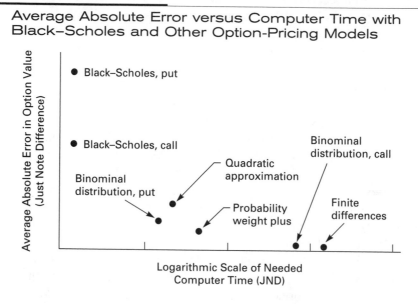

Many improvements of the Black–Scholes formula are possible, and they may be welcome. But the reader should also recognize that anything that looks better is incompatible with what already existed. There are already a number of incompatible versions of this production algorithm.

6. LEVELS OF CONFIDENCE AND THE SHARPE INDEX

The fact that there are always approximations built into models makes even more important the use of levels of confidence in association to their usage. Other things being equal, a bank that chooses a higher confidence level is essentially more conservative because it wants to be sure its worst-case scenario is exceeded only in a rare number of cases.

Regulators advise guarding against disaster scenarios that lack the level of assurance that should be associated with them. Knowing the confidence level is important inasmuch as the changes, say, in currency rates or the interest rate can have the effect of shocks to the cash flow profile. Banks must be able to find out ahead of time how much the present value changes and how much they can depend on this prognosis.

Though the concept of level of confidence has been discussed in Chapters 9 and 10 in connection to value-at-risk, it is applicable throughout the domain of mathematical analysis. The notions underpinning this statistical approach to putting limits on uncertainty are fundamental to all functions involving estimation and therefore speculation, from management to lending, investing, and trading.

As has been already explained, the approximation we are making in calculating levels of confidence rests on the hypothesis of the normal distribution. There is also the fact that the tools we have available don't account for panics. Therefore, let's be conservative.

I have already explained the reason why when the Basle Committee says that the 99 percent level of confidence should be used, it is better to take 2.60 standard deviations, not 2.33 as should be taken with a one-tailed distribution. Being conservative in the choice of confidence levels can, in the longer run, be the better policy by far.

This being said, I am not particularly enthusiastic about mathematical models on whose outcome I can place no level of confidence. For example, the Sharpe Index is one of the metrics banks use to evaluate portfolios for which no dependability estimates can be made.

Like any other measure, the Sharpe Index is approximate and in practical usage exhibits several deficiencies, instability being one of them. The Sharpe Index algorithm is:

$$I = \frac{\overline{R}}{\sqrt{s_R^2}} = \frac{\overline{R}}{s_R}$$

where:

I = the index

$\overline{R}$ = average return

s_R^2 = variance of the return

The Sharpe formula for calculating s_R^2 is

$$s_R^2 = \frac{n}{n-1}\left(\overline{R^2} - \overline{R}^2\right)$$

where:

n = number of returns entering the computation

$\overline{R^2}$ = average of squared returns

$\overline{R}^2$ = square of average of returns

Not only are there no confidence intervals associated with this algorithm, but the fact that the Sharpe Index put the s_R^2 in the denominator makes the metric unstable when the variance is near zero. Besides this, the

Index is unable to consider the clustering of profit trades and loss trades. At the same time, it measures realized losses, but it neglects unrealized losses.

Frequent calculations, for instance hourly or daily based on intraday data, partially remedy this deficiency, particularly in connection to evaluating a portfolio's performance. This, however, does not correct the model's instability. I am not really impressed with the results the Sharpe Index can provide, but would not drop it altogether from the library of algorithmic solutions.

7. WHERE THE OLSEN UTILITY FORMULA MAY BE OF HELP

Another algorithm I would keep in the applications library is the utility formula developed by Olsen and Associates.[8] It is a better risk-management model than the Sparpe Index, and it is based on the R. L. Keeney and H. Raiffa formalisms[9]:

$$R(x) = \frac{U''(x)}{U'(x)} = C$$

where:

R(x) = return function

U(x) = utility function

C = level of risk aversion

U'(x) and U''(x) are, respectively, the first and second derivatives of the utility function U(x). Dr. Richard Olsen mentioned during our meeting that by empirically balancing risk and return, $0.08 < C < 0.15$ seems to be a reasonable range. The factor C can, however, vary outside these limits. With $C > 0$, this algorithm tends toward:

$$U(x) = -e^{-Cx}$$

The way it is used in this utility function, x is a stochastic variable of mean x and variance s^2 over a testing interval Δt. The expected utility of such variable can be computed as:

$$E(U(x)) = \int_{-\infty}^{\infty} U(x) P(x) \, dx$$

---

8 M. M. Dacorogna, U.A. Müller, and O.V. Pictet, *A Measure of Trading Model Performance with a Risk Component* (Zurich: O&A Research Group, 1991).

9 R. L. Keeney and H. Raiffa, *Decisions with Multiple Objectives: Preferences and Value Tradeoffs* (New York: Wiley, 1976).

where:

$$P(x) = \text{the probability distribution of } x$$

Assuming for a moment that this algorithm might be applied in connection to each investor, trader, desk, or the whole bank—but for a specific financial instrument in a given market—we can approach its implementation via the hypothesis that x must be related to return R, for instance, through the formula:

$$R(\Delta t) = R(t) - R(t - \Delta t)$$

where:

$$R(t) \;=\; \text{the total return of past trades up to time } t$$
$$R(\Delta t) \;=\; \text{return in time interval } \Delta t$$
$$\Delta t \;=\; \text{time horizon on which measurements are made}$$

If R(t) represents the realized return in profit and loss, we can introduce another factor:

$$R_C(t) = R(t) + r(t)$$

where:

$$R_C(t) \;=\; \text{cummulative realized and unrealized return}$$
$$r(t) \;=\; \text{unrealized return on current position}$$

Part of the importance I perceive in connection to the Olsen formula, as compared to other algorithms, is its ability to estimate unrealized returns on current positions. This fits well with the calculations to be provided in the comprehensive statement in the United States, and STRGL in the United Kingdom. We have spoken of both in Part One.

Attention should be paid to the fact that, as in the case of the new regulations by the Swiss National Bank about integrating derivatives risk into the balance sheet,[10] one or more elements in r(t) may move to R(t) after a trade. If $R_E(t)$ is a measure of trading model performance comparable to the yearly average return, then over a particular time horizon Δt:

$$R_{E,C}(t) = R_C - \frac{Cs^2}{2}$$

The $R_{E,C}$ metric expresses the average return R_C, which includes realized and unrealized profits and losses, diminished by a factor proportional to Cs^2.

---

10 See Chapter 9.

The R_E measure depends on the time interval Δt, and it is difficult to compare its values for different intervals. This, however, could be achieved through *annualization*—by multiplication with the annualization factor:

$$R_{E,C,A} = \frac{1 \text{ year}}{\Delta t} R_{E,C}$$

Notice that this formula includes the risk aversion embedded in $R_{E,C}$, transformed into a function independent of Δt. The reader should be aware that these recently developed algorithms require a great deal of formal work for real-life testing, which is still to be done.

Dr. Olsen suggests that beyond the annualization formula it is possible to implement multihorizon measures through the introduction of weights:

$$R_E = \sum_{i=1}^{n} w_i R_{E,A}\left(\Delta t_i\right)$$

where:

$\quad w_i$ = weights chosen according to relative importance of
$\qquad\quad$ different time horizons

The latter algorithm takes advantage of the fact that the annualized return values have no systematic dependence on the horizon Δt. The formula helps to create a *metautility* function that also has to be tested in a real-life sense. I would also advise the development and use of confidence intervals in connection to the Olsen formula.

8. THE EVOLUTION OF MODELS AND THEIR APPLICATION IN RISK CONTROL

Models are made neither forever nor for all occasions. This is true of any construct, including the popular Black–Scholes formula for pricing options, which is appreciated by many banks but also criticized by a number of financial analysts because of overpricing or underpricing options due to its error rate shown in Figure 11–2.

Who is right, those who believe in Black–Scholes or those who don't? To answer this query, we must first understand that it is not just the model and its strengths that make a valid implementation, nor a model and its shortcomings that destroy it. The issue of how well or how poorly a model fits in its applications domain is complex. The answer depends not only on the model itself but also on the data we feed it *and* on what we are after.

What we are after with Black–Scholes is the evaluation of a price structure that cannot be directly measured no matter what the reason is. With other models, such as the demodulator of the notional principal amount that I introduced for stress analysis in Chapter 10, the goal is to establish a *risk equivalence.*

The interactive computation of the results we wish to attain is as important as the precision the model may provide. As we have seen in Figure 12–3, much more precise models than Black–Scholes require three orders of magnitude more computing time.

Something similar happens with risk equivalence. We can have a much more exact demultiplier than the general factor for all derivatives. With a very precise demultiplier by instrument, the notional principal amount of each financial transaction can be examined in light of its most critical characteristics:

- Overall payoff profile.
- Volatility curve.
- Yield curve.
- Time to maturity.
- Initial rate.
- Frequency of payments.

It can also be examined in terms of *liquidity* conditions prevailing in the market. But the goal of a general demodulator is not precision; it is the ability to generate a figure that rather accurately reflects the potential risk embedded in the trading book.

As Figure 12–4 suggests, a general demodulator may permit real-time computation of a bankwide exposure profile, taken intraday. The upper and lower control limits are those explained in Chapter 10 in connection to a quality-control chart and its contribution to risk management. Similarly, through a generalized demodulator, we can judge the risk profile of traders. We can also compare traders A, B, and C against one another on an intraday basis.

Risk-adjusted exposure should include both credit risk and market risk. But models written to measure potential and actual market risk are not cast in stone. They should evolve:

- As longer-term experience accumulates,
- As shortcoming show up in daily usage, and
- As function of changes taking place in instruments—and in the market.

F I G U R E   12–4

Intraday Follow-Up on Exposure, Trader-by-Trader
and Bankwide

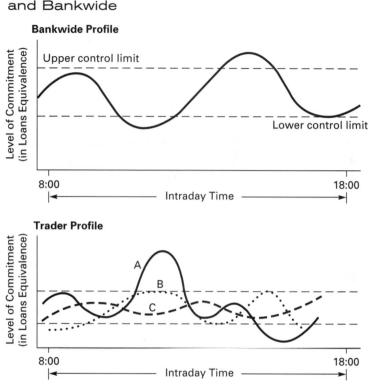

Indeed, these three items above describe the whole sense of interactive computational finance, which can be seen as an attempt to apply to the markets some of the complex mathematical techniques developed in physics and engineering.

Let's not underestimate cross-fertilization and technology transfer. The 1973 breakthrough by Fischer Black and Myron Scholes was an adaptation of heat-transfer equations from physics. In the background of their work was a method of studying Brownian motion, that is, the movements of tiny particles buffeted by gas or liquid molecules.[11]

In a span of a quarter century, but most particularly during the last few years, the Black–Scholes formula has become a cornerstone in the

---

11 D. N. Chorafas, *How to Understand and Use Mathematics for Derivatives,* Volume 2 (London: *Euromoney,* 1995).

field of financial engineering and the propellant for an explosive growth in options trading.

But let's not overlook the fact that Black–Scholes is just a formula. What has changed is the way bankers think. Modeling has been instrumental in the growth and potential of financial exploration. The process includes the following:

- Algorithms for optimizing complex portfolio strategies.
- The analysis of tick-by-tick behavior of prices, a process of great significance for traders and investors.
- Improved methods for analyzing and evaluating risk for any instrument, at any time.
- New techniques for visually representing complex portfolio performance, using three-dimensional interactive graphics.
- Computational techniques that help develop new financial products and emulate marketing experience.

This is an evolutionary process; therefore, model maintenance is not only wise but mandatory. For instance, one of the basic Black–Scholes assumptions is that price movements in financial markets follow the same kind of lognormal distribution that applies to natural phenomena. Is this hypothesis valid in all cases where the model is used?

The answer is no. This is an approximation. Current experience suggests that few financial distributions literally follow this model. Some exhibit frequent extreme outcomes, or fat tails, due to outliers, which we spoke about in Section 5. Therefore, in usual circumstances, there will be awkward price jumps. Sometimes volatility is higher than assumed under normal conditions, and risks cannot be entirely hedged away, as implied by Black–Scholes options pricing.

Improvements are needed. It is, for instance, possible to handle residual risks by applying a sophisticated mathematical treatment to the tails of the distribution. What is necessary in this connection is to develop robust mathematical techniques able to handle extreme circumstances and integrate them into the model.

The application of models from the natural sciences to the financial markets is good, as long as we remember that markets are not just controlled by natural laws. They are controlled also, if not primarily, by human psychologies of greed, lust, and fear. Hence, correct modeling requires understanding the behavior of traders, bankers, and investors. Not everything is in the numbers.

CHAPTER 13

Hedge Accounting and Delta, Gamma, Theta, Kappa, and Rho

1. INTRODUCTION

While many applications domains benefit from the use of models, the majority require much more ingenuity than algorithms alone can provide. I bring up this subject to caution the reader that not everything is done through models—though algorithmic solutions can help focus management's attention as well as prioritize the list of exposures.

Policies and procedures make the difference between a successful use of models and a trivial one. Top management policies are necessary both before the development (or adoption) of models and after their implementation and usage. One of the crucial policies has to do with *hedging*. Hedging is used by bankers, treasurers, and traders with all financial instruments—quite often, in connection to the *macromarkets*.

Currency-exchange, stock index, and bond futures as well as all sorts of derivatives trades are the macromarkets. Their size and their dynamism are believed to be able to satisfy the requirements of very demanding investors with a global market view. Though these financial products are diverse, they have in common their *macro* dimension in instruments and in a geographic sense.

The macromarkets are large enough to accommodate many investment opportunities. But there is a significant difference between maintaining momentum and regaining momentum after adversity hits because the size of each one of the big players hinders the regaining of momentum following a profitless period.

Not only may starting anew be tough, momentum must also be gained with profits commensurate to the risks being taken. Therefore, the measurement of risk and return taken with hedging is important in providing management with a compass.

The more the bank or fund and its clients move in capitalizing from the macromarkets, the more the tools being used as risk metrics must be state-of-the-art, and the ingenuity quotient by managers and professionals must be higher.

In this chapter, we will first define hedging and review the basic rules underpinning *hedge accounting.* Then, we will examine the use that can be made of advanced tools for the measurement of exposure, with emphasis placed on delta, gamma, theta, kappa, and rho.

Delta measures the sensitivity of a derivative instrument to changes in the underlier; *gamma* is the derivative of delta; *theta* is the anticipated value of an option given a change in expiry time; *kappa* (vega, lambda, or beta plus) measures the impact on the value of an option of a 1 percent change in volatility; and *rho* is the metric of the sensitivity of option value to changes in interest rates.

2. WHAT'S THE REAL SENSE OF HEDGING?

Many financial analysts believe that even if hedging were adequately defined in connection to risk management and everyone had a clear hedging policy, the majority of banks and treasuries would not have systems in place to effectively use hedging policies. The skilled use of hedging requires identifying and accumulating the portion of earnings generated from hedging activities in order to counterbalance risks.

Some of the people I spoke to in this research suggested that accounting for gains and losses currently associated with hedges is incomplete and possibly misleading. While this observation is correct, it is beyond doubt that first comes the understanding of an instrument or procedure and then systems support. Any effective hedging policy rests on four pillars:

1. Knowing what we want to do.
2. Understanding what we are doing.
3. Having systems to support our policy.
4. Having in place the appropriate regulation and supervision.

Hedging-related accounting should provide timely and accurate information for management. Hedging-related disclosure must enable investors, creditors, government supervisors, and other users of financial statements to appreciate an entity's risk exposure and its strategy for managing risks. Hedging through complex transactions requires appropriate disclosures of the transactions themselves and of the instruments used to hedge anticipated transactions.

This means a description of anticipated transactions whose risks are hedged with derivative financial instruments. Our understanding of what we do should include the period of time of firmly projected future financial moves and the amount of hedging gains and losses explicitly deferred.

Just as necessary is a description of the transactions or other events that result in the recognition of gains or losses deferred by hedge accounting. This is not common policy, both because only recently has regulation begun looking into future gains and losses—as is the case with the comprehensive statement and with STRGL—and because few bankers, treasurers, traders, and investors take care to distinguish between speculating and hedging.

Sometimes management takes hedges by means of diversification outside the company's main business. Like other moves, these hedges can turn sour. In 1966, Nomura Securities was placed on Standard & Poor's CreditWatch list (with negative implications) after it said it would provide 371 billion yen ($3.39 billion) to help its Nomura Finance unit deal with bad real estate loans.

In other cases, the board micromanages a hedge, but a market gyration turns it on its head. In late 1995, after the dollar's turnaround against the yen, the chairman of Mitsubishi Motors, Hirokazu Nakamura, said, "Mitsubishi has been long and wrong on the direction of the yen." While the yen passed the 100 bar to the U.S. dollar, Mitsubishi had hedged at 90 yen to the dollar, until March 31, 1996.[1]

As a result of this wrong hedge, the dollar's appreciation did not show in Mitsubishi Motors' bottom line for about seven months. True enough, market prognostication is a tough business. Therefore, while the calculations leading to a hedge may be sound and the hedge can initially work, as the market changes a hedge may become counterproductive.

This underscores the need for *dynamic hedging*. Models, systems, and procedures must see to it that we rehedge sufficiently often through real-time input to minimize risk. But we should not do so in such a way

---

1 *The Asian Wall Street Journal,* September 12, 1995.

that the execution of small transactions significantly increases dealing expenses and settlement costs.

Attention should also be paid to not losing the natural smoothing effect that the longer term can have on market prices, and to not missing the effects of an increase in volatility—either marketwide or toward the end of the life of an option.

Delta hedges and gamma hedges, which we examine in Sections 4 and 5, do provide the algorithmic approach necessary for real-time monitoring. Once the model of the derivative instrument we wish to control has been built, we can produce the means for handling delta and gamma in a skillful manner.

Computers should be used in real time to monitor exposure very carefully, supporting the financial analyst and the trader as well as the bank's management as a whole in judging if and when potentially risky positions are being accumulated. This is an integral part of interactive computational finance, which is indispensable to every company doing hedges.

An example of what I mean by first-class computer support for hedging is provided by Phibro, the world's biggest commodity trading firm, now nominally owned by Salomon Brothers. In the 1973–74 time grame, under its old name Phillips Brothers, Phibro cornered all the oil on the spot market using a computer system that rivals the best in business applications.

Phibro's computers can track a metal shipment on any boat on the high seas and identify which mine in the world has sold what metal to any wholesaler on any day. This capability exceeds the systems capabilities of most governments and of the large majority of financial institutions, but high technology is a required support when one is doing hedging or operates in the macromarkets.

3. THE FIRST BASIC RULE IN HEDGING: KNOW YOURSELF

The first basic rule in hedging is no different than the one Sun Tzu has written: "If you know the enemy and know yourself, you need not fear the result of a hundred battles."[2] Knowing ourselves begins by identifying our strengths and our weaknesses as well as where our greatest risks are.

The study of our strengths and weaknesses requires us to perceive, qualify, and quantify vulnerabilities in our portfolio prior to advancing or

---

2 Sun Tzu, *The Art of War* (New York: Delacorte Press, 1983).

recommending a hedging strategy. As I explained in Part One, a hedge is similar to buying insurance. Before we buy the policy, we must decide how much we are willing to lose in relation to what the protection will cost.

One of the problems is that many derivative instruments can be hard to value unless we have both skills and an array of analytical tools and high-performance computers. Without appropriate supports, we may end up paying too much and taking inordinate risks in making hedges.

One of the first principles for understanding and following a hedging strategy is that we have to be selective. We don't need to hedge everything. For instance, producers of precious metals, Mobil Oil protects itself against swings in interest rates and currencies, but not in petroleum prices.

By contrast, Barrick Gold effectively uses its gold price-hedging program to minimize gold price risk and lock in rising earnings and cash flows. The difference from other players is that its hedging program is matched to its prevailing production profile. Production is fully hedged for two years forward and partially hedged for another couple of years.

This allows Barrick to minimize the return from its production while leveraging to the gold price through the unhedged portion of reserves and the flexibility of the program. Flexibility is gained through the extensive use of spot deferred contracts.

Depending on which price is higher at the time, Barrick may either deliver its gold against contracts or roll the contracts forward and sell on the spot market instead. This permits getting the best price for gold by decoupling the timing of production and the timing of gold sales.

Because of its existing gold reserves, the continuous acquisition of new reserves, and its underlying financial strength, Barrick has calculated that it can roll a contract forward for up to 10 years.

One of the advantages of the rather conservative hedging strategies by Mobil Oil and Barrick Gold is that they avoid exotic products that have brought trouble to many companies. Let's keep that in mind when in Sections 4 and 5 we talk of delta hedge and gamma hedge.

If the strength and weakness of Mobil is oil and of Barrick is gold, banks have a major exposure to interest income. This is shown in Figure 13–1, through five years of operating income statistics from a major money-center bank. In Part One, we discussed how some large banks take the interest-rate risk out of the banking book through an internal interest-rate swap. They bring it to the trading book, where it will be hedged.

The second basic rule in hedging is figuring out in advance not only the risk but the cost. Both must be commensurate with what we aim to protect in terms of financial or other resources. Therefore, as advised in

F I G U R E   13–1

Operating Income by a Major Money-Center Bank over a Five-Year Period

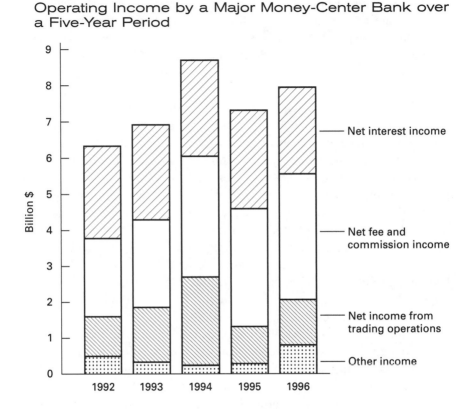

the opening paragraphs of this section, before choosing any strategy, we must perform a thorough examination of our company to unearth where its biggest vulnerabilities lie. We must also write down the goals we wish to reach through hedging. We cannot target unspecified goals.

Do we need to hedge revenues, cash flows, profits, or dividends? Where are our biggest foreign-exchange risks? What exactly are we hedging in terms of interest rates? What's our target duration?

The third rule is the avoidance of fuzzy policies. Any self-respecting company needs to implement a clear corporate strategy on hedging. Do we have written guidelines? Do we know whether we hedge for profit or just to offset changes in the market value?

In a way, the lack of such guidelines is not surprising if we take account of the fact that, in spite of lip service to strategic planning, few companies are enthusiastic about setting their policy in black and white. Yet, doing so can eliminate a lot of confusion and ward off the trader's temptation to cross over into speculation.

The fourth basic rule is to avoid confusion between the legacy functions of the treasury and hedging. This can be done by making sure traders have a separate pool of capital for hedging and that they have been given well-defined limits on how much they can risk. At the same time, the board should always know what the treasury is trying to achieve, and how it is doing it. Hedging must be audited by an independent auditor that can examine risk-management activities and make recommendations for corrective action.

In terms of currency exchange policy, for instance, some companies, like the Bechtel Corporation, the global engineering group, sometimes arrange to be paid in a basket of currencies that mirrors what it must lay out to cover its costs. And in regard to interest rates, some companies guard against sudden spikes by hedging the maturities of their debt.

In conclusion, success stories in hedging converge to the same point: the importance of clear cut hedging strategies and the ability to calculate the values, maturities, costs, and risk of every hedge. Our hedging system must be able to alert us to possible losses and give us the information we need to test our portfolio with worst-case scenarios. Hedging must also benefit from the calculation of value-at-risk, as explained in Chapters 9 and 10.

4. DELTA AND DELTA HEDGING

Delta, gamma, kappa, and other metrics used for hedging reasons and for the evaluation of hedges have been briefly defined in the chapter introduction. These metrics are applicable to derivatives trades and constitute some of the best algorithms available for risk evaluation in connection to underliers and derivative instruments. Yet, a surprisingly large number of banks and investors don't master them—and therefore don't use them.

Mathematically, delta is the first derivative of the price function $F(x)$ of the underlying asset:

$$\text{Delta} = \frac{dF(x)}{dx}$$

In an applications sense, delta measures the sensitivity of a derivative instrument to a change in underlying variables. It represents the change in premium because of a small change in the underlying spot market.

The value of delta ranges from zero to one. Because it reflects the probability that the option will expire in-the-money, delta indicates the amount of hedge that the option seller has to buy (or sell).

The value of zero would result from a far out-of-the-money option, which has no need to hold a hedge in the underlying asset since the probability of exercise is virtually nil. By contrast, a value of one would come from a far in-the-money option, which is virtually certain to be exercised. Therefore, the option writer would have to hold the underlying asset as a hedge against the option he has sold.

In real life, delta measures would often be midrange. The value of 0.65 indicated in Figure 13–2 would arise from an option at-the-money with a 65 percent probability of being exercised.

Notice that in Figure 13–2 the price of the underlier varies from 90 percent to 110 percent. In the same figure, the delta changes from 40 percent to 50 percent and 65 percent. A mathematical model tracking delta for

F I G U R E   13–2

Delta Slope and the Target Options:
A Payoff Diagram

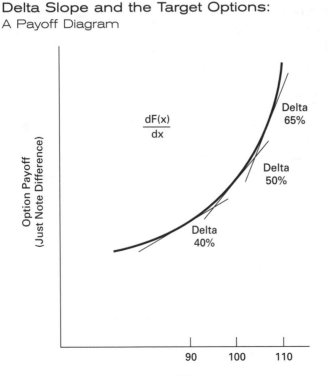

Price of Underlier

a particular underlier and its options would be able to alert us to this change. The advisable approach is intraday.

This is very important in managing hedges because delta is the risk that the price of an option changes because of changes in the price of the underlier. If the underlier's price moves more than a small amount, delta also changes, altering the factors that have entered into the hedge.

Critical to an investment decision is the way delta changes. In the case of a call option, if the price of the underlier rises, the delta rises: A rise in the underlying asset increases the probability of exercise. Therefore, the writer must be covered with the asset as a hedge.

If the price of the underlier falls, the probability of the call option being exercised also falls. Hence, the writer can sell part of his holding in the asset. Typically, the delta value of a position is used to estimate the value-at-risk for small changes in prices. Delta is helpful because it gives the price change in the option for a 1 percent change in the underlying asset.

With this in mind, we can see that delta expresses the ratio of underlying contracts to option contracts required to establish a *neutral hedge*. For instance, if an option has a delta of 0.40 (as in Figure 13–2), a neutral hedge will require a hedge of 0.40 of an underlying contract for each option contract. If the delta is 50 percent and two option contracts are written, one underlying contract can be sold. That's why delta is sometimes referred to as the *hedge ratio*.

An option with a delta of 50 can be expected to change its value at 50 percent of the rate of change in the price of the underlier. If the underlying security changes by 30, the option's theoretical value can be expected to change by 15. This hedge ratio specifies the number of underlying contracts that the purchaser (seller) of a call is long (short) or that the purchaser (seller) of a put is short (long).

For example, if a trader buys a call with a delta of 20, he is in theory long 0.20 of an underlying futures contract. The delta identifies the theoretical or equivalent futures position and therefore the rate of change in the theoretical value of an option with respect to the change in the price of the underlying contract.

The delta assists in appropriately defining the probability that the option will finish in the money. It could also be helpful to think of delta as the speed with which an option moves with respect to its underlier. The maximum speed is 100 percent for very deeply in-the-money options, and the minimum speed is zero for very far out-of-the-money options.

Because of these relationships between an option and its underlier, the *delta hedge* has become the most common type of option replication.

The delta of any financial instrument, be it an option, a forward-rate agreement, or an interest-rate swap, is the partial derivative of this instrument's market value with respect to the spot. In terms of foreign-exchange markets, for example, delta is the change in the instrument's value given a unit change in the exchange rate. In a delta hedge position, contracts are constructed so as to match the delta of the target option.

Experts, however, contend that static delta hedges can be unreliable, especially in volatile markets. The delta of the hedge might drift from the delta of the target option as the target option's delta changes with movements in the spot exchange rate because of interest rates or simply due to the passage of time.

This is one of the reasons delta hedges are implemented with instruments such as forward contracts and currency futures contracts, which are not that sensitive to changes because of movements in spot exchange rates.

An improvement to a static delta hedge is the dynamic hedge. It is obtained by adding or subtracting to the forward or future position to track the changing delta of the target option.

Hedges require significant skill. If improperly done, they can get financial analysts and traders into trouble. Not only must the calculation of hedges be analytical, factual, and documented, they must also must be dynamically adjusted for changes in operating conditions such as changes in the underlier's price and a drift in the option's delta. Look at delta as being only a tool.

The *delta-plus* method and *scenario writing* are being advanced by the Market Risk Amendment to provide stepping stones to the use of internal evaluation models. Because, however, such implementation is new, at least at the level of supervisory authorities, the Basle Committee intends to keep these issues under review and plans to continue monitoring financial industry practices for measuring options risk.

5. GAMMA, THETA, KAPPA, AND RHO

There is also a way of measuring the change in delta. This is done through *gamma,* its first derivative. Gamma is the second derivative of the underlier's price function $F(x)$:

$$\text{Gamma} = \frac{d^2 F(x)}{dx^2}$$

The risk of delta changing is referred to as *gamma risk,* a significant risk common to all options. There are also other types of risk associated with options, which are referred to as *higher-order risks.* The term reflects the mathematical concept of higher-order differentiation rather than the magnitude of risk.

If an option has a delta of 70 and a gamma of 10, the option's expected delta will be 80 if the underlyer goes up one point, and 60 if the underlier goes down one point. Another way of looking at gamma is as expressing the sensitivity of delta to changes in the underlying spot market.

A low gamma reflects deltas that are stable. A high gamma reflects deltas that are unstable. This difference materialized because delta itself changes as the underlier's spot rate changes in a nonlinear fashion. If the price rises, the delta of a call option also rises; if the underlier's price falls, the delta falls. In both cases, the degree of change is expressed by gamma.

Gamma is often referred to as the option's curvature. The measure of the acceleration of the option it provides tells how fast the option picks up or loses speed (hence delta) as the price of the underlying contract rises or falls. Gamma for options is analogous to convexity for bonds.

While the target option may have a positive gamma, currency forward and futures contracts have gamma equal to zero. Among currency options, those with the shortest remaining time to expiration have the largest gamma. These characteristics permit making hedges that use options near to expiration for convexity, for example, taking a position in forward and futures contracts to match the delta of the target option.

In the spot currency-exchange rate, for example, the effect of changes on the option's delta is captured by gamma which critically depends on the time remaining until expiration. Close-to-expiration options tend to be *gamma neutral.* Such options can be found easily in the market, and they can be incorporated into a hedging strategy. Three approaches are used to hedge gamma.

The more evident way is to buy back options identical to the ones that have been sold. But such back-to-back deals are not making profits and, therefore, are rare in the OTC market.

The second method is to buy deep out-of-the-money options, known as *buying the tails.* This applies to portfolios with at-the-money or slightly out-of-the-money options. The third approach is to do a horizontal spread.[3]

A strategy often sought after is a delta-gamma hedge. In this case, the trader may take a position in a short-lived call to match the gamma of the target, longer-lived option. Given that short-lived calls have much larger gammas than long-lived calls, few of them will be required.

---

3 See D. N. Chorafas, *Rocket Scientists in Banking* (London: Lafferty, 1995).

Another metric, *theta,* measures the anticipated change in the premium value of an option because of a change in time to expiration. More precisely, it measures the decay in the time value of the option, showing how its value changes from one day to the next, under the hypothesis that all other variables stay the same.

Theta is always negative. As such, it benefits the writer and erodes the value held by the buyers of an option. Theta becomes zero at the expiration of the option, decaying most rapidly towards the end of an option's life. Theta graphs for 30-day and 120-day options are shown in Figure 13–3.

Kappa (also known as lambda, vega, or beta plus) measures the impact on the premium value of an option for a 1 percent change in volatility. A particular characteristic of this metric is that it will equally affect puts and calls set at the same strike value.

Only the *time value* component of an option is affected by volatility. This results from the fact that time value derives from the possibility of further movement in the underlying asset.

- The *intrinsic value* depends on the strike rate compared with the forward rate.

If volatility is zero, the option will have no time value and will be valued exactly the same as an off-market forward. Another way of looking at

FIGURE 13–3

Theta Graphs for 30-Day and 120-Day Options

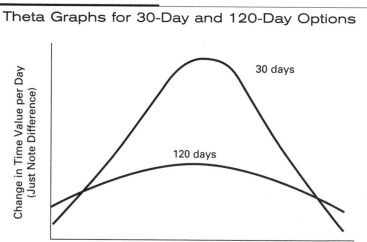

Spot Price of Underlier

F I G U R E   13-4

Kappa Graphs for 30-Day and 120-Day Options

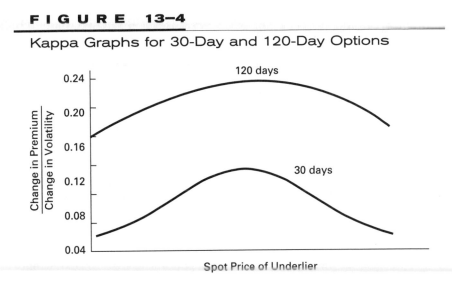

Spot Price of Underlier

kappa is that it expresses the sensivity of an option's computed value to a change in volatility. An option with a kappa of .30 can be expected to gain (lose) 30 percent in theoretical value for each percentage point increase (decrease) in volatility. Kappa graphs for 30-day and 120-day options are shown in Figure 13–4.

Finally, *rho* reflects the sensitivity of the option premium to changes in interest rates. Some traders think that since interest rates are relatively unimportant in the evaluation of options on futures, rho is also the least important of the option sensitivities. This is not necessarily true.

Rho can be quite helpful. In the case of currency options, for example, there are two separate interest rates to be measured: the base currency and the quoted currency. Movements in either will affect the value of the option because the forward exchange rate depends on the ratio between the two interest rates. Every trader would like to know if the intrinsic value component changes.

6. PROCEDURAL SOLUTIONS FOR HEDGE ACCOUNTS

We have looked at hedging as a protective procedure designed to minimize losses that may occur because of price fluctuations. The point has also been made that very often hedging is confused with speculation.

Properly used, investment instruments available in the financial markets enable the hedger to shift the risk of price fluctuations with the goal of protecting the hedger's position. But this is true only up to a point, and it also has as a prerequisite the existence of valid procedural solutions for *hedge accounting*.

Acceptable hedge-accounting procedures are established by standards bodies and approved by regulators. Usually, prior to approval they are issued as discussion papers. For instance, in the United Kingdom, the Accounting Standards Board (ASB) has elaborated the following two alternative procedural solutions for *hedge accounting*:

1. Measure the hedge at current value in the balance sheet and put the resulting gain and loss to the Statement of Total Recognized Gains or Losses (STRGL).[4] In accounting terms, this is a good approach because it sees to it that gains and losses are recycled from STRGL to the P&L account. It also has the advantage of reporting a gain or loss without biasing the balance sheet.

By means of alternative 1, in a later period the gain or loss would then be transferred from STRGL to the profit and loss account, precisely when the hedged transaction occurs. Such an approach is similar to the one proposed by FASB, in the United States, for hedges of uncontracted future transactions.

The disadvantage of this solution is that there might be some accounting issues because of recycling in a later period—since this procedure has not yet been widely tested in court. For this reason, the discussion paper by ASB[5] presents an alternative acceptable hedge accounting procedure:

2. Measure the hedge at current value in the balance sheet and record resulting gains with assets and losses with liabilities.

This is roughly the directive by the Swiss National Bank, which has been mandatory in Switzerland since 1996. Some experts consider it a better solution in terms of capital measurements. The problem it presents is that, depending on market risk (current value), a transaction would change sides in the balance sheet from assets to liabilities, and vice versa.

The careful reader will remember that this has already been explained in Chapter 9. The solution advanced by the British Accounting Standards Board is roughly similar to the one proposed by the FASB for hedges of firm contracts. The concept underpinning the FASB solution is that of reporting:

---

4 See also Chapter 6.
5 *Derivatives and Other Financial Instruments* (London: ASB, 1996).

- Losses as assets and
- Gains as liabilities.

Supposing the hedge is connected to a recognized asset or liabilbility, is measured at cost, and represents a firmly contracted future transaction, this approach could be justified on the grounds that a loss on the hedge will be offset by a gain on the hedged position.

In other words, deferring the loss on the hedge as an asset can be seen as a surrogate for recognizing the hedged position and measuring it at current value. If, on the contrary, the hedge is of an uncontracted future transaction, then what has just been stated is no longer valid.

Because the notions described in the preceding paragraphs have not yet been established as a regulatory requirement, ASB was careful to also outline what in its judgment constitutes nonacceptable solutions for hedge accounting. There are essentially two:

1. Leave the hedge at cost. The assets and liabilities solution is also better than leaving the hedge at cost, which is a fairly wide practice. The practice has the disadvantage that many derivatives are not shown in the accounts since their initial cost is zero, or they are shown at minimal cost.

2. Measure the hedge at current value at the balance sheet and put the resulting gain/loss to equity. With this approach, all derivative trades will be at the liabilities side of the balance sheet, which is not a recommended practice.

Both ASB and FASB stress that apart from the need for standards permitting the handling of accounts in a consistent and uniform manner, the process of hedge accounting requires support from *modeling*. This permits going beyond the so-called bean counting into evaluation procedures that mark-to-market the trading book and the banking book, but also make marking-to-model feasible when there is no active market for the assets and liabilities to be valued.

This essentially amounts to reengineering the accounting methodology established by Luca Paciolo, who in 1495 invented the system we now call classical accounting. Five hundred years after Paciolo, it is correct to rethink and revamp the accounting procedures—a job that needs to be done in a rigorous manner, with a generalized methodology.

In conclusion, interest in hedge accounting has evolved as banks and treasuries use hedging to reduce risk. The whole concept rests on the fact that risk is a chance with both an upside and a downside—through gains and losses resulting from changes in market values and cash flows. The challenge is to establish valid universal solutions. Otherwise, it will not be hedge accounting but chaos.

7. INVESTORS, SPECULATORS, AND HEDGING POLICIES

The point was made in Section 6 that many bankers, treasurers, traders, and others tend to confuse hedging with speculation. It is not enough to say that hedgers can be investors or speculators. We must also define what these terms mean. Typically, investors risk their own capital with the hope of making profits from price volatility in derivatives and other contracts.

By hedging, they seek to offset some potential losses, which is not what speculators do. Speculators risk the capital of others—usually borrowed or trusted money—and their aim is short-term profits rather than long-term hedges.

This is what the hedge funds do. They assume the risks that other investors seek to avoid. But both investors and speculators rarely take delivery of the actual physical commodity in the futures market. They close out their positions by entering into offsetting purchases or sales of futures contracts.

Because investors and speculators may take either a long or short position, it is possible for them to earn profits or incur losses whether the direction of price trends is up or down. P&L depends on how they have been betting their chances, that is, on their market outlook.

In addition to classes of investors and speculators, there is a group of commodities market participants that, while not literally hedging their cash positions or requirements, use the futures, forwards, options, and swaps markets in following strategies designed to reduce risk.

Investors, speculators, and risk managers can benefit from delta hedges, gamma hedges, and the other metrics we studied in Sections 4 and 5 because all these processes involve financial exposure, albeit of a different type. By means of hedging, producers, processors, salespeople, and users of commodities, or treasurers handling financial instruments, try to obtain a form of price insurance. This helps take the guesswork out of projected future costs and helps one hold onto property without sustaining losses as a result of volatility.

The motivations behind each form of trading can also be different, but as exposures mount it becomes increasingly difficult to distinguish an investment contract from one that is speculative.

In its genuine form, a hedge involves establishing a position in the futures market that is equal and opposite to a position in the actual commodity. The concept of taking such equal and opposite positions in cash and futures is that a loss in one market should be offset by a gain in the other market, and a hedge can fix a futures price for a commodity in today's market by using a derivative instrument.

In theory, this process of hedging works because cash prices and futures prices tend to move in tandem, converging as each delivery month reaches expiration because of the basis risk. In practice, it does not work out that way because very few hedges are pure hedges.

Also in theory, if the difference between the cash and futures prices of a given commodity widens or narrows as they fluctuate independently, the risk of an adverse change in this relationship is considered generally less than the risk of going unhedged. In practice, hedging has a cost. Therefore, we must find a balance between the cost of an operation and the protection it provides.

These two differences between theoretical and practical aspects of hedging can be bridged by means of sound procedural solutions to hedge accounting, which we spoke about in Section 6. The solution we establish for true hedging reasons can be optimized and steadily tracked through the delta, gamma, theta, kappa, and rho metrics we discussed in Sections 4 and 5. When I say optimized, I do not necessarily mean trying to predict price movements before they occur and thereby profit from market volatility—though prognostication is necessary for an optimization.

Let me also add this afterthought. Though a hedge is generally applied against a corresponding position in a given commodity, it is not necessarily a substitute for a later cash market transaction. Like speculative positions, hedges are generally closed out prior to contract expiration, and there are bound to be profits and losses.

CHAPTER 14

The Assessment of Counterparty Risk, Interest-Rate Risk, Currency Risk, Country Risk, and Equity Risk

1. INTRODUCTION

What kind of assistance are the central banks providing to commercial banks confronted with compliance to the 1996 Market Risk Amendment? According to the Federal Reserve of San Francisco, it is encouragement, skill in advising and discussing the development and use of models, and systems know-how in examining the model's adequacy.

Equally important in terms of assistance by the central bank is the development of a methodology for the evaluation of models developed by commercial banks, in terms of compliance to the Basle Committee directives for the control of market risk. In the United States, a great deal is being done in connection to modeling by the Federal Reserve Bank of Chicago because many of the U.S. capital markets are in Chicago, and because of the quantitative capital market skills this reserve bank has available. The proximity of know-how in econometrics at the University of Chicago also plays a role.

Another issue discussed with the Fed of San Francisco is how American banks are facing the modeling challenge. The answer is that they take one of two approaches: Either they develop the models in-house or they buy them from software houses. In both cases, the reserve bank has a role to play in terms of assistance to the commercial banks—and of control of compliance.

It was the sense of the meeting that, as far as commercial banks are concerned, buying ready-made models is far from the optimal approach.[1] Bought software tends to be rather inaccurate, and even if accurate it is static. By contrast, for management purposes, the greater value of the model is in its dynamic characteristics.

This reference to dynamics goes beyond market forces, though this is a crucial factor. Just as important are the *operating characteristics* of the bank and the *products* it supports as well as the skills it has available and the solutions it has adopted for hedging.

This chapter addresses the product lines that require an assessment of risks and a system to control exposure. In Chapter 14, we will examine what bought software can provide. Then, in Chapter 15, we will follow the process of studying and developing eigenmodels for business opportunity analysis, optimization, and risk management.

2. UNDERSTANDING AND MODELING THE KEY COMPONENTS OF MARKET RISK

Typically, board members don't understand the instruments their bank is using. This is true all the way from derivative products to interactive computational finance. It is a cultural issue that, in many commercial banks, constitutes a salient problem—because only top management decisions can provide the necessary initiative and momentum for a radical change. Quantitative illiteracy at the board level reduces the ability to implement the Market Risk Amendment. Hiring and effectively using rocket scientists helps to significantly improve this ability.

As every rocket scientist knows from his or her academic training and experience in engineering or physics, the process of modeling a real-life situation in order to map it into the computer is based on an orderly process. First we conceive and understand the world we wish to model. Then we simplify what we get because our model will be that much more accurate if it is based on the essentials.[2]

For instance, rather than targeting a detail that might lack accuracy, we may choose to develop a system that treats market risk as having four key components: *Interest-rate* risk, *currency-exchange* risk, *country* risk, and *equity* risk. In doing so, we know that there are a number of other

---

1 See in Chapter 15 the discussion about buying and using commodity software.
2 See also in Chapter 16 the discussion of abstraction and idealization.

exposures and that all risks our bank takes are influenced by the underlying forces of *volatility* and *liquidity.*

This is a different ball game than tracking credit risk. The more clear-eyed bankers appreciate that there are several reasons why so much attention has been paid to credit risk and not enough to market risk. Credit risk is well understood in the financial industry, and over the years grading schemes have been developed that help to classify the counterparty according to its dependability. By contrast, market risk has been an elusive concept when approached in a general manner or, alternatively, when we try to apply credit-risk approaches to market risk.

If anything, the banker should be working the other way around, bringing into credit risk concepts that are proper to market risk. A good example is *counterparty risk,* which we consider in Section 3. Counterparty risk is credit risk plus other factors influenced by market conditions.

But if the rocket scientist and the banker differ in the way they confront the problem of market risk, chances are their approaches will also have several issues in common. For instance, they will try to comprehend the problem by adopting a simplified structure of, say, currency risk—from spot transactions to derivative financial instruments.

It is not true that all rocket scientists look at risk-management problems the same way. A different analyst developing a model of market exposure might disagree with the thesis of a simplified approach and suggest greater detail. Or he or she might point out that some other risks are also pervasive and may morph themselves into critical factors affecting a trading book's value.

The block diagram in Figure 14–1 identifies 16 risks, including the 4 of the simplified model and the classical credit risk. Whether we consider the simplified model or the more complex approach with many variables, any analysis and modeling of market risk worth its salt must take *volatility* and *liquidity* into account. The market risks we choose to analyze must be studied both as independent variables and in conjunction with one another. Covariance is a critical issue. It is also a subject that not every banker, treasurer, or investor readily understands.

Both rocket scientists and bankers must consider in their analytical approach what is stipulated by the 1988 Capital Adequacy accord, the 1996 Market Risk Amendment, and (for banks operating in Europe) the European Union's Capital Adequacy Directive of 1993. These regulations require banks to have available capital equivalent to a percentage of their holdings in different asset classes. A valid solution will also be influenced by the systems of capital requirements operated by American and British securities regulators.

F I G U R E   14–1

A Consolidated Exposure Involves Many Risks and
Their Synergy: These Are Only an Example

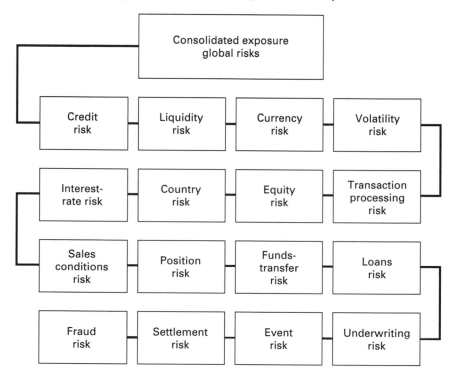

Astute developers of risk models will not fail to notice that from the bank's perspective, a major advantage of eigenmodels is that they are better fit for experimentation, and they can be made more global. As a result, they do not generate excessive capital requirements for market risk the way a simpler standard method of BIS does through the additive approach it uses.

3. WHAT'S THE DIFFERENCE BETWEEN COUNTER-PARTY RISK AND CREDIT RISK?

Counterparty risk is the possibility that a loss may occur from the failure of the other party to perform according to the terms of a contract. This contrasts to market risk, which concerns the chance that ongoing changes in market prices may make a financial instrument less valuable or more onerous to the holder, but it also differs, in some respects, from the classical credit risk.

With both counterparty risk and market risk the risks of accounting loss are not easily quantifiable. The accounting loss from credit risk is better known, and it is usually quantified through a credit-rating assessment that results in a credit-risk premium.

Beyond that premium, which essentially covers default, counterparty risk includes delays in the other party's execution of its obligations and, in general, accounting loss not due to the other party's failure. This is an important consideration with large contracts, such as the examples we will see in this section. Therefore, our risk-management model must not only consider but also estimate the likelihood of possible accounting loss.

As Figure 14–2 suggests, the model we develop should reflect the fact that counterparty risk includes credit risk but also incorporates some elements of market risk. This, for instance, may come from country risk (discussed in Section 5) or from other factors.

Like credit risk, counterparty risk is well embedded into banking practice. The associated premium can be seen as a sense of financial responsibility connected to a given product or service, resulting from the fact that banking instruments impose contractual obligations, not just rights.

Even when a risk premium is present in the transaction, something might change more significantly than originally thought in terms of

F I G U R E   14–2

Counterparty Risk Includes Credit Risk and Partly
Overlaps with Market Risk

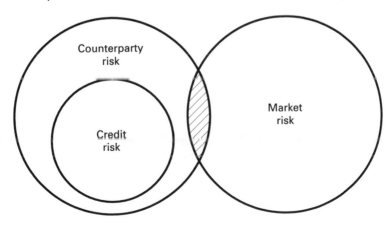

counterparty risk. A nontraditional factor entering this reference is the size of the transaction.

To better explain the question of size, let's think in terms of the *notional principal amount* involved in the deal the two parties enter into. To refresh the reader's memory, let me repeat that this is a term borrowed from the swap business: Notional principal (not to be confused with nominal) is an amount never actually paid or received. But it constitutes the contractual reference on which will be calculated, for instance, interest-rate swaps (IRS) or forward-rate agreements (FRA).

Some banks take *$1 billion* in notional principal as the cutoff for an important derivatives contract. This $1 billion transaction level is nothing rare or extraordinary. It is a unit of measurement devalued with time, as more and more banks enter the macromarkets.[3] As we saw in Chapter 8, today each of the top 10 money-center banks has a derivatives exposure in notional principal of more than $2.7 trillion. $1 billion corresponds, on average, to some $30 to $40 million in real money risk; $2.6 trillion will amount to between 1,500 and 2,200 important contracts.

This is only a hypothesis; however, it can serve in estimating default risk, and by extension counterparty risk, as defined in this chapter. What this statistic essentially means is that more than 1,000 derivatives contracts, even more than 1,500, with one major counterparty is in the realm of possibilities.

A different way of looking at the same statistics is that because of macro-opportunities that can be found in macromarkets, the world's top 10 banks with over $2.7 trillion notional principal in derivatives exposure have taken upon themselves an inordinate amount of default risk, transaction risk, and position risk. In the cumulative, this is at the level of over $80 billion in real money for each of the 10 top international banks.

The next 20 global banks are not much better off. The guesstimate in Chapter 9 indicates that each has $1.0 trillion or more in notional principal exposure, which corresponds to more than $30 billion in real money. These conditions are also examined by the 1993 European Union Capital Adequacy Directive (CAD), which defines *large exposure* as one connected to a client (or group of clients) that equals 10 percent of the bank's funds.

A large exposure is made up of large commitments, and large commitments magnify counterparty risk. The $1 billion in notional principal as cutoff of a large derivatives contract would represent about $33 million

---

3 See Chapter 13.

in loans equivalent risk in the bank's portfolio but concentrated in the macromarkets and in the hands of a few counterparties.

Neither the European Union's Capital Adequacy Directive nor the Market Risk Amendment talk of the macromarkets. This is a pity because it leaves uncovered a large chunk of default risk. Though the macro-opportunities domain has several players, their number tends to be rather limited. Therefore, it approximates the "group of clients" defined in CAD.

Not many banks and funds have the skill and the stomach to be in the macromarkets. Among those who are players, only a few know how to manage risk and return. As a result, counterparty risk in the sense defined in this chapter is alive and well. Bought software may not account for it, but eigenmodels should consider it—both for pricing and in the management of exposure. When they do so, they will be much more accurate.

In conclusion, the demand for a rigorous and uniform assessment of counterparty risk is substantiated by the need to calculate exposure in a way that is consistent with current banking practices, particularly in connection to derivative financial products. A simple rudimentary inclusion of counterparty risk in calculating operating results is no satisfactory long-term solution. Banks need a much more fundamental approach that integrates well with the other market risks they confront.

4. FACING THE CHALLENGES OF INTEREST-RATE RISK

Interest-rate risk can adversely affect a bank's financial condition in a very important way. This is the market risk banks are exposed to whenever the interest-related sensitivity of their assets does not match the interest-related sensitivity of their liabilities from loans to off-balance sheet positions.

This is known as mismatch risk. For instance, if a bank has liabilities that reprice faster than its assets, a rise in interest rates reduces net interest income by increasing the cost of funds relative to its yield on assets.

Interest-rate risk is well known to the banking industry, and there are many models written to account for its impact. One of the more popular approaches to the evaluation of interest-rate risk is a sensitivity analysis that considers the effects on the bank's exposure through a change of one, two, three, or more basis points. We have spoken of this approach.

Simple sensitivities, however, fail to account for the fact that fundamentally interest-rate risk is more complex than it is generally considered to be. Indeed, we can effectively distinguish between three types of interest rate risk:

1. With *fixed interest rates* there is a possibility of reduction of income or even a loss due to fixed cash inflows, while cash outflows for deposits and bought money may be larger than the inflows.

It should be noted in this connection that fixed interest-rate risk exists both in the loans business, hence in the banking book, and in the trading book. Examples from trading are bonds and capital market swaps.

2. With *interest-rate structures,* there exist limited possibilities of adjusting interest rates for a specific type of credit or funds.

Fixed interest rates and interest-rate structures often tend to be confused—which is wrong. One of the better-known examples in the structural reference is mortgages, but interest-rate structure risk exists with many financial products.

3. With liquidity extremes, there is *excessive liquidity* or *insufficient liquidity* thereby guaranteeing payments as well as the reconstitution of legally required reserves.

Basically, liquidity risk has the character of a constraint that has to be observed in accounting for interest-rate risk. If and when a bank can buy liquidity on the money market, this risk may be eased. Generally, however, the maintenance of liquidity is a question of interest rates.

Neither profits and losses nor issues connected to exposure can be separated from any of these considerations. Typically, banks control interest-rate risk by allocating *limits* to trading lines and to the loans business. Such limits should not be confused with limits because of counterparty risk. They are motivated by the fact that changes in interest rates affect an institution's current earnings, future earnings, and economic value of its capital.

If a bank has liabilities with interest rates that change faster than those of its assets, its *net present value*[4] will decline in case interest rates rise. For this reason, BIS suggests that for the measurement of interest-rate risk, banks should classify interest-rate-sensitive assets, liabilities, and off-balance sheet instruments according to their maturities or repricing characteristics.

This leads to the method of time buckets we have spoken of on several occasions, or slotting various instruments into maturity bands. The next step is to compute the difference between maturity- or duration-weighted assets and liabilities, subject to certain adjustments.

In terms of interest-rate swaps that are risk-embedded into the loans book, the Financial Accounting Standards Board (FASB) believes that

---

4 See Chapter 2.

fixed-rate loan commitments have characteristics similar to option contracts because they provide the holder with benefits of favorable movements in the price of an underlying asset or index, but they feature limited or no exposure to losses from unfavorable price movements.

However, like option contracts, they subject the issuer to market risk. For this reason, FASB decided that those financial instruments should be included within the definition of derivatives products and be subject to the disclosures required by Statement 119.

By extension, variable-rate loan commitments and other variable-rate financial instruments may also include terms that subject the issuer to market risk. For instance, contract rate adjustments may fall behind changes in market rates or be subject to caps and floors.

All these references concerning interest-rate risk are most important to the development and use of algorithms for marking-to-model. Most of the points I have made are generic and therefore applicable to all markets. Others are specific to only one market but have been refined by a regulatory authority.

For example, in the case of the United States, the Financial Accounting Standards Board has concluded that disclosures of derivative financial instruments should be separated into two classes based on the reasons that parties write and buy derivatives:

1. Instruments held or issued for trading purposes measured at fair value. These include dealing or other activities reported in a trading book.

2. Instruments for purposes other than trading, including hedging.

Not every bank may agree with this classification. Some respondents to the Board's Exposure Draft stated that those two classes did not accurately reflect derivatives activity, suggesting that the disclosures would be more realistic if separated into three classes:

1. Dealing.
2. Speculative position taking.
3. Risk management.

However, after considering this alternative, FASB concluded that regulatory reporting must also be concerned about the difficulty in defining and distinguishing between speculative position taking and risk management. This, as I stressed in Chapter 12 in connection to hedging, is one of the major issues confronting the computation and simulation of market risk.

5. CURRENCY RISK AND COUNTRY RISK

Currency risk and country risk are two distinct subjects that, for a number of reasons, tend to be confused. As shown in Figure 14–3 there is some overlap between the two notions. There is also overlap between currency risk and interest-rate risk.

So that you can appreciate *currency risk* in its pure form, let me begin with the reference that currency products are, in a very large majority, traded over-the-counter. Their dealing includes spot, futures, forwards, swaps, options, and options on futures.

The foreign-exchange market is global. Worldwide currency-exchange trading amounts to about $1.5 trillion per day, which represents some $380 trillion per year. By contrast, merchandise trade stands at about $8.5 trillion per year, or less than 3 percent of foreign exchange.

This global currency-exchange market is characterized by important regulatory, operational, and structural differences among national markets. To a large extent, these reflect diverse approaches of local authorities, with rules and informal arrangements defining the following:

F I G U R E   14–3

Currency Risk and Country Risk Are Distinct Entities That Only Partially Overlap

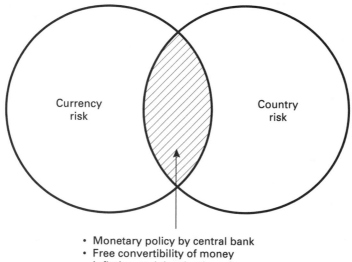

• Monetary policy by central bank
• Free convertibility of money
• Inflation and devaluation of currency

- Who is authorized to participate in the currency-exchange markets.
- How local banks can trade with each other and with foreign banks.
- What types of transactions can be conducted.

Therefore, I personally do not believe in bought software for the control of currency-exchange risk. Not only do national authorities impose different constraints and reporting characteristics—and each bank has its own limits structure—but there are also important cultural and operational differences among financial institutions in foreign-exchange trade.

The currency business is not just a matter of following exchange risk through statistics, like those in Figure 14–4, though this is necessary. The currency business requires a significant amount of bid–ask data streams to come up with a basis for prognostication. Forecasting the direction of changes in currency rates is most important in making money in a dynamic

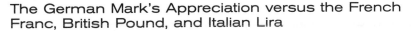

F I G U R E   14–4

The German Mark's Appreciation versus the French Franc, British Pound, and Italian Lira

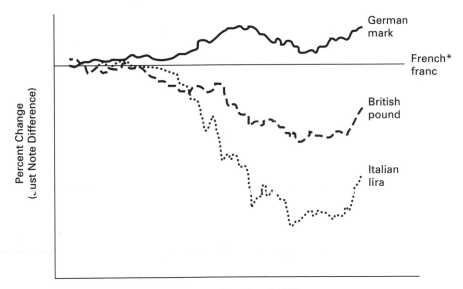

First Four Months of 1995

*Taken as reference level for real average

market such as forex. Tick-by-tick, therefore intraday, recording is the only sound approach in exploiting business opportunity and in controlling currency risk.

For business opportunity purposes, since the mid-1980s many banks have built expert systems that operate online as assistants to traders. Now the challenge is to develop and implement *agents*[5] able to watch after the observance of limits by each individual dealer and desk.

Given the frequency of forex trades and the fact that the large majority of contracts are over-the-counter, agents are one of the better risk-control strategies. Knowledge-enriched software is also necessary to measure currency risk in terms of positions per currency and counterparty, reporting interactively in real time and through ad hoc requests.

The online mining of databases is also crucial because on a daily basis banks exercise risk management in foreign exchange by allocating limits to the trading lines. While a central department establishes the limits and assuming positions within these limits, it is the responsibility of the parties receiving the limits to come up with the profits.

In the case of currency-exchange trading, the bank's expert systems can calculate risk and return through the *net present value* (NPV) method.[6] By contrast, with interest business, the discounted squaring result is often used. The different approaches to be taken with different instruments suggest that the eigenmodels policy should closely follow the bank's own policies and practices. An internal model written for foreign exchange will most likely not be able to accurately serve other product lines. Each major banking product has its own perspectives and requirements.

Attention should also be paid to nontrading lines. Nontrading lines do not receive any limits and therefore have to close their foreign currency positions. Positions from other businesses in foreign currencies, such as commissions or fund transfers, are closed through internal transactions with the currency-trading line. A good practice is to convert cash flows in foreign currencies into local currency. A cost-effective solution would see to it that this, too, is supported through agents.

In terms of *country risk,* what we target is the exposure related to a country of operations; its laws and bylaws; business ethics and practices; effectiveness of law enforcement agencies; and government policies, monetary, fiscal, and others. For money-center banks, country risk is

---

5 D. N. Chorafas, *Agent Technology Handbook* (New York: McGraw-Hill, 1997).
6 See Chapter 2.

inherent in their business. It is determined in the country ratings assessment, charged as a country-risk premium, and taken into account when establishing pricing policies.

The usual way country risk is assessed is by comparing the difference between the country premium contracted at the conclusion of the deal and the country-risk premium required on the basis of current valuation of such risk. The risk premium forms the foundation for calculating provisions and sharpening the algorithm(s) associated with country exposure.

The models that we build must reflect the fact that an integral part of country risk is that a counterparty, while willing to make payment, is prevented from fulfilling its commitments due to intervention on the part of the government of a sovereign state. We have spoken of this fact in connection to counterparty risk.

Whether an action leading to country risk is due to the sovereign state itself or another state, such action might render the bank's claims completely or partially worthless. For instance, a sovereign state or its central bank might suspend payment on its own obligations with the result that the bank's branches and subsidiaries abroad cannot fulfill their commitments to clients, or the bank's own operations in other countries suffer a prejudice, including the delivery of profits.

The so-called *risk domicile,* or the place where the risk occurs, is the determining factor for country risk. Notice that the risk domicile might be quite different than the domicile of the debtor.

Let me conclude this section by bringing to the reader's attention the fact that, generally, country risk has two main components. One is exposure-specific to the country to be taken into account in country rating. The other is risks associated with the instrument, usually accounted for by means of credit equivalents. Each component requires its own model, plus a systems approach making integration of the outputs feasible.

6. AN ADVISABLE PROCEDURE FOR THE ASSESSMENT OF EQUITY RISK

By definition, an *equity instrument* is a contract that provides ownership interest in an entity. Typically, it entitles its holder to a pro rata share of all distributions made to the class of equity holders he or she belongs to, but entails a right to receive cash or other financial assets only upon declaration of a dividend or the issuing entity's liquidation.

Usually, equity trading is done in connection with a business policy that may involve emphasis on blue chips (stock of prime companies), midcaps, small caps, or new issues on which the bank takes an under-writing position. All of these investments are subject to *equity price risk,* but its control may vary according to the time horizon.

Banks take positions in equities for one of two reasons: as *an invest-ment,* in which case the equities are in the banking book, and for *short-term profits.* In this case, banks are parking the equities in their trading book. Also in the trading book are *equity derivatives,* including deals done for short-term profits.

As with all other investments and trades, the essence of short-term positions is to exploit the business opportunity connected to rising equity prices. These positions, however, are subject to equity price changes that may move in the opposite direction of the one the banker, treasurer, or investor expects.

Because practically all banks, with the possible exception of very small ones, make equity investments in many countries (including emerg-ing markets that have a weak currency), commitments to equities also involve currency risk. In other words, not only do currency risk and coun-try risk overlap, as we saw in Section 5, but currency risk and equity risk do as well.

An investment made in stock exchange A may have provided signif-icant profits. But because the currency of the country where this stock exchange is located lost a good deal of its value, the overall result (con-verted back into the original currency) might be a loss. The possibility of a reduction in profits may be due to equity price fluctuations, currency-exchange fluctuations, or both.

Neither the bond markets not the stock markets like inflation. Inflation also hits the currency value, but nothing guarantees that these risks move in the same direction. Alternatively, the performance of a spe-cific market may be wanting because of illiquidity. The position in equi-ties and equity-like securities (such as participation in warrants and other certificates) may show good, average, or disappointing performance.

All equity market characteristics must be reflected in the model we build for the control of equity risk. The better approach is to use intraday data streams. Figure 14–5 helps illustrate the pattern we can obtain through high-frequency financial data. Fuzzy engineering provides a good tool for the exploitation of this information.[7]

Several different models may be necessary for the control of equity risk. Among the trades that banks enter into regarding equities are securities

---

7 See D. N. Chorafas, *Chaos Theory in the Financial Markets* (Chicago: Probus, 1994).

F I G U R E   14–5

A Three-Day Correlogram of S&P 500 Time Series;
Volatility Characteristics with Intraday Patterns

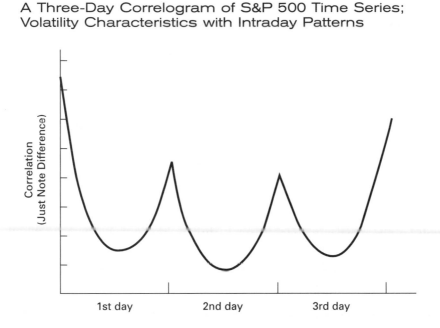

lending and borrowing as well as delta-weighted options per individual equity. Each of these has its own algorithmic requirements.

There are also transactions in equity index instruments, which may be broken down into their individual components and integrated into the net position of an equities exposure. Alternatively, the index may be considered a separate, individual equity that is included in the portfolio position. This may be done independently of the individual equities comprising its constituent parts.

All five examples we have considered in this chapter—counterparty risk, interest-rate risk, currency risk, country risk, and equity risk—pose important challenges for the development and use of eigenmodels able to help the bank's management control exposure. And as Part One has stressed, there are also organizational and structural requirements for risk management.

Indeed, the most important weakness of the 1996 Market Risk Amendment is that it made no provision for the organizational and structural requirements that banks should observe in order to effectively control market risk. The best solution is that suggested by Dr. Alan Greenspan, the chairman of the Federal Reserve, for the American financial industry:

The functions and responsibilities of a *chief risk management officer* (CRMO) should be handled at the executive board level.

Because it is in their own interest in terms of the control of exposure, a growing number of U.S. banks create the CRMO as an independent management position. In a banking environment, the CRMO's authority is combining credit risk, derivatives risk, and other market risks. Even the manufacturing industry follows this line of a new, independent risk controller.

In a recent meeting in Boston, the State Street Bank mentioned one of its clients, a manufacturing company specializing in building materials, whose CRMO is in the treasury unit. He is looking at commodity prices globally and auditing procurement practices and projects from the viewpoint of price evolution. But he also evaluates the company's dependence on information technology and the risks of vendor failures it is taking.

About 50 percent of the business of this company is in the United States; the other 50 percent is international. Management was decentralized, and P&L was good until a rigorous audit found that there was no effective global control over the many types of risk the company was taking; hence the new CRMO position.

Similarly, in a banking environment, equity limits may be established by the chief risk management officer, who also has responsibility for the allocation of risk-premium limits. If the bank does not have a CRMO, equity risk limits may be established by the credits division. This approach, however, has a glaring weakness, as any knowledgeable banker would appreciate. Risk management should never depend on a division that might develop a conflict of interest.

CHAPTER 15

Starting with RiskMetrics and Moving Toward an Expanding Risk Horizon

1. INTRODUCTION

In discussing the technical details of the 1996 Market Risk Amendment, Chapter 2, 3, and 4 made the point that the Basle Committee offers the banks an option: They can develop and use their own models for marking their trading book to fair value, or they can employ the so-called *standard method.*

Eigenmodels and standard method are two worlds apart, though banks lacking the know-how in rocket science, and most particularly lacking the will to build proprietary models, could adopt the less sophisticated solution. One of the drawbacks of the standardized approach is the additive nature of the capital required for broad asset classes, with requirements computed market-by-market for the following:

- Interest-rate risk,
- Currency exchange, and
- Equities.

Subsequently, the separate requirements are summed. While the capital requirement for a long position in, say, U.S. equities takes into account hedging in the same market, it does not accept any offset from holding, for instance, a short position in German equities. Nor does it consider possible diversification effects from holding long and short positions in both markets.

As a result, the standard method tends to favor market makers at the expense of diversified money-center banks. The latter run global portfolios and have pressed the Basle Committee to consider approaches to capital requirements that take into account diversification. In a nutshell, this is the background of the Basle Committee's *alternative approach* with eigenmodels.

Proprietary models, however, are not the only option left with the alternative approach. As I have already mentioned, there is also the option of *bought software,* for instance, the RiskMetrics system the Morgan Bank makes available to correspondent banks and other entities. We will be talking about RiskMetrics in this chapter.

As Figure 15–1 suggests, there are three options for marking-to-model: the standard method, bought software, and eigenmodels. These three alternatives overlap.

RiskMetrics is a value-at-risk approach and therefore different than netting, which characterizes the standard method. But for those banks that use it, RiskMetrics has many aspects of a de facto standard, like in old times Visicalc was a de facto spreadsheet standard.

It is quite different with eigenmodels. The fact that a bank's proprietary models form the basis for the calculation of capital requirements permits us to align capital calculation with the risk-measurement approach of *our* bank and the specific conditions that it encounters in the market it is working.

FIGURE   15–1

A Commercial Bank Has Three Alternatives for Marking-to-Model

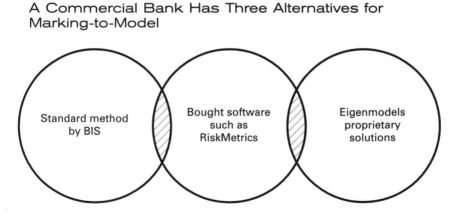

These alternatives only partly overlap

2. PLAYING WITH EQUATIONS OR ANALYZING THE FINANCIAL MARKETS?

"Chance," Voltaire once wrote, "is a word void of sense. Nothing can exist without a cause." It took time for management to learn that lesson. This happened painfully over the years, as banks and other companies continued to feel the pinch of "unexplained coincidences" with derivative financial instruments.

Everything has a cause. Therefore, we should search for that cause. That's one of the missions we attempt to accomplish through financial analysis and the use of algorithms. Another goal is to position ourselves to do a more rigorous pricing of financial products, while developing a system that is better able to analyze exposure and manage risk.

"A great deal of my work is playing with equations," said physicist Paul A. M. Dirac. "I look for beautiful mathematical relations which don't seem to have any physical meaning, but sometimes they do."[1] Indeed, Dirac's equations made a number of predictions. One stated that electrons have spin. Another unearthed a new particle: an electron with a positive charge.

Dirac called the new particle an "anti-electron." Some years down the line, bigger accelerators confirmed that for every particle there was an antiparticle. Yet, originally, the discovery was made through *abstraction* and *idealization*,[2] not by means of *physical testing*. Besides this, the symmetry Dirac established between matter and antimatter created new perspectives in research.

Contrary to what is commonly thought, that modeling first developed in physics and engineering and then migrated to finance, modeling originated in economic theory in the late 19th century, through the work of Dr. Leon Walras and Dr. Vilfredo Pareto. Both Walras and Pareto worked through abstraction and simplification in formulating financial models.

By contrast, aircraft design and dam construction has been based on scale models. Scale models first appeared in the 1930s, followed by mathematical models of power-distribution systems developed in the 1940s on analog computers. Subsequently, mathematical models were ported to digital differential analyzers and from there to digital computers in the late 1950s and early 1960s.[3] Whether in science, engineering, or finance, modern modeling efforts are to a large part concerned with functional analysis

---

1 John Berslough, *Master of Time* (London: J. M. Dent, 1992).
2 On the role of abstraction and idealization in model development, see Chapter 16.
3 See D. N. Chorafas, *Systems and Simulation* (New York: Academic Press, 1965).

and morphology. A significant part of our task lies in the comparison of related forms rather than in the precise definition of each.

Also of primary concern is the study of possible deformations of a complex system, be it a market or an aircraft. When this task is properly approached, it can lead to comprehension of the process of transformation—even if the underlying entity itself continues to hold its secrets. This is an issue of great importance in financial analysis. Based on *hypotheses,* therefore on tentative statements, we can construct a block diagram that represents this process of transition in, say, $/DM exchange rates. The study of this transition begins with analysis of financial data streams and with database mining.[4] It ends with the justification of a prediction of possible course(s).

Because modeling is based on know-how and experience, eigenmodels can integrate in a much better way with the bank's own risk-management policies. But the bank supervisors are now faced with a much greater challenge than if the standard method were widely used.

Even if risk-management models are built by financial institutions belonging to business lines that are more or less similar to one another, the way to bet is that they use different parameters:

- Some cover $/DM price changes weekly; others focus on intra-day datastreams.
- Some take bid/ask midpoints; other concentrate on the bids.
- Some choose a higher level of confidence than the Market Risk Amendment specifies; others don't.

Also, in making their calculation, banks may assume stronger or weaker correlations between markets. It will take some time for the different eigenmodels to converge towards greater homogeneity, which will permit effective comparisons—and even this convergence is not certain.

A greater homogeneity will be helped by the fact that among banks and securities houses there is a body of experience concerning pricing by means of models—particularly experience on the pricing of options. At the same time, however, an eigenmodel procedure raises a number of issues for supervisors regarding the safeguards that should be put in place to assure that the model-generated capital requirements are adequate.

Part One explained that the Basle Committee has left to each central bank the mission of establishing standards for model construction and for

---

4 D. N. Chorafas and H. Steinmann, *Database Mining* (London: Lafferty, 1994).

the backtesting of eigenmodels. In turn, the central banks look at the commercial banks for incorporating into their models all crucial variables for product pricing and risk management.

With this background, the question posed in the title of this section can be answered. While the goal of developing and using financial models is analysis, this goal is best reached by a process akin to playing with equations. This is the Paul Dirac way, but also the Albert Einstein way, and generally the way of all great physicists.

The commercial banks that will be better positioned to cooperate with central banks in structuring a long-lasting procedure for marking-to-model are those that have in-house expertise with proprietary solutions—from conception to the development of algorithms, rigorous testing, and real-life applications. This does not make bought software useless, but as the chapter introduction underlined, using someone else's artifact is not synonymous with developing one's own skill and expertise.

3. J. P. MORGAN'S RISKMETRICS

J. P. Morgan's RiskMetrics is a parametric value-at-risk model, like those we discussed in Chapter 10. It is based on a normal distribution of values, and as a bank representative states: "Despite recent attempts to produce alternatives to the normal distribution assumption, we believe that [it] is a viable alternative. In fact, empirical results from applying normality assumptions to risk management confirm this."

Other people do not necessarily agree with this statement. Chapter 11 explained the reasons nonparametric value-at-risk models are superior. It is also true, however, that the more sophisticated a model is, the less it can be generalized. Bought software has its place, as Figure 15–2 suggests. In terms of sophistication and complexity, over and above bought software are the bank's own proprietary solutions.

The Morgan Bank made RiskMetrics public in October 1994. Quite likely, the foremost goal sought out by the bank's management in taking that step was to show the technique that should be used, as well as the historical data necessary on a daily basis to do the following:

- Estimate risk exposure.
- Set position limits.
- Refine asset-allocation strategies.

As we saw in Chapter 12 in connection to the SMI research project, for volatility estimates RiskMetrics uses a time series of historical

F I G U R E   15–2

Layers of Open and Proprietary Solutions from a
Financial Institution's Viewpoint

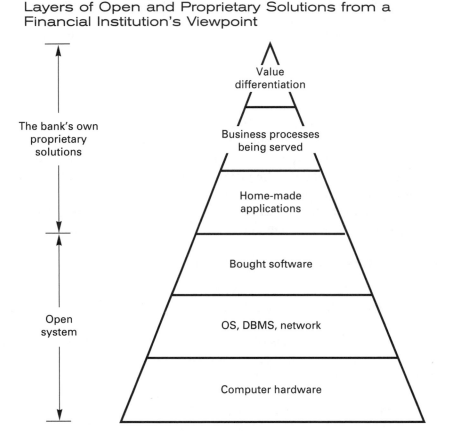

volatilities, specifically, the exponential moving weighted average
(EMWA) model.

The values in this time series are exponentially weighted to assure
that past volatility influences the calculation of actual volatility. Morgan
says that compared to other methods, this approach has the advantage of
mathematical simplicity and, therefore, of a shorter calculation time for
real-time modeling.

Some of the banks that have worked with RiskMetrics buy this argument and like RiskMetrics. Others are not so enthusiastic. Still others have
choosen to develop their own models after having gained some initial
experience.

While the reason for this switch is largely functional, some knowledgeable bankers think that RiskMetrics is more oriented towards operations

risk than market risk. However, while the Morgan model is far from being ideal, this is not a fair criticism:

- *Operations risk* is in itself a fuzzy notion, and
- RiskMetrics does address *market risk;* like CreditMetrics, also by J. P. Morgan, addresses *credit risk.*

True enough, because commodity software tries to appeal to a wider possible market, it has its shortcomings. RiskMetrics cannot, for example, generate a value-at-risk exposure for a number of derivative products including options. Yet, options are the security most likely to worry the regulators.

Critics also say that RiskMetrics cannot take into account the influence derivatives now have on underlying cash markets. Because of this, the banks using it are exposed to losses that might arise through basis risk. J. P. Morgan answers that its release of RiskMetrics has a dual goal to encourage banks to use a number-crunching methodology as a base from which to develop a new generation of risk-management systems and to hasten the development of an industrywide de facto standard.

I believe in the first of these objectives much more than the second. In fact, as already mentioned, some banks that used RiskMetrics did so to acquire experience for the development of eigenmodels. At least three different banks were to comment that (1) there is really no other substitute for the acquisition of the necessary new culture than to develop proprietary models, and (2) in terms of compliance to the Market Risk Amendment by the Basle Committee, the key phrase is "back to fundamentals" for the acquisition of basic analytical skill.

We can better appreciate the importance of a polyvalent approach to analytical skill if we recall the gyrations financial markets are going through, which at times seem to be chaotic. The movement through a number of temporary short-lived equilibria has been fed by:

- The globalization of financial markets,
- The rapid transfer of liquid capital through networks, and
- The uncertainty about interest rates and fluctuating currency rates.

What can be considered chaotic behavior[5] is as much a characteristic of capital markets as it is of money markets and currency exchange. Figure 15–3 shows the chaotic pattern of the yen/DM exchange rate, particularly at

---

5 See D. N. Chorafas, *Chaos Theory in the Financial Markets* (Chicago: Probus, 1994).

F I G U R E   15–3

Intraday Yen/DM Exchange-Rate Volatility in Five-Minute Intervals

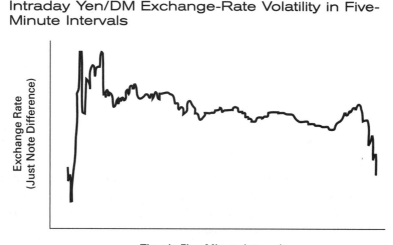

Time in Five-Minute Intervals

the beginning and closing intervals. This plot uses five-minute data input, which helps capture microsecond volatility.

RiskMetrics cannot track that sort of exchange-rate volatility. Nor does it have the algorithms or the ability to accept tick-by-tick input. For this purpose, the Morgan Bank has an eigenmodel that uses *heteroschedasticity*[6] and high-frequency financial data, developed through sponsored research at the Industrial Liaison program at MIT.

In conclusion, in a time when know-how about marking-to-model is still thin, RiskMetrics might be of assistance to the bank that uses it. If nothing else, it can help as a demonstrator, learning tool, and test environment. But banks that think they can solve their risk-management problems through bought software are mistaken. There is no substitute for internal experience and know-how.

4. IS THERE A REASON TO QUESTION THE VALUE-AT-RISK APPROACH?

The Morgan Bank is offering RiskMetrics free of charge. By contrast, Bankers Trust has put a significant price on its Risk Adjusted Return on Capital (RAROC) risk model. A one-off run costs around $75,000, while on-site licenses at client premises start at $1 million.

---

6 D. N. Chorafas, *How to Understand and Use Mathematics for Derivatives,* Volume 2 (London: *Euromoney,* 1995).

Despite this price, however, Bankers Trust says that there is no shortage of willing takers. It has already signed up leading U.S. institutional fund managers (including the $15 billion Chrysler pension fund), an international insurer, and a European utility company.

As with all investments, this is a cost-and-return evaluation. When Chrysler's pension fund ran its $400 million currency exposure through RAROC, it uncovered a natural hedge that reduced the incremental risk exposure in the portfolio to less than 5 percent. This optimization was estimated to provide the fund with a $20 million gain.

RAROC and RiskMetrics are not directly comparable, but they are both examples of commodity software. From spreadsheets to more complex modeling approaches, when we buy programming products we must be aware that their developers worked on a number of assumptions that condition the software's behavior. The use of a programming product is inseparable from the de facto acceptance of the developer's hypotheses. The most basic hypothesis behind RiskMetrics is that, generally, parametric VAR offers a good approximation to real-life risk.

However, a number of financial analysts and rocket scientists question the approach behind parametric value-at-risk, even if it has been embraced by many bankers and regulators. In their opinion, VAR in general and VAR/P in particular have two serious drawbacks. The primary drawback is that it relies heavily on past volatility as a guide to future volatility. Past volatility, however, has proven to be a poor predictor of a portfolio's future behavior.

Another of the value-at-risk shortcomings discussed in the financial industry meetings is that it is of limited use at a strategic decision-making level. This is because it does not permit meaningful comparisons across financial markets. Yet today many bankers, treasurers, and other investors target a global allocation of capital.

The knowledgeable reader will appreciate that this second constraint is, to a large extent, possible to overcome if we develop a conceptual model that offers cross-market metrics and into which VAR integrates. It is more difficult is to overcome CAR's absence of *liquidity* measures, in the sense that investments must not only consider volatility but market liquidity as well. As a matter of principle, the future behavior of risk factors is never one-dimensional. Each market differs from another in both volatility and liquidity.

Future market behavior, and therefore the amount of risk, depends on more than just historic correlations. This becomes VAR's third shortcoming, because risk is also a function of the period over which it is measured and the trader's corresponding assessment of market responses.

To measure performance across markets, we use benchmarks, such as an index, which reflect the pecularities of each market. In no market is there a sort of riskless trade that will yield return at no costs. Eigenmodels available today at tier-1 banks pay attention to this factor.[7]

Some experts in risk management suggest that value-at-risk also has the disadvantage of being little known among investors, creditors, and even financial institutions that are not mathematically oriented. Others think that, though VAR could be an appropriate measure, the fine grid in measurements and the reporting systems to support effective VAR use are not yet available.

The fact that I am reporting these criticisms does not necessarily mean I agree with them. Some of the negative comments contradict the positive ones. As for the shortcomings in measurements and reporting systems that exist in many banks, it is evident they have to be corrected. But this is *not* VAR's problem. The correction of shortcomings in the measurement and reporting system of *our* banks is a never-ending business. In a dynamic market environment, competitive disadvantages grow like the heads of the mythical Hydra.

But throwing money at the problem is not the way to solve it. A short time ago, for example, the General Bank of Luxembourg hired 50 consultants from Arthur Andersen to revamp its information technology. That huge crowd is expected to work at the bank for three years! This reminds me of an old joke at IBM about a farmer who had to sell his one and only cow to make the down payment for a machine to milk it. Whether it is to develop eigenmodels or restructure their IT, banks that hire a large team of outsiders are in for high costs and low results. It is in this sense that bought software, like RiskMetrics, might prove a good intermediate solution.

Banks that develop proprietary algorithms or use RiskMetrics should also appreciate that while modeling is well established in finance, we should always be sure to measure return on investment. We should also be ready to recognize that changing market conditions can see to it that what was a good return at one moment might be a poor return at another, or even an altogether unwarranted risk.

Let me close this section with this advice. If the bank starts with a simple model, it should always strive to improve its technology. Tier-1 banks are steadily reassessing current models. They are evaluating their shortcomings—such as the hypotheses of normality and linearity—and are using

---

7 D. N. Chorafas, *How to Understand and Use Mathematics for Derivatives,* Volume 2 (London: *Euromoney,* 1996).

fuzzy engineering, Latin squares hypercube sampling, and Monte Carlo simulation to build realism into VAR or any other approach they choose to follow. They are also identifying and overcoming computational and database bottlenecks that exist with mainframes, moving into high-performance computing that can render greater benefits at lower cost.

5. MAKING RISKMETRICS AVAILABLE ON THE INTERNET

A short time after having introduced the model to the financial market, the Morgan Bank decided to make RiskMetrics available free of charge via the Internet. This made it possible to put risk-analysis techniques at the disposal of firms that could scarcely afford to develop them on their own.

J. P. Morgan says there have been thousands of downloads of the RiskMetrics data to companies that use the system. Among the most popular applications is that of investment managers applying the concepts of volatility and correlation to asset allocation.

Will RiskMetrics give these investment managers a benchmark that lets them tell their clients that the portfolio run has this much risk attached to it? There are reasons to doubt this will be the case because of the existence of cultural and algorithmic barriers, which were discussed in Section 4.

Will data streams flowing through the Internet make RiskMetrics a success? I doubt it for two reasons. First, the cultural factor. A new culture develops over time through steady effort and experience; it cannot be downloaded through a network.

Second, the most useful financial statistics are a bank's own. They are not provided by someone else. Granted, the intention of downloading financial statistics is to determine how well the risks are diversified. But for diversification purposes, the mathematics is complex, and the output, though comprehensible by expert financial analysts, is not for general use.

A risk-oriented programming product must go beyond the amount of capital that regulators force banks to set aside to cover potential trading losses. It must integrate with and promote the quality of the bank's risk-management system, which may run on intranet or other software, but which may also be in shambles.

The quality of the bank's risk-management system as a whole has an important impact on the banks' profits and competitiveness. And while RiskMetrics may be too much to comprehend for the average investor or investment advisor, software that runs through the Internet offers too little in terms of the sophistication necessary to balance risk and return at the bank's level.

The major weakness of RiskMetrics, critics say, is that the user must mark-to-market all investments in a given portfolio. This is not as easy as it sounds since with many OTC derivatives, which are the more risky, there is rarely an active market to use for pricing.

The Internet does not carry that sort of information, at least for the time being. Nor can it assist bankers in estimating probable changes in asset values. For its part, RiskMetrics provides some estimates of volatility. But many bankers think this is not enough.

Better solutions are possible, but they are also contingent on the existence and interactive use of rich databases. No bought software provides that. Databases are a bank's internal resource and responsibility. This is another reason I have stressed on several occasions that it takes much more than algorithms to develop a sound risk-management system.

Cultural factors also play a role in the ability of the user of a model to work with successive software releases. A model that stays put will not survive. Within its financial analysis goals and orientation, J. P. Morgan is adjusting RiskMetrics to help banks calculate the impact of new central-bank guidelines concerning trading risks and bank capital.

In other words, the user bank must also be able to comprehend the new releases of commodity software and improve its skills to meet their requirements. New releases come fast. Six months after its public introduction, Morgan expanded RiskMetrics by adding commodities and extending the program's coverage.

The individual bank that uses RiskMetrics must also be aware that the multidiversity of risk in a complex portfolio can rarely be studied through packages. One of the lessons of the past few years is the degree to which standard statistical and mathematical risk-measurement techniques fall short of describing *real life.*

For this reason, J. P. Morgan is expanding the databases currently included in RiskMetrics. Its goal is to make its programming product a gauge for measuring risk across major asset classes, such as stocks, government bonds, short-term interest rates, commodities, and currencies for a variety of geographic markets.

The Internet initiative fits well within this perspective, but it may not be enough. Commercial banks that use RiskMetrics or other bought software must also be able to sharpen the interactive visualization tools at their disposal.

As an example, Figure 15–4 presents in a nutshell a system built for risk management that permits real-time response to ad hoc queries about exposure.[8]

6. CAPITALIZING ON THE EXPANDING HORIZONS OF RISK MANAGEMENT

During the 1980s and early 1990s, enterprising brokers and bankers as well as most of the boiler rooms created tons of options. Wall Street's rocket scientists generated anything from options, futures, and swaps to synthetic stocks. The city's financial engineers further exploited the potential of innovation connected to such instruments.

F I G U R E   15–4

Real-Time Response Should Be Available at Any Time through a Six-Dimensional Frame of Reference

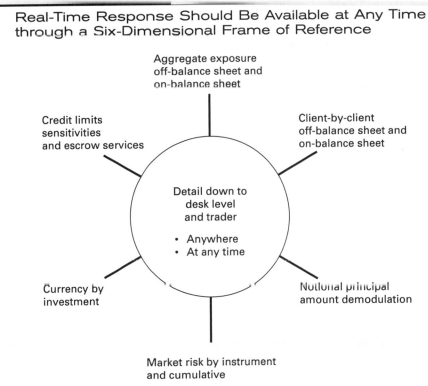

8 See D. N. Chorafas and H. Steinmann, *Virtual Reality: Practical Applications in Business and Industry* (Upper Saddle River, NJ: Prentice-Hall, 1995).

With deregulation, there is nothing surprising about this thrust for innovation in financial products and markets. In every country, banks compete with each other to offer more sophisticated services to customers. Yet, at the same time, they must cooperate to contain systemic risk, particularly when it comes to trading on new financial instruments, 24 hours per day anywhere in the world, and facing the exposure of a follow-the-sun overdraft, which might hit the financial industry at any time.

This is the background for why Section 5 insisted that the mathematical models rocket scientists built are necessary but not enough. The other pillars of a real-time system that should be built with the dual objective of enlarging the bank's business opportunity and controlling its risks are as follows:

- Distributed deductive databases, with algorithms and heuristics for interactive database mining.

- Intelligent networks connecting the bank with its clients, at any time and for any product.

- Agile, user-friendly interfaces capitalizing on three-dimensional, color computer graphics.

A properly architectured system will provide a real-time response that should be available throughout the day interactively and ad hoc at the disposal of all authorized users. Figure 15–4 has given a multidimensional frame of reference for risk-management reasons.

The expanding horizon of risk management sees to it that a most important aspect that combines the trust for new financial products and risk containment is the tradeoffs between profits and exposure. Not only is this issue highly connected to *financial innovation,* it also underpins future gains and losses. No matter how good a financial product is, it is only 12 to 18 months away from losing the market's interest. But steady innovation poses challenges that very few banks are able to handle.

This statement is just as true of proper pricing as it is of risk containment. Proper pricing makes the difference between gain and loss. Risk containment can be basically reduced to a cost factor, like an insurance premium. We spoke of this concept in Part One.

Both product-pricing and risk-management solutions depend very much on the perspective of the risk taker with financial products. This perspective varies by payer, payee, banker, settlement system, or regulator. Exposure is also a function of how clearly we perceive current risks and their peculiar characteristics:

1. Today banks tend to allocate to off-balance sheet operations about two-thirds of their credit line toward counterparties.
2. Fifty percent or more of derivatives trades are made between correspondent banks, not with other parties.
3. Some forecasts indicate that by the end of this decade, or right after, there will be a shakedown among financial players. From 30, the top team will be reduced to 5 or 6.

The market where the largest risk is taken is New York—not only by U.S. financial institutions but by foreign banks as well. Australian banks, for example, have more exposure in New York than in Sydney.

As far as U.S. financial institutions are concerned, there is a concentration of off-balance sheet trades, with the top seven banks representing 90 percent of total U.S. exposure to derivative instruments. Much of this exposure has been created in the name of hedging, and therefore hedging practices and risk-reducing policies are not necessarily synonymous.

Moving toward the containment and control of the expanding risk horizon is necessary because leveraging in the financial markets is further increased as, at current levels of trading and exposure, there are not enough underlying securities to go around. Therefore, some investors lend while other investors borrow, and some investors go long while other investors go short.

A good risk-management system for one bank may not be good for another bank because of their idosyncratic differences. But the aggregate of risk-management systems by financial institutions can be good for the global economy because it helps to contain the follow-the-sun overdraft.

There is a theory that states that an uncontrolled volume of transactions will act, by its sheer volume, as a risk-management system. Investments carry different levels of risk. Some are higher and some are lower. The more transactions there are, the more the risk of offset. There is a flaw in this logic. Anything that runs out of control is dangerous. Hence the reason for feedback, which we look at in Chapter 16.

Some financial analysts believe that the 1996 Market Risk Amendment by the Basle Committee does not answer all of the exposure problems embedded into the different portfolios of financial institutions. They consider the Amendment unsatisfactory in terms of market risk because it measures the risk in the *trading book* alone. But, in reality, emphasis should be on the whole *banking account,* including the *banking book.*

Behind this thesis lies the fact that commercial banks have huge mismatches in the interest rates embedded into their loans portfolio and bond portfolio that magnify exposure. This problem, as well as the projected solutions, were discussed in Part One.

7. FINANCIAL THEORIES ARE NOT FOREVER

Like raw materials, all of the bank's assets and liabilities have to be analyzed as though they are products to purchase, inventory, and sell. This is indeed the sense of the 1996 Market Risk Amendment; therefore, I consider it a most valuable document. Whether money is bought or sold, inventoried or transformed, it is subject to the whims of the market, with opportunities for appreciation and risk of depreciation.

Both appreciation and depreciation have a significant probability in markets with high volatility and uncertainty about future course. Because they act as investors, bond issuers, and loan takers, all companies need to permanently manage their treasury, which obliges them to have an arsenal of analytical tools ready for use.

These tools cannot be paper, pencil, and personal memory. They have to be high-technology based, involving financial analysis models, intelligent distributed databases, corporate memory facilities, database mining algorithms, and heuristics as well as any-to-any intelligent networks and high-performance computers.

The market has its own dynamics that we aim to analyze. For instance, short-term interest rates are set by the reserve bank. But short-term and long-term rates are not always related. For any two currencies, or triangular relation, the market sets the exchange rate, but the reserve banks influence the market's behavior through their intervention.

Invariably, the analysis we do is based on assumptions, hypotheses, and theories. Whether in science or in finance, a theory can only be acceptable in the longer run if it is testable in practice and gives reliable results. The cemetery of science is full of dead theories that, in their time, had the upper hand.

Does this mean that at some point all of our theories will be incorrect or that incorrect beliefs that somehow escape scrutiny are the dominant force in science? In engineering? In finance? It means neither, and for good reason. In the short run, some of our theories are correct—because they represent a state-of-the-art discovery. But in the long run, practically all of our theories are wrong because our knowledge has gone beyond the old state-of-the-art.

This is true not just of economic and financial theories, but also of those physics, chemistry, engineering, and other fields. Theories are based on hypotheses, and hypotheses are by definition tentative. They remain valid up to a point, until they are disproved—or their expected documentation fails to materialize.

When we accept a theory—which, so to speak, is the derivative of a hypothesis—all we are saying is that we have found *so far* no reason to reject its underlying hypothesis. In principle, we are much more confident when we reject a theory than when we accept it. That's the way science works.

Science is a tough critic. If just one of the hypotheses or the subsystems supported by the theory fails the test, this is enough to falsify the theory and eliminate its possible impact. The same is true of prognosis. Let's keep this in mind when we mark-to-market or mark-to-model the trading book, and when we develop and use models and systems for risk management.

CHAPTER 16

The Development and Use of Proprietary Models for Pricing the Trading Book

1. INTRODUCTION

Every chapter in this book emphasized the development and use of models for pricing the trading book. But though the notion of marking-to-model has been used on many occasions, this chapter will explain how a model can be built. Remember, however, that while this chapter will guide the reader's hand in the art of model making by providing the guidelines, it is personal experience that primarily helps one to shape a model.

This hands-on experience is of the utmost importance because in the financial industry the development and use of models is both challenging and urgent. Professor Charles A. R. Goohart, of the London School of Economics, and Maureen O'Hara, of Cornell University, said that much in their joint lectures to the First International Conference on High Frequency Data in Finance.[1] They also lamented that financial institutions pay a lopsided interest in their modeling practice. While the fixed-interest market, Treasury bills market, and money market vastly exceed the equity market in turnover, the theories that have been developed and used by academics and banks are much more oriented to equities than to any other domain of transactions.

Trading in the interest-rate market, Treasury bills market, currency-exchange market, and money market is of greater macroeconomic importance than trading in the more classical securities. But, ironically, the

---

1 Zurich, March 29–31, 1995.

number of really rigorous analytical studies is surprisingly small in these four markets, as it is in the derivatives market at large.

Though, as we have seen in Chapters 12 and 13, there are some well-accepted models for derivatives, much more is necessary given the size and growth rate of that market. Creative solutions must also involve the effectiveness of the organization as a whole and unearth the conflicts of interest of the functional units of a bank.

A bank's internal conflict of interest is not that different than the one faced by an automobile manufacturer whose clients want fast, safe, powerful, economical, sleek, roomy, comfortable, and attractive vehicles.

This chapter does not address the organizational conflicts of interest in the banking industry. This is a subject so vast it could fill a library. Instead, it concentrates on the background concepts necessary for developing, testing, and using models. Therefore, it fulfills the *how-to* aspects of a concept thoroughly discussed in the preceding 15 chapters.

2. APPRECIATING THE POWER OF ABSTRACTION AND OF SIMPLIFYING ASSUMPTIONS

As financial analysts, engineers, or scientists, we have always made sense of the world around us by simplifying abstractions. Abstractions concentrate on the underpinning principles in our knowledge and experience—as well as the observed order, or lack of it, in our perceptions. Abstraction allows us to express a conceived structure of certain phenomena and cast aside detail irrelevant to the issue at hand.

Abstraction and *modeling* essentially come after *perception* and *conception* and are followed by calculation, response, and *feedback.* This process is shown in Figure 16–1. In relatively simple cases, this is informally and unconsciously done in our brain, but we need a formal discipline when addressing problems that are relatively complex.

In its way, the process of abstraction leads to a theory or theories that enable us to investigate the kernel of observed phenomena, whether through standalone analysis or by means of correlations or covariance among variables. This is what scientists do with zeal, even if—as Chapter 15 stated—the final result may mean that the theory underpinning the research is eventually cast aside.

Whether we talk of modeling in finance, engineering, or physics, the key words to keep in mind are *abstraction* and *simplification* followed by an algorithmic expression. Abstraction means to suppress all finer points, making it possible to consider a simplified system.

F I G U R E   16–1

From Perception to Response: Seven Successive
Layers in Intelligent Organisms

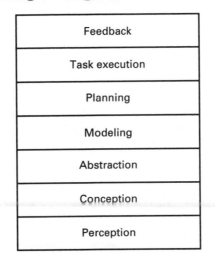

Feedback
Task execution
Planning
Modeling
Abstraction
Conception
Perception

The concept of idealization applies to conditions prevailing in the financial market, and it is particularly important to the study of those situations that are fairly complex. A paradigm can be taken from the animal kingdom. With very few exceptions, the bodies of all animals can be visualized as living cylinders, pierced by two tubes or passages: one for the breath of life, the other for food and water.

The reason for this parallelism lies deep in the secret of life: The cells of any animal require a steady, uninterrupted double uptake. We routinely breath through one compound passage, while we eat and drink through the other, the two processes proceeding in parallel.

This is a good example of the power of abstraction, and it has a counterpart in human-made systems. Both tubes are vital to the sustenance of systems functions, which are better served through this approach than by means of interrupts in one shared channel.

Like trading in a financial market, the one cylinder works in real time. Practically every second, an animal draws a new breath. Although no less essential, input and output through the second cylinder, for instance food and liquids, enter in timed batches. This might be compared to a financial payments and settlements system.

This allegory is powerful and helps explain the difference between *real time* (the breath of life) and *real-enough time* (the timed batches). But there is another way to look at the the financial market's two cylinders if we abstract—as in the case of animals—the limbs, wings, fur, and fins. The knowledgeable reader will perceive:

- *Volatility,* which works in real time, and
- *Liquidity,* which acts in timed batches.

Volatility has a great deal to do with trading. Liquidity is both the prerequisite and the result of the payments system. When we abstract and idealize, as is the case with this example, we don't try to micromanage the object of our research. Our goal is to comprehend how the system works.

The process of abstraction in financial analysis follows the same principle. In finance, as in physics, abstraction is associated with the power to simplify the world analytically, visually, or both. This is the only way obscure phenomena or their origins can be successfully defined and, in some cases, explained.

Matters become more complex when we deal with multiple states, which in financial analysis, happens quite often. The pervasiveness of multiple stable outcomes has broad implications. Some economists talk as if there is only one correct way to solve a problem, such as inflation, unemployment, or rising healthcare costs. This is, however, a misconception.

What chaos theory teaches is that the range of possibilities is enormous, and it may be possible to shift from one arrangement of economic and financial activities—however stable it may look—to a different one, which might be better. In other words, there are not only *equilibrium* and *instability,* there are also multiple equilibria, and we may be fixed on a bad one.

There is another benefit from modeling, along the animal cylinders paradigm. Abstraction is the interface between complexity and simplicity, as shown in Figure 16–2. It is a process that works in both ways because we build complex systems from what we already know but also investigate unknown factors or domains through simple idealizations. This is the way science has found to stand at the edge between *reality* and *mind.* Abstraction eases the perpetual tention between the need to simplify and the need of explaining perceived complexity.

Because of the complexity of modern finance, when we apply ideas of abstraction and idealization to global markets and sophisticated financial instruments, we need much more elaborate models than those that macroeconomics has used in the past, which have been largely based on matrix analysis. It is also necessary to examine similarities at different scales, and

F I G U R E   16–2

Abstraction Is the Two-Way Interface
between Complexity and Simplicity

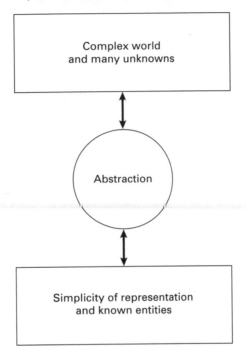

to find an approximate generating function that can be applied to each scale in a recursive manner.[2]

The very essence of modeling lies in the examination of similarities and finding the generating functions. In finance, as in physics, the parameter space that bounds a given set of values can be treated as a mathematical domain populated by different forms and values that, up to a point, can be derived from one another. In this space, we can experiment, using patterns whose forms we access, analyze, and evaluate.

Computers are laboratories for visualizing form, which presents great potential for furthering our understanding, clarifying ideas, and turning from abstraction to concretization. The visualization of data streams

---

2 See also the discussion on Brownian motion in D. N. Chorafas, *How to Understand and Use Mathematics for Derivatives,* Volume 2 (London: *Euromoney,* 1996).

can significantly enhance our understanding as well as help communicate in a clear, manageable form[3]—provided that the financial data we use is worth visualizing.

3. USING INTRADAY DATA STREAMS FOR A MORE FUNDAMENTAL UNDERSTANDING OF MARKETS

The careful reader will recall the statement made by James J. Darr, of Boston's State Street Bank, that during the coming years the difference in competitiveness will depend much more on the financial data streams we can establish and exploit than on any other single factor in the realm of information technology. I have also on several occasions stressed the importance of intraday information and high-frequency financial data (HFFD), which are the means for doing what Darr is advising.

Whether a bank plans to develop and use its own models (an issue we will concentrate on in Sections 4, 5, and 6) or employ bought software, the importance of high-frequency financial data is inescapable. Yet, not many banks today know how to establish and use *intraday* data streams, as opposed to the classical *interday* financial series. The skillful exploitation of five-minute intervals in terms of data capture is absolutely doable with current technology. The constraint is that few financial institutions have a culture that permits them to use this opportunity.

A practical example from currency exchange is given in Figure 16–3. It reflects the fractal dimension in DM/$ intraday average absolute returns with input forex prices at five-minute intervals.

Along the same frame of reference, other quite significant analytical results have been produced using a Fourier transform with S&P 500 intraday average absolute returns.[4] Commenting on this analysis of the Dow Jones Industrial Average (DJIA), Ralph J. Acampora stated in a report by Prudential Securities that the eight market corrections witnessed in the early 1960s averaged 5.5 percent over a four-week period:

> I was very careful when calculating these patterns. I specifically avoided using DJIA closing prices; I used the absolute intraday highs and the absolute intraday lows in my study. I wanted to capture all of the greed on the way up and all of the fear on the way down.[5]

---

3 D. N. Chorafas, *Visual Programming Technology* (New York: McGraw-Hill, 1996).

4 D. N. Chorafas, *How to Understand and Use Mathematics for Derivatives,* Volume 2 (London: *Euromoney,* 1996).

5 *Strategy Weekly,* July 26, 1996.

F I G U R E 16–3

Fractal Dimensions in DM/$ Intraday Average
Absolute Returns

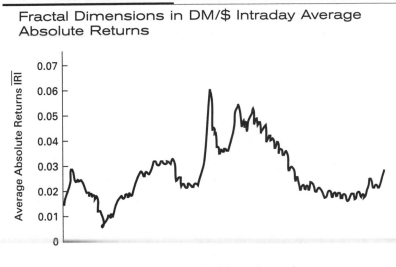

Time, in Five-Minute Intervals

Forty-four years ago, I had a professor of banking at the Graduate School of Business, University of California, Los Angeles, who lectured his students that greed and fear is what moves the market. But is the financial market an adaptive system? This is a query many rocket scientists labor to answer, and they look at *microseasonality* for a factual and documented response.

According to Dr. Murray Gell-Mann of the Santa Fe Institute, if we are dealing with complex adaptive systems such as organisms, human beings, and so on, and we are looking at composite complex adaptive systems like villages made of people, markets made of investors, ecological communities made of organisms, *then* a serious simulation would involve schemata not only at the level of the adaptive agents out of which the composite complex adaptive systems are composed, but also the schemata at the higher level.

The more complex the real world we're studying gets, the harder it is to analyze. It is no less true that without high-frequency financial data we cannot even formulate a clear concept of the behavior of the system we're studying. There are many levels of sophistication when we talk of the visualization of these data streams.

Most bankers, investors, and treasurers keep working with two-dimensional representations because that's what they have been trained to do. Yet an interactive, three-dimensional visualization is by far the better alternative. It is technology's cutting edge.

Figure 16–4 gives an example of how much better the data stream is represented by three dimensions (the graph at the bottom level of the figure) as contrasted to a traditional two-dimensional (top level) mapping. It usually takes three two-dimensional graphs to render the information contained in one three-dimensional picture.

- But in some cases, even three dimensions can be inadequate because many problems confronting us in finance are n-dimensional, with n a lower two-digit number.

If we wish to develop models for pricing the trading book—which is the subject of this text—and we wish to do so in a fairly accurate and comprehensive manner, we have to use a whole family of interactive three-dimensional color graphics, personalized to the requirements and the decision type of each user.

Whether it is properly appreciated or not, the banking industry sometime ago left the familiar two-dimensional frame of reference and moved to a six-dimensional structure. Table 16–1 explains its key components. Notice that even six dimensions is rather coarse grain. A more fine-grain approach involves (according to the latest count) 23 dimensions in the financial market, and therefore much greater complexity.

Granted, some of the information may be harder to obtain in very fine detail. For instance, in connection to market volatility, while data on bid/ask and deals is generally available from most exchanges, this is not true of over-the-counter deals. To compensate for this, however, additional data can be profitably exploited by analytical studies regarding market behavior and/or performance. Such information is less commonly available and includes the following:

- Size or depth of the deal for which the market maker provides the best quotes.

- Supporting schedule of limit orders that may drive the market.

- Change in prices required to persuade market makers to fill an order.

- Size of order increases or decreases as they take place.

The availability of such information would permit more realistic real-time simulation, enhancing the ability to study not only volatility but also liquidity and *depth of the market*, the latter being the price change

F I G U R E   16–4

Gamma of 100•100 Time Spreads–View over Price Movement: Futures-Style Margin, 56 Days and 28 Days to Go, 10% Volatility, and .01% Interest

(From Charles M. Cottle, *Options: Perception and Deception* [Chicago: Irwin Professional Publishing®, 1996, p. 251, © Charles M. Cottle, 1996]).

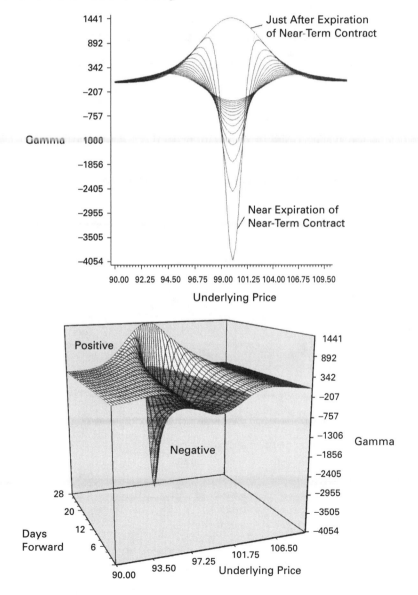

T A B L E   16–1

Factors Entering Financial Modeling and Resulting Representation Dimensions

1. *Volatility*
   - Relative volatility
   - Volatility ratio
   - Directional change of volatility

2. *Liquidity*
   - Relative liquidity
   - Tick frequency
   - Bid–ask spread
   - Level of business activity

3. *Seasonality*
   - Microseasonality
   - Business time
   - Intrinsic time

4. *Product Characteristics*
   - Design factors
   - Market factors
   - Customization

5. *Contract Characteristics*
   - Counterparty
   - Currency
   - Notional principal
   - Duration

6. *Cumulative Exposure*
   - Risk assumed with this deal
   - Cumulative risk with this instrument
   - Cumulative risk with this counterparty
   - Cumulative risk in this interest rate
   - Cumulative risk in this currency
   - Cumulative risk in this country
   - Cumulative risk in this equity
   - Cumulative risk on-balance sheet
   - Cumulative risk off-balance sheet

that makes the market tick. Other things being equal, the greater the price change, the less the depth of the market, which is another dimension that should be added to Table 16–1.

4. MODELS OF DYNAMIC SYSTEMS IN THE FINANCIAL INDUSTRY

The reason we develop models of financial systems is to help ourselves in the analysis of business opportunity, the design of new instruments, a specific market test, the right pricing of new financial product, and the control of risk. All of these goals require the simulation of dynamic systems, this being most particularly true of the management of exposure.[6]

Dr. Murray Gell-Mann has long been a proponent of modeling. "With very complex systems, analytic study of what's going on is often difficult," he says. "Computer modeling or simulation is often the best way to learn something."[7] This is as true in finance as it is in physics.

From his professional experience, Gell-Mann describes a spectrum of simulation activities, ranging from models with extremely simple rules, which usually operate in conjunction with chance, to models with more information. The latter often come in the form of details corresponding to what has actually happened. One of the challenges is to establish whether these details represent real or apparent complexity.

Dr. Gell-Mann's principle is that complexity often emerges from very simple rules, usually with the addition of chance phenomena. Therefore, he suggests, the analysis of data streams is a very exciting activity, even addictive. He also suggests that, while most of the modeling done today is at the simple end of the spectrum, the time has come to move more toward middle complexity.

The difficulty, according to Gell-Mann, comes in reconciling the actual observations with what might emerge in the model. This makes it necessary to add information about what may be involved in midrange complexity or at a higher level, without removing the potential for generating this higher level.

To describe dynamic systems algorithmically means to acknowledge and express in a mathematical form the characteristics of nonlinear behavior, which are discussed in Section 6. Combining the algorithmic and

---

6 See also Chapter 10 on simulation in connection to value-at-risk.
7 *The Bulletin of the Santa Fe Institute,* Spring 1995.

heuristic (trial and error) approaches, which we examine in Section 5, suggests new methods for addressing the following problems:

- Measurement,
- Adaptation, and
- Stability.

All three bullets are relevant to the control of complex, nonlinear systems. The advised solution requires new concepts addressing observability and controllability as well as trade-offs, including the identification of sampling rates and scales at which dynamics systems are observable and can therefore be controllable. Of particular interest is what we can do with natural scales and sampling rates.

The concept of sampling rates was introduced in Section 3 in connection to microseasonality and the five-minute intraday intervals. As technology advances, we can increase the sampling frequency. One-minute rates are feasible today, and second-level frequency in data capture is becoming doable.

As the financial analyst goes to finer and finer scales and to more and more frequent sampling, the case will arise than an uncontrollable system suddenly becomes better known, hence controllable. This is the reason we are eager to study microseasonality in the financial markets.

As for natural scales of measurement and the analysis of distributions in data streams, in Chapter 9 we spoke about the normal distribution but also said that in most real-life cases the normal distribution is an approximation that we use because of the rich statistical tables associated with it. Other distributions used in financial series are the lognormal (examined in Chapter 11), binomial, Poisson, and Weibull,[8] the last being very important in connection to risk-management studies.

When represented algorithmically, data streams about the dynamics of a financial system, market, or instrument can be combined with other forms of information to encompass both deterministic and apparently stochastic frames of reference. The behavior of any system, whether a turbulent fluid, a robot's behavior, a stock index, interest rates, or currency-exchange rates, exhibits some orderly and therefore regular features that are predictable.

Chaos theory suggests that such behavior may be deterministic according to some set of rules. By contrast, features that complexity theory fails to predict are apparently random, or at least we believe so until there is proof to the contrary.

---

8 See D. N. Chorafas, *Derivative Financial Instruments: Strategies for Managing Risk and Return in Banking* (London: Lafferty, 1995).

5. ALGORITHMS, HEURISTICS, AND THE MANAGEMENT OF RISK

Both predictable, regular features and unpredictable ones can be described through models. The amount of information required to specify the regular features can be identified through appropriate study, which will also permit us to make plausible guesses as to the type of model we should be using for greater accuracy. If a suitable computer program leads from variable inputs to expected results, *algorithmic* approaches should be used. If the amount of information required to describe different features is stochastic and unpredictable, the approach to be used is *heuristic.*

With the exception of very simple linear models, we must be very careful in establishing whether the behavior of the financial system, market, or instrument is algorithmic or heuristic. Fuzzy engineering and genetic algorithms (GA) are good examples of applications in heuristics. Polynomials, difference equations, and differential equations are algorithmic solutions.

Both algorithmic and heuristic approaches must be supported through visual programming,[9] leading to end-user software development because the end user is the best person to do a meaningful analytical study. Knowledge-enriched software is necessary to track, measure, and filter financial data streams as well as to do database mining, for example, to mine information on credit exposure, market spreads, developing trends, and assumed risk.

The analytical system we develop and implement may work well in theory but utterly fail in practice if high technology is unavailable to support real-time managing of oncoming financial data streams and database information.

The dynamic management of market risk and credit exposure is impossible without sophisticated technological solutions. If advanced systems are available, dynamic risk management becomes doable. The fundamental requirements include the following:

- Real-time database management of current credit exposure by counterparty.
- The ability to visualize both the portfolio of derivatives and balance-sheet items.
- Simulation tools that permit online experimentation at the end user's discretion.

---

9 D. N. Chorafas, *Visual Programming Technology* (New York: McGraw-Hill, 1996).

Erik Banks advises that real-time access to current credit-exposure information forms the core of a valid technology.[10] A communications- and computer-based system should permit, say, the credit officer to inter- actively call up by counterparty all references to credit exposure. For a derivatives portfolio, these references should, at a minimum, include the following:

- Gross actual exposure.
- Net actual exposure.
- Net actual exposure, net of collateral.
- Gross fractional exposure.
- Gross potential exposure.
- Net potential exposure.
- Expected and unexpected credit losses.

Defining necessary information elements is the banker's job. The provision of modern technological supports is the responsibility of the information systems specialist. The advanced mathematical tools to be used for a rigorous analysis of market data streams and for database min- ing are the responsibility of the rocket scientist(s).

Historically, though they developed in parallel, dynamic systems theory and the mathematical treatment of information are often seen as distinct subjects. But although the backgrounds and methods of dynamic systems theory and information theory look as if they are distinct, in prac- tice the two fields work in unison and, up to a point, overlap.

Some historical background will clarify this relationship. After its beginnings in the work of Lyapunov and Poincaré a century ago, the the- ory of dynamics went through a 50-year lull before exploding, in the last few decades, to provide a mathematical understanding of both linear sys- tems and nonlinear systems.

The way they are used in connection to the study of complexity, the methods of *dynamic systems theory* derive largely from deterministic, classical mechanics. By contrast, the methods of information theory derive from statistical mechanics, which is probabilistic and at its base quantum-mechanical.

Let's recall that information theory originated in the 19th century when Maxwell, Boltzmann, and Gibbs developed successful statistical treatments of thermodynamic problems. Fifty years later, their work

---

10 Erik Banks, *Credit Risk with Complex Derivatives* (London: Macmillan, 1997).

formed the mathematical basis for Dr. Claude Shannon's work for the purposes of communications.

Over the years, Shannon's theory has expanded to encompass a variety of subjects in artificial intelligence, computation, control, robotics, and the analysis of the financial markets. This synergy between applications fields, which might have been seen as distinct, arises from the concurrent development of nonlinear systems theory, as Section 6 demonstrates.

Analytics and computation play a complementary role in investigative and discovery processes, particularly in the study of nonlinear systems. Financial analysis has a great deal to gain from this approach because the only practical way to follow the individual trajectories of a nonintegrable system is to simulate its dynamics.[11]

6. LINEARITIES, NONLINEARITIES, AND FEEDBACKS

Scientists studying nonlinear dynamics, the equations that describe irregular motion, have found that predictions about the future are greatly dependent on initial conditions—and on the present. Two situations identical in all but the smallest detail will result in utterly different conclusions. This is the principle behind what is often called *deterministic chaos,* and it constitutes the foundation of *chaos theory,* which is very helpful in complexity studies.

Classical financial theory perceives a company as a black box that has inputs and outputs, the latter being the result of production functions. The relations characterizing inputs to outputs are taken to be mostly linear, which of course, is an approximation. In reality, such input-to-output relations are nonlinear.

Standard texts in accounting and in banking perceive the cash flow as a compensation for the company's output, which looks as if it is linear. But they fail to relate the value of the firm to the prognosis of its future cash flow (hence, the company's intrinsic value) and of its profitability. Future cash flow compensating a company's output is no linear function of quantity and unit price. It is nonlinear because of unpredictable events, discounts, special conditions, illiquidity, payment delays, and so on.

Simplified and linearized approaches may be easier to comprehend and map into a model. But, at the same time, they provide an incomplete theoretical basis, leading to erroneous practical results.

---

11 See D. N. Chorafas, *Systems and Simulation* (New York: Academic Press, 1965).

One lesson that can be learned from rocket science is that not only complex mathematical models and high-performance computers but also ingenious sampling techniques must be used to cope with torrents of data. A crucial question that is not being asked often enough is how much information has been lost through sampling procedures. The amount of information being lost will be small if we weed out the noise level and if the procedure we follow helps capture even low activity in the market.

This is what Section 3 said should be done through *intraday* financial series. As will be remembered, I have advised using five-minute intervals in data capture, progressing towards one-minute or subminute intervals, rather than using interday time series.

Both high-frequency financial data and nonlinear financial research are important competitive advantages because they can be instrumental in uncovering significant areas of fitness or, alternatively, of risk. They also bring to the banker's attention the fact that, quite often, the total is worth much more than its parts because of nonlinear relationships among its components.

"Anything linear is probably wrong," says Dr. Joel Moses, Dean of the School of Architecture and Planning, MIT. "In complex systems you usually have feedback loops. In R&D, we've long had this notion of a linear chain from basic research to product development, and we know that that's wrong. Unfortunately, not enough people operate as if they know it's wrong."[12] This concept of feedback characterizing a nonlinear system was demonstrated in Chapter 12, Figure 12–2.

Engineers trained in servomechanisms and control systems appreciate the feedback's impact and aftermaths. But many bankers, investors, and even financial analysts are not sensitive to the concept of feedback and of nonlinearities or their impact on the study of financial markets.

The theory of nonlinear dynamics represents the wave of the future. Whether in science or in finance, a theory can only be acceptable if it is testable in practice and gives reliable results. As we saw at the end of Chapter 14, even if one of the subsystems supported by the theory fails the test, this will be enough to falsify the theory or at least render it questionable and discard its possible effects in terms of evaluation or prognosis.

Feedback mechanisms help to demonstrate that basically nonlinearity means that an effect is not proportional to its cause. If for no other reason than this, financial markets are nonlinear. But financial data also have

---

12 *The MIT Report,* June/July 1996.

a lot of noise. Because of nonlinearities, the same-size cause can have different effects, depending on the circumstances.

A 10-basis point rise in interest rates will affect financial market A differently than market B or C, depending on how the players in each market interpret the authorities' objectives and on what the psychology is when interest rates rise. This makes the mathematics of cause and effect complex but also provides a lot of opportunities for profit.

Because of psychology and of initial conditions, financial markets are nonlinear adaptive systems whose behavior can become unpredictable. Both trading prices and transaction velocity tend to change in real time, with the result that complexity increases and so does the system's ability to go out of control.

There is talk among knowledgeable bankers and technologists that real-time networks may create unforeseen kinds of systemic risk,[13] apart from the more evident result that they will redefine competition among the main players in the financial industry. A basic but little appreciated fact is that technology increases both the efficiency and the complexity of the financial system. It helps to manage risk and at the same time it amplifies exposure. It also blurs the boundaries between retail and wholesale banking, as well as commercial, investment, and retail banking activities.

A similar statement can be made about new financial products that were originally thought to be hedging mechanisms, but whose nonlinear behavior bankers have not understood very well. In fact, the reason this section on nonlinearities has been included is to increase the reader's awareness of the impact that nonlinear financial systems have, all the way from market opportunity to the management of risk.

7. CASE-BASED REASONING IN PRICING THE TRADING BOOK

The whole process, from idealization of a real-life situation to the concretization of the model we have under development, depends on our perceptual ability in connection to the problem we are addressing and on our skill in mapping the real world into the computer. In regard to the Market Risk Amendment, this mapping involves the contents of the bank's trading book and subsequently the pricing of assets and liabilities contained

---

13 See Chapter 9.

in the trading book, and the calculation of the exposure the bank has taken because of its transactions.

Both processes can be significantly assisted through *case-based reasoning*. Even without formal modeling methods, the banker, investor, and treasurer should appreciate that when reasoning by analogy he or she improves the chances of benefitting from past experience.

Case-based reasoning starts with indexing of the cases stored in a network of reference nodes and proceeds with the evaluation of past experiences by comparing the significance of cases versus rules. Hence, to begin with, appropriate references must be recovered in the indexing phase. A significant role in this approach is played by knowledge engineering; knowledge robots, or *agents,* can be used to advantage in connection with a case-based reasoning methodology.[14]

The algorithms for indexing, reuse, and storage of the cases depend on the structure of the knowledge bank. The aim of an optimization is to make fast, appropriate generalizations based on distinctions specified by the expert in the construction of an ephemeral classification tree.[15]

This differs from classical control theory, which requires formulation of a single evaluation function expressing the closeness of actual behavior to the desired one. The exploration of an episodic memory by means of agents is crucial because many practical problems are impossible to model in a predetermined way.

The rocket scientist who has been given the mission of modeling the processes represented in the trading book for pricing and the evaluation of exposure must give some degree of freedom to the end user. As Erik Banks suggests, depending on the approach employed, for instance, in the management of limits, it may be necessary to include critical information on the following:

- Gross/net potential exposure.
- Actual exposure limit(s).
- Maximum maturity limit(s).
- Maximum expected credit loss(es).

The way to bet is that database mining will include information on the status of the master agreement and associated documentation; collat-

14 D. N. Chorafas, *Agent Technology Handbook* (New York: McGraw Hill, 1997).
15 See D. N. Chorafas, *Intelligent Multimedia Databases* (Upper Saddle River, NJ: Prentice-Hall, 1994).

eral and its current market value (whether incremental or pooled); covenants such as a mark-to-market agreement, including dollar or time trigger points; the existence of credit derivatives hedges (if any); termination/ downgrade option dates or trigger points; internal and external ratings (credit scores); and the like.

Analogical reasoning will be instrumental in constructing the model in a way that supports both a detailed and an overall view of trading-book exposures as well as specific exposures, transaction by transaction, counterparty by counterparty, instrument by instrument, and location by location.

Not only should the pricing model provide ad hoc information at the end user's request, but it should also be possible to interactively define a combination of factors with impact on exposure. It is bad policy to look at individual risks from loans, derivatives, or other instruments in isolation from other exposures with the same counterparties. While different banks have different means of highlighting and aggregating risks, both market risk and credit risks should certainly be interactively investigated within the analogical reasoning perspectives offered by an online exposure system.

This strategy can be assisted through a process of model-based diagnosis to translate a set of similitudes into a combination of factors that can be used to express the behavior of the trading book. The solution to be adopted should offer the ability to choose between functions and constraints.

Finally, one of the objectives of case-based reasoning is to develop learning systems. In principle, an artifact learns as more experiences are added to its knowledge bank. But we should not overcrowd or swamp memory and indexing capabilities. Hence, it is necessary to have a method for removing redundant data using agents and filtering algorithms.

8. THE OVERWHELMING CASE OF MODEL TESTING

Both natural and human-made systems undergo tests. Models for pricing the trading book or banking book, as well as algorithms and heuristics for risk management, are no exception to this rule. Natural artifacts have been tested over millions of years of evolution by means of crossovers, mutations, and survival of the fittest, resembling genetic algorithms in a way.[16]

Models and other human-made systems must be tested through a rigorous methodology that reveals their weaknesses and confirms their

---

16 See D. N. Chorafas, *Rocket Scientists in Banking* (London: Lafferty, 1996).

strengths. Testing is not only the way to prove whether or not the model conforms to objectives. It also provides a means for the artifact's evolution.

Testing can take several forms. For instance, one way to test whether a model fits the pattern in implied volatilities is to do a comparison with spot prices. This is what the Market Risk Amendment requires in terms of backtesting.

Researchers with experience in backtesting have found sizeable biases in Black–Scholes' model prices. To the contrary, stochastic volatility option-pricing models seem to adequately describe the patterns in implied volatilities.

As a way of testing models, other financial analysts have looked into lead-lag relationships between movements in prices and volatility regarding the equity and derivatives markets. One of the hypotheses being tested is whether the higher leverage available in option markets might induce informed traders to transact in options rather than stocks.

Many projects have investigated the relation between option prices and equity prices by testing prognostication models. Some have focused on whether particular option volumes might have information about future price movements, which should be reflected in the model. For example, with derivatives, traders would:

- Write a put or buy a call if they knew there was good news.
- Write a call or buy a put if they heard bad news.

Because option-writing patterns and effective trade volume could provide information on the future movement of equity prices, it is proper to test whether the model has this sensitivity. Using intraday option data, certain results show that option volumes tend to lead equity prices, which may provide evidence that option markets have introduced special characteristics into financial trading activities.

Sensitivity to market evidence is a good way to test the fitness of a model. For instance, increasing evidence tends to suggest the role of futures in providing a broader market. This market tends to have a quicker, more efficient price discovery and greater liquidity and depth than the spot market. One hypothesis is that volatility in the spot market might even be dampened by the coexistence of a futures market. Can our model withstand the test of this hypothesis? If not, what are the necessary value-added characteristics?

It is just as important to develop methods that permit one to test how volatility in the spot market would have varied if there had not been a related futures market. The use of low-frequency financial data does not permit such discovery, but high-frequency financial data might.

Some research has addressed the subject of volatility in the spot market in connection to measures of activity in both the spot and futures markets. At least one of the projects I know of did so by using data for *expected* and *nonexpected* volumes in both the spot and futures markets as well as the open interest in the futures market.

Not only is model testing an integral part of its development, testing is also an integral part of model usage. This has begun to be generally appreciated, and the Market Risk Amendment specifies backtesting throughout the life cycle of the model.

One way of looking at the evolutionary aspect of model testing is that it would require considerable coinvolvement by the Basle Committee, the G–10 central bankers, and other regulatory authorities. In the years to come, a major job by supervisory authorities will be to validate the models that banks use to do the following:

- Value positions.
- Compute risks.
- Project cash flow.
- Develop value-added instruments.

It is also appropriate to bring the reader's attention to the fact that models not only can be profitably used for training, but their use in training helps test them. One of the interesting features of the Options Training and Trading (OTT) model developed in Tokyo by Nikko Securities is its dual purpose. It has been designed in such a manner that it can serve as a tutor to both novice and mature options traders.

The simpler model helps one understand the very basic level of dealing, through strategy selection supported by simulation. The sophisticated model helps the experienced trader set up positions, load and run tests, and simulate results. We will hear more and more about knowledge-supported approaches to training and trading in the years to come.

ACKNOWLEDGMENTS

The following organizations, their senior executives and system specialists, participated in the recent research projects that led to the contents of the present book and its documentation.

UNITED STATES

Federal Reserve Bank of Boston

William N. McDonough, Executive Vice President–Legal
Richard Kopcke, Vice President and Economist
Peter Fortune, Senior Economist
George Alexakos, Examiner
Katerina Simons, Economist
Joanna Stavins, Economist
Jane Katz, Editor, Regional Review

600 Atlantic Avenue, Boston, MA 02106–2976, USA

Seattle Branch, Federal Reserve Bank of San Francisco

Jimmy F. Kamada, Assistant Vice President
Gale P. Ansell, Assistant Vice President, Business Development

1015 2nd Avenue, Seattle, WA 98122–3567, USA

Federal Reserve Bank of San Francisco

Matthew Foss, Manager, Capital Markets
Nigel Ogilvie, Banking Supervision and Regulation

101 Market Street, San Francisco, CA 94120, USA
(Teleconferencing from the Seattle Branch of the Federal Reserve Bank of San Francisco)

State Street Bank and Trust

James J. Darr, Executive Vice President, US Financial Assets Services

225 Franklin Street, Boston, MA 02105–1992, USA

307

Bankers Trust

Dr. Carmine Vona, Executive Vice President for Worldwide Technology
Shalom Brinsy, Senior Vice President, Distributed Networks
Dan W. Muecke, Vice President, Technology Strategic Planning
Bob Graham, Vice President, Database Manager

One Bankers Trust Plaza, New York, NY 10006, USA

Citibank

Colin Crook, Chairman, Corporate Technology Committee
Dr. Daniel Schutzer, Senior Vice President, Information Technology
Jim Caldarella, Manager, Business Architecture for Global Finance
Nicholas P. Richards, Database Administrator
William Brindley, Technology Officer
Michael R. Veale, Network Connectivity
Harriet Schabes, Corporate Standards
Leigh Reeve, Technology for Global Finance

399 Park Avenue, New York, NY 10043, USA

Morgan Stanley

Gary T. Goehrke, Managing Director, Information Services
Guy Chiarello, Vice President, Databases
Robert F. DeYoung, Principal, Information Technology

1933 Broadway, New York, NY 10019, USA

Eileen S. Wallace, Vice President, Treasury Department
Jacqueline T. Brody, Treasury Department

1251 Avenue of the Americas, New York, NY 10020, USA

Goldman Sachs

Peter T. Hoversten, Vice President, Information Technology
Leo J. Esposito, Vice President, Information Systems
David Flaxman, Advanced Technology Group
Malcolm Draper, Architect, Communications Systems
Fred M. Katz, Applications Architect, Equity Sales and Trading
Vincent L. Amatulli, Information Technology, Treasury Department

85 Broad Street, New York, NY 10004, USA

J. J. Kenny Services Inc.

Thomas E. Zielinski, Chief Information Officer

Ira Kirschner, Database Administrator, Director of System Programming and of the Data Center

65 Broadway, New York, NY 10006, USA

Merrill Lynch

Kevin Sawyer, Director of Distributed Computing Services and Executive in Charge of the Mainframe to Client-Server Conversion Process

Raymond M. Disco, Treasury/Bank Relations Manager

World Financial Center, South Tower, New York, NY 10080–6107, USA

Teachers Insurance and Annuity Association/College Retirement Equities Fund (TIAA/CREF)

Charles S. Dvorkin, Vice President and Chief Technology Officer

Harry D. Perrin, Assistant Vice President, Information Technology

730 Third Avenue, New York, NY 10017–3206, USA

Financial Accounting Standards Board

Halsey G. Bullen, Project Manager

Jeannot Blanchet, Project Manager

Teri L. List, Practice Fellow

401 Merritt 7, Norwalk, CN 06856, USA

Teknekron Software Systems, Inc.

Vivek Ranadive, President and CEO

Robert Rector, Senior Vice President, Client Technical Services

Martin Luthi, Senior Director, Client Technical Services

Gerard D. Buggy, Vice President, Global Financial Sales and Marketing

Norman Cheung, Director, Quantum Leap Group

Bradley C. Rhode, Vice President, Core Technology Engineering

Tugrul Firatli, Director, Network Consulting Services

John E. McDowall

Tom Jasek, Director, Market Sheet

Glenn A. McComb, Senior Member of Technical Staff, New Technologies

Murat K. Sonmez, Member of Technical Staff

Murray D. Rode, Member of Technical Staff

530 Lytton Avenue, Suite 301, Palo Alto, CA 94301, USA

Evans and Sutherland

Les Horwood, Director, New Business Development
Mike Walterman, Systems Engineer, Virtual Reality Applications
Lisa B. Huber, Software Engineer, 3-Dimensional Programming

600 Komas Drive, P.O. Box 58700, Salt Lake City,
Utah 84158, USA

nCUBE

Michael Meirer, President and Chief Executive Officer
Craig D. Ramsey, Senior Vice President, Worldwide Sales
Ronald J. Buck, Vice President, Marketing
Matthew Hall, Director of Software Development

919 East Hillside Blvd., Foster City, CA 94404, USA

Visual Numerics

Don Kainer, Vice President and General Manager
Joe Weaver, Vice President, OEM/VAR Sales
Jim Phillips, Director, Product Development
Dr. Shawn Javid, Senior Product Manager
Dan Clark, Manager, WAVE Family Products
Thomas L. Welch, Marketing Product Manager
Margaret Journey, Director, Administration
John Bee, Technical Sales Engineer
Adam Asnes, VDA Sales Executive
William Potts, Sales Manager

6230 Lookout Road, Boulder, Colorado 80301, USA

Massachusetts Institute of Technology

Prof. Dr. Stuart E. Madnick, Information Technology and Management Science
Prof. Dr. Michael Siegel, Information Technology, Sloan
School of Management
Patricia M. McGinnis, Executive Director, International
Financial Services
Prof. Peter J. Kempthorne, Project on Non-Traditional Methods
in Financial Analysis
Dr. Alexander M. Samarov, Project on Non-Traditional Methods
in Financial Analysis
Robert R. Halperin, Executive Director, Center for
Coordination Science
Prof. Amar Gupta, Sloan School of Management

Prof. Jean-Luc Vila, Finance Dept., Sloan School of Management
Prof. Bin Zhou, Management Science, Sloan School of Management

292 Main Street, Cambridge, MA 02139, USA

Eric B. Sundin, Industrial Liaison Officer
David L. Verrill, Senior Liaison Officer, Industrial Liaison Program

Sloan School of Management
50 Memorial Drive, Cambridge, MA 02139, USA

Henry H. Houh, Desk Area Network and ViewStation Project, Electrical
Engineering and Computer Science
Dr. Henry A. Lieberman, Media Laboratory
Valerie A. Eames, Media Laboratory
Prof. Dr. Kenneth B. Haase, Media Arts and Sciences
Dr. David Zeltzer, Virtual Reality Project

Ames St., Cambridge, MA 02139, USA

University of Michigan

Prof. John H. Holland, Electrical Engineering and
Computer Science
Dr. Rick L. Riolo, Systems Researcher, Department of Psychology

Ann Arbor, MI 48109–2103, USA

Santa Fe Institute

Dr. Edward A. Knapp, President
Dr. L. Mike Simmons, Jr., Vice President
Dr. Bruce Abell, Vice President, Finance
Prof. Dr. Murray Gell-Mann, Theory of Complexity
Prof. Dr. Stuart Kauffman, Models in Biology
Dr. Chris Langton, Artificial Life
Dr. John Miller, Adaptive Computation in Economics
Dr. Blake Le Baron, Non-Traditional Methods in Economics
Bruce Sawhill, Virtual Reality

1660 Old Pecos Trail, Santa Fe, NM 87501, USA

School of Engineering and Applied Science, University of California, Los Angeles

Dean A. R. Frank Wazzan, School of Engineering and Applied Science
Prof. Richard Muntz, Chair, Computer Science Department
Prof. Dr. Leonard Kleinrock, Telecommunications and Networks

Prof. Nicolaos G. Alexopoulos, Electrical Engineering
Prof. Dr. Judea Pearl, Cognitive Systems Laboratory
Prof. Dr. Walter Karplus, Computer Science Department
Prof. Dr. Michael G. Dyer, Artificial Intelligence Laboratory
Susan Cruse, Director of Development and Alumni Affairs
Joel Short, Ph.D. Candidate
David Chickering, Ph.D. Candidate

Westwood Village, Los Angeles, CA 90024, USA

School of Business Administration, University of Southern California

Dr. Bert M. Steece, Dean of Faculty, School of Business Administration
Dr. Alan Rowe, Professor of Management

Los Angeles, CA 90089–1421, USA

Prediction Company

Dr. J. Doyne Farmer, Director of Development
Dr. Norman H. Packard, Director of Research
Jim McGill, Managing Director

234 Griffin Street, Santa Fe, NM 87501, USA

NYNEX Science and Technology, Inc.

Thomas M. Super, Vice President, Research and Development
Steven Cross, NYNEX Shuttle Project
Valerie R. Tingle, System Analyst
Melinda Crews, Public Liaison, NYNEX Labs

500 Westchester Avenue, White Plains, NY 10604, USA

John C. Falco, Sales Manager, NYNEX Systems Marketing
David J. Annino, Account Executive, NYNEX Systems Marketing

100 Church Street, New York, NY 10007, USA

Microsoft

Mike McGeehan, Database Specialist
Andrew Elliott, Marketing Manager

825 8th Avenue, New York, NY 10019, USA

Reuters America

Robert Russel, Senior Vice President
William A. S. Kennedy, Vice President

Buford Smith, President, Reuters Information Technology
Richard A. Willis, Manager, International Systems Design
M. A. Sayers, Technical Manager, Central Systems Development
Alexander Faust, Manager, Financial Products USA (Instantlink and Blend)

40 E. 52nd Street, New York, NY 10022, USA

Oracle Corporation

Scott Matthews, National Account Manager
Robert T. Funk, Senior Systems Specialist
Joseph M. Di Bartolomeo, Systems Specialist
Dick Dawson, Systems Specialist

885 Third Avenue, New York, NY 10022, USA

Digital Equipment Corporation

Mike Fishbein, Product Manager, Massively Parallel Systems (MAS-PAR Supercomputer)
Marco Emrich, Technology Manager, NAS
Robert Passmore, Technical Manager, Storage Systems
Mark S. Dresdner, DEC Marketing Operations

146 Main Street, Maynard, MA 01754, USA
(Meeting held at UBS New York)

Unisys Corporation

Harvey J. Chiat, Director, Impact Programs
Manuel Lavin, Director, Databases
David A. Goiffon, Software Engineer

P.O. Box 64942, MS 4463, Saint Paul, MN 55164–0942, USA
(Meetings held at UBS in New York)

Hewlett-Packard

Brad Wilson, Product Manager, Commercial Systems
Vish Krishnan, Manager, R&D Laboratory
Samir Mathur, Open ODB Manager
Michael Gupta, Transarc, Tuxedo, Encina Transaction Processing
Dave Williams, Industry Account Manager

1911 Pruneridge Avenue, Cupertino, CA 95014, USA

IBM Corporation

Terry Liffick, Software Strategies, Client-Server Architecture
Paula Cappello, Information Warehouse Framework

Ed Cobbs, Transaction Processing Systems
Dr. Paul Wilms, Connectivity and Interoperability
Helen Arzu, IBM Santa Teresa Representative
Dana L. Stetson, Advisory Marketing IBM New York

Santa Teresa Laboratory, 555 Bailey Avenue, San Jose, CA 95141, USA

UBS Securities

A. Ramy Goldstein, Managing Director, Equity Derivative Products

299 Park Avenue, New York, NY 10171–0026, USA

Union Bank of Switzerland

Dr. H. Baumann, Director of Logistics, North American Operations
Dr. Ch. Gabathuler, Director, Information Technology
Hossur Srikantan, Vice President, Information Technology Department
Roy M. Darhin, Assistant Vice President

299 Park Avenue, New York, NY 10171–0026, USA

UNITED KINGDOM

Bank of England

W. D. R. Swanney, C. A., Head of Division, Supervision and Surveillance
Patricia Jackson, Special Advisor, Regulatory and Supervisory Policy
Mark Laycock, Banking Supervision

Threadneedle Street, London EC2R 8AH, UK

British Bankers Association

Paul Chisnall, Assistant Director

Pinners Hall, 105–108 Old Broad Street, London EC2N 1EX, UK

Accounting Standards Board

AVC Cook, Technical Director
Sandra Thompson, Project Director

Holborn Hall, 100 Gray's Inn Road, London WC1X 8AL, UK

Barclays Bank

Alan Brown, Director, Group Credit Policy
Brandon Davies, Treasurer UK Group

54 Lombard Street, London EC3P 3AH, UK

Peter Golden, Chief Information Officer, Barclays Capital Markets, Treasury, BZW

David J. Parsons, Director, Advanced Technology

Christine E. Irwin, Group Information Systems Technology

Murray House, 1 Royal Mint Court, London EC3N 4HH, UK

Abbey National Bank

Mac Millington, Director of Information Technology

Chalkdell Drive, Shenley Wood, Milton Keynes MK6 6LA, UK

Anthony W. Elliott, Director of Risk and Credit

Abbey House, Baker Street, London NW1 6XL, UK

Natwest Securities

Sam B. Gibb, Director of Information Technology

Don F. Simpson, Director, Global Technology

Richard E. Gibbs, Director, Equity Derivatives

135 Bishopsgate, London EC2M 3XT, UK

Credit Swiss Financial Products

Ross Salinger, Managing Director

One Cabot Square, London E14 4QJ, UK

Credit Swiss First Boston

Geoff J. R. Doubleday, Executive Director

One Cabot Square, London E14 4QJ, UK

Bankgesellschaft Berlin

Stephen F. Myers, Head of Market Risk

1 Crown Court, Cheapside, London, UK

British Telecom

Dr. Alan Rudge, Deputy Managing Director

BT Centre, 81 Newgate Street, London EC1A 7AJ, UK

Association for Payment Clearing Services (APACS)

J. Michael Williamson, Deputy Chief Executive

14 Finsbury Square, London EC2A 1BR, UK

Oracle Corporation

Geoffrey W. Squire, Executive Vice President, and Chief Executive
Richard Barker, Senior Vice President and Director, British Research Laboratories
Giles Godart-Brown, Senior Support Manager
Paul A. Gould, Account Executive

Oracle Park, Bittams Lane, Guildford Rd., Chertsey, Surrey
KT16 9RG, UK

E. D. & F. Man International

Brian Fudge, Funds Division

Sugar Quay, Lower Thames Street, London EC3R 6DU, UK

Prudential-Bache Securities

Stephen Massey, Regional Director—Euorope

9 Devonshire Square, London EC2M 4HP, UK

SCANDINAVIA

Sveriges Riksbank

Göran Zettergren, Economics Department

Brunkebergstorg 11, 3–103 37 Stockholm, Sweden

Vaerdipapircentralen (VP)

Jens Bache, General Manager
Aase Blume, Assistant to the General Manager

61 Helgeshoj Allé, Postbox 20, 2630 Taastrup, Denmark

Swedish Bankers' Association

Bo Gunnarsson, Manager, Bank Automation Department
Gösta Fischer, Manager, Bank-Owned Finanical Companies Department
Göran Ahlberg, Manager, Credit Market Affairs Department

P.O. Box 7603, 10394 Stockholm, Sweden

Skandinaviska Enskilda Banken

Lars Isacsson, Treasurer
Urban Janeld, Executive Vice President, Finance and IT
Mats Andersson, Director of Computers and Communications

Gösta Olavi, Manager, SEB Data/Koncern Data

2 Sergels Torg, 10640 Stockholm, Sweden

Securum AB

Anders Nyren, Director of Finance and Accounting
John Lundgren, Manager of IT

38 Regeringsg, 5 tr., 10398 Stockholm, Sweden

Sveatornet AB of the Swedish Savings Banks

Gunar M. Carlsson, General Manager

(Meeting at Swedish Bankers' Association)

Mandamus AB of the Swedish Agricultural Banks

Marie Martinsson, Credit Department

(Meeting at Swedish Bankers' Association)

Handelsbanken

Janeric Sundin, Manager, Securities Department
Jan Aronson, Assistant Manager, Securities Department

(Meeting at Swedish Bankers' Association)

Gota Banken

Mr. Johannsson, Credit Department

(Meeting at Swedish Bankers' Association)

IRDEM AB

Gian Medri, Former Director of Research at Nordbanken

19 Flintlasvagen, 19154 Sollentuna, Sweden

AUSTRIA

Bank Austria

Dr. Peter Fischer, Senior General Manager, Treasury Division
Peter Gabriel, Deputy General Manager, Trading
Konrad Schcate, Manager, Financial Engineering

2, Am Hof, 1010 Vienna, Austria

Creditanstalt Bankverein

Dr. Wolfgang G. Lichtl, Director of Foreign Exchange and Money Markets

Dr. Johann Strobl, Manager, Financial Analysis for Treasury Operations

3, Julius Tandler-Platz, 1090 Vienna, Austria

Association of Austrian Banks and Bankers

Dr. Fritz Diwok, Secretary General

11, Boersengasse, 1013 Vienna, Austria

Wiener Betriebs- Und Baugesellschaft mbH

Dr. Josef Fritz, General Manager

1 Anschützstrasse, 1153 Vienna, Austria

Management Data of Creditanstalt

Ing. Guenther Reindl, Vice President, International Banking Software

Ing. Franz Necas, Project Manager, RICOS

Mag. Nikolas Goetz, Product Manager, RICOS

21–25 Althanstrasse, 1090 Vienna, Austria

GERMANY

Deutsche Bundesbank

Eckhard Oechler, Director of Bank Supervision and Legal Matters

14, Wilhelm Epstein Strasse, D-6000 Frankfurt 50, Germany

Deutsche Bank

Peter Gerard, Executive Vice President, Organization and Information Technology

Hermann Seiler, Senior Vice President, Investment Banking and Foreign Exchange Systems

Dr. Kuhn, Investment Banking and Foreign Exchange Systems

Dr. Stefan Kolb, Organization and Technological Development

12, Koelner Strasse, D-6236 Eschborn, Germany

Dresdner Bank

Dr. Karsten Wohlenberg, Project Leader, Risk Management, Simulation and Analytics Task Force, Financial Division

Hans-Peter Leisten, Mathematician

Susanne Loesken, Organization and IT Department

43, Mainzer Landstrasse, D-6000 Frankfurt, Germany

Commerzbank

Helmut Hoppe, Director, Organization and Information Technology
Hermann Lenz, Director Controllership, Internal Accounting and Management Accounting
Harald Lux, Manager, Organization and Information Technology
Waldemar Nickel, Manager, Systems Planning

155, Mainzer Landstrasse, D-60261 Frankfurt, Germany

Deutscher Sparkassen and Giroverband

Manfred Krueger, Division Manager, Card Strategy

4 Simrockstrasse, D-5300 Bonn 1, Germany
(Telephone interview from Frankfurt)

Media Systems

Bertram Anderer, Director

6, Goethestrasse, D-7500 Karlsruhe, Germany

Fraunhofer Institute for Computer Graphics

Dr. Ing. Martin Geobel
Wolfgang Felber

7, Wilhelminerstrasse, D-6100 Darmstadt, Germany

GMD FIRST—Research Institute for Computer Architecture, Software Technology and Graphics

Prof. Dr. Ing. Wolfgang K. Giloi, General Manager
Dr. Behr, Administrative Director
Dr. Ulrich Bruening, Chief Designer
Dr. Joerg Nolte, Designer of Parallel Operating Systems Software
Dr. Matthias Kessler, Parallel Languages and Parallel Compilers
Dr. Friedrich W. Schroer, New Programming Paradigms
Dr. Thomas Lux, Fluid Dynamics, Weather Prediction and Pollution Control Project

5, Rudower Chaussee, D-1199 Berlin, Germany

Siemens Nixdorf

Wolfgang Weiss, Director of Banking Industry Office
Bert Kirschbaum, Manager, Dresdner Bank Project
Mark Miller, Manager, Neural Networks Project for UBS and German Banks
Andrea Vonerden, Business Management Department

27, Lyoner Strasse, D-6000 Frankfurt 71, Germany

UBS Germany

H.–H. v. Scheliha, Director, Organization and Information Technology
Georg Sudhaus, Manager, IT for Trading Systems
Marco Bracco, Trader
Jaap Van Harten, Trader

52, Bleichstrasse, D-6000 Frankfurt 1, Germany

FRANCE

Banque de France

Pierre Jaillet, Director, Monetary Studies and Statistics
Yvan Odonnal, Manager, Monetary Analyses and Statistics
G Tournemire, Analyst, Monetary Studies

39, rue Croix des Petits Champs, 75001 Paris, France

Secretariat Général de la Commission Bancaire–Banque de France

Didier Peny, Head of Supervisory Policy and Research Division
Michel Martino, International Affairs
Benjamin Sahel, Market Risk Control

115, rue de Reaumur, 75002 Paris, France

Ministry of Finance and the Economy, Conseil National de la Compatibilité

Alain Le Bars, Director, International Relations and Cooperation

6, rue Louise Weiss, 75703 Paris Cedex 13, France

ITALY

Banca d'Italia

Eugenio Gaiotti, Research Department, Monetary and
Financial Division

Banca d'Italia, Rome, Italy

Istituto Bancario San Paolo di Torino

Dr. Paolo Chiumenti, Director of Budgeting
Roberto Costa, Director of Private Banking
Pino Ravelli, Director, Bergamo Region

via G. Camozzi 27, 24121 Bergamo, Italy

LUXEMBOURG

Banque Générale du Luxembourg

Prof. Dr. Yves Wagner, Director of Asset and Risk Management

Hans-Jörg Paris, International Risk Manager

Dirk Van Reeth, Manager, Department of Companies and Legal Structures

Dr. Luc Rodesch, Investment Advisor

27, avenue Monterey, L-2951, Luxembourg

CEDEL

André Lussi, Chief Executive Officer

Ray Soudah, Chief Financial and Investment Officer

67 Bd Grande-Duchesse Charlotte, L-1010, Luxembourg

SWITZERLAND

Swiss National Bank

Robert Fluri, Assistant Director, Statistics Section

Dr. Werner Hermann, Risk Management

Dr. Christian Walter, Representative to the Basle Committee

15, Börsenstrasse, 8022 Zurich, Switzerland

Bank for International Settlements

Claude Sivy, Director, Controllership and Operational Security

Frederik C. Musch, Secretary General, Basel Committee on Banking Supervision

2 Centralbankplatz, Basel, Switzerland

Swiss Bank Corporation

Dr. Marcel Rohner, Director, IPD Controlling

Swiss Bank Center, 8010 Zurich, Switzerland

BZ Bank Zurich

Martin Ebner, President

Peter Sjostrand, Finance

Olivier Willi, Analyst

Roger Jenny, Analyst

50 Sihlstrasse, 8021 Zurich, Switzerland

BZ Trust Aktiengesellschaft

Dr. Stefan Holzer, Financial Analyst

24 Eglirain, 8832 Wilen, Switzerland

Ciba-Geigy AG

Stefan Janovjak, Divisional Information Manager
Natalie Papezik, Information Architect

Ciba-Geigy, R-1045, 5.19, 4002 Basle, Switzerland

Ecole Polytechnique Fédéral de Lausanne

Prof. Dr. Jean-Daniel Nicoud, Director, Microinformatics Laboratory
Prof. Dr. Bo Faltings, Artificial Intelligence
Prof. Dr. Martin J. Hasler, Circuits and Systems
Dr. Ing. Roman Boulic, Computer Graphics

1015 Lausanne, Switzerland

EURODIS

Albert Mueller, Director
Beat Erzer, Marketing Manager
B. Pedrazzini, Systems Engineer
Reto Albertini, Sales Engineer

Bahnhofstrasse 58/60, CH-8105 Regensdorf, Switzerland

Olsen and Associates

Dr. Richard Olsen, Chief Executive Officer

232 Seefeldstrasse, 8008 Zurich, Switzerland

JAPAN

Bank of Japan

Harry Toyama, Counsel and Chief Manager, Credit and Market
Management Department
Akira Ieda, Credit and Market Management Department

2–1–1, Kongoku-Cho, Nihonbashi, Chuo-Ku, Tokyo 103, Japan

DAI-ICHI Kangyo Bank

Shunsuke Nakasuji, General Manager and Director, Information
Technology Division
Seiichi Hasegawa, Manager, International Systems Group

Takahiro Sekizawa, International Systems Group
Yukio Hisatomi, Manager, Systems Planning Group
Shigeaki Togawa, Systems Planning Group

13–3, Shibuya, 2–Chome, Shibuya-ku, Tokyo 150, Japan

Fuji Bank

Hideo Tanaka, General Manager, Systems Planning Division
Toshihiko Uzaki, Manager, Systems Planning Division
Takakazu Imai, Systems Planning Division

Otemachi Financial Center, 1–5–4 Otemachi, Chiyoda-ku, Tokyo, Japan

Mitsubishi Bank

Akira Watanabe, General Manager, Derivative Products
Akira Towatari, Manager, Strategic Planning and Administration, Derivative Products
Takehito Nemoto, Chief Manager, Systems Development Division
Nobuyuki Yamada, Systems Development Division
Haruhiko Suzuki, Systems Development Division

7–1, Marunouchi, 2–chome, Chiyoda-ku, Tokyo 100, Japan

Nomura Research Institute

Tomio Arai, Director, Systems Science Department
Tomoyuki Ohta, Director, Financial Engineering Group
Tomohiko Hiruta, Manager, I-STAR Systems Services

9–1, Nihonbashi, 1–Chome, Chuo-ku, Tokyo 103, Japan

Mitsubishi Trust and Banking

Nobuyuki Tanaka, General Manager, Systems Planning Division
Terufumi Kage, Consultant, Systems Planning Division

9–8 Kohnan, 2–Chome, Minato-ku, Tokyo 108, Japan

Sakura Bank

Nobuo Ihara, Senior Vice President and General Manager, Systems Development Office VIII
Hisao Katayama, Senior Vice President and General Manager, System Development Office VII
Toshihiko Eda, Senior Systems Engineer, Systems Development Division

4–2, Kami-Osaki, 4–Chome, Shinagawa-ku, Tokyo 141, Japan

Sanyo Securities

Yuji Ozawa, Director, Systems Planning Department
K. Toyama, Systems Planning Department

1–8–1, Nihonbashi, Kayabacho, Chuo-ku, Tokyo 103, Japan

Center for Financial Industry Information Systems (FISC)

Shighehisa Hattori, Executive Director
Kiyoshi Kumata, Manager, Research Division II

16th Floor, Ark Mori Building, 12–32, 1–Chome Akasaka,
Minato-ku, Tokyo 107, Japan

Laboratory for International Fuzzy Engineering Research (LIFE)

Prof. Dr. Toshiro Terano, Executive Director
Dr. Anca L. Ralescu, Assistant Director
Shunichi Tani, Fuzzy Control Project Leader

Siber Hegner Building, 89–1 Yamashita-Cho, Naka-ku, Yokohama-shi 231, Japan

Real World Computing Partnership (RWC)

Dr. Junichi Shumada, General Manager of RWC
Hajime Irisawa, Executive Director

Tsukuba Mitsui Building, 1–6–1 Takezono, Tsukuba-shi, Ibarahi 305, Japan

Tokyo University

Prof. Dr. Michitaka Hirose, Dept. of MechanoInformatics, Faculty of Engineering
Dr. Kensuke Yokoyama, Virtual Reality Project

3–1, 7-Chome, Hongo Bunkyo-ku, Tokyo 113, Japan

Tokyo International University

Prof. Dr. Yoshiro Kuratani

9–1–7–528, Akasaka, Minato-ku, Tokyo 107, Japan

Japan Electronic Directory Research Institute

Dr. Toshio Yokoi, General Manager

Mita-Kokusai Building–Annex, 4–28 Mita, 1–Chome, Minato-ku, Tokyo 108, Japan

Mitsubishi Research Institute (MRI)

Masayuki Fujita, Manager, Strategic Information Systems Dept.
Hideyuki Morita, Senior Research Associate, Information Science Dept.

Akio Sato, Research Associate, Information Science Dept.

ARCO Tower, 8–1 Shimomeguro, 1–Chome, Meguro-ku, Tokyo 153, Japan

NTT Software

Dr. Fukuya Ishino, Senior Vice President

223–1 Yamashita-Cho, Naka-ku, Yokohama 231, Japan

Ryoshin Systems (Systems Developer Fully Owned by Mitsubishi Trust)

Takewo Yuwi, Vice President, Technical Research and Development

9–8 Kohman, 2-Chome, Minato-ku, Tokyo 108, Japan

Sanyo Software Services

Fumio Sato, General Manager, Sales Department 2

Kanayama Building, 1–2–12 Shinkawa, Chuo-ku, Tokyo 104, Japan

Fujitsu Research Institute

Dr. Masuteru Sekiguchi, Member of the Board and Director of R & D
Takao Saito, Director of the Parallel Computing Research Center
Dr. Hiroyasu Itoh, R & D Department
Katsuto Kondo, R & D Department
Satoshi Hamaya, Information Systems and Economics

9–3 Nakase, 1-Chome, Mihama-ku, Chiba-City 261, Japan

NEC

Kotaro Namba, Senior Researcher, NEC Planning Research
Dr. Toshiyuki Nakata, Manager, Computer System Research Laboratory
Asao Kaneko, Computer System Research Laboratory

3–13–12 Mita, Minato-ku, Tokyo 108, Japan

Toshiba

Dr. Makoto Ihara, Manager, Workstation Product Planning and Technical Support Dept
Emi Nakamura, Analyst, Financial Applications Dept.
Joshikiyo Nakamura, Financial Sales Manager
Minami Arai, Deputy Manager, Workstation Systems Division

1–1, Shibaura, 1-Chome, Minato-ku, Tokyo 105, Japan

Microsoft

James LaLonde, Multinational Account Manager, Large Accounts Sales Dept.

Sasazuka NA Bldg, 50–1 Sasazuka, 1–Chome, Shibuya-ku, Tokyo 151, Japan

Apple Technology

Dr. Tsutomu Kobayashi, President

25 Mori Bldg., 1–4–30 Roppongi, Minato-ku, Tokyo 106, Japan

Digital Equipment Japan

Roshio Ishii, Account Manager, Financial Sales Unit 1

2–1 Kamiogi, 1-Chome, Suginamiku, Tokyo 167, Japan

UBS Japan

Dr. Peter Brutsche, Executive Vice President and Chief Manager
Gary P. Eidam, First Vice President, Regional Head of Technology
Charles Underwood, Vice President, Head of Technical Architecture and Strategy
Masaki Utsunomiya, Manager, IT Production Facilities

Yurakucho Building 2F, 1–10–1 Yurakucho, Chiyoda-ku, Tokyo 100, Japan